The English Whippet

Frontispiece: 'Misse et Turlu', by Jean-Baptiste Oudry, (1686-1755). Musée Nationale du Chateâu, Fontainebleau; see Appendix 6.

THE ENGLISH WHIPPET

E. G. Walsh and Mary Lowe

SECOND EDITION

COCH-Y-BONDDU BOOKS

First published by The Boydell Press 1984
Reprinted by Coch-y-Bonddu Books 2004

ISBN 1 904784 03 8

Published & distributed by
COCH-Y-BONDDU BOOKS
MACHYNLLETH, POWYS, SY20 8DJ
Tel 01654 702837 www.anglebooks.com

To

Susie and Mousse

Tessa, Amber, Sophie, Blue,

Cleo, Souffle, Spider, Sylla, Windle,

Pecker, Owly, Honey, Poodle, Ruff, Bella, Dinah,

Stickit, Wiv, Wissie, Colditz and Minnie,

Blini, Honey, Dishy, Matilda

&

Angel,

who all contributed.

Contents

List of Illustrations

Acknowledgements And Thanks

We could not have written this book without help from many people both in and out of the whippet world.

For whippet material, memories, anecdotes and details we are, above all, indebted to the comprehensive and beautifully kept records of the late Mrs Cleeve which were bequeathed to the Author by her husband, Major David Cleeve. Our thanks are also due, in particular for details and photographs, to Mr R. M. James, Mrs Anne Knight, Mrs Bobbie Cooke, Mrs M. B. Garrish and Mrs Kay Chapman on whippets in England; to Mrs Vanessa Mather for information about whippets on the Continent; to Mr Bo Bengtson for information about whippets in Scandinavia and America and to Mrs Marilyn Reynolds for information about whippets in New Zealand and Australia; and to Mrs Edward Russell and Miss Gay Robertson for certain information about the W.C.R.A.

We wrote the 'Looking After' chapter with some trepidation but we were heartened when it was passed by Mrs J. A. James, BVMS, MRCVS, to whom we are grateful, not only for this service but also for the miracles which she has performed on our dogs from time to time.

Although, after nearly two years of research, we know that there are areas which could be much more fully investigated and documented, we hope that our coverage is sufficiently detailed to provide an adequate record of the progress of whippets during the last twenty years. In particular, lists of Group and BIS winners have proved illusive since these are not available in the Kennel Club Stud Books; changes of addresses have prevented us from compiling a complete record.

We would like to express our gratitude to all the owners and breeders who have responded so generously with photographs. Inevitably there are dogs and bitches whom we would have liked to include but of whom it has proved impossible to acquire suitable pictures and, since illustrations must necessarily be limited, there are a number of absences which we regret.

Our special thanks must go to Mr Harry Whimpanny, whose superb portrait photographs have added substantially to our pictorial records. We are very grateful to the Musée du Chateau, Fontainebleau, the Fitzwilliam Museum, Cambridge, and the Leeds City Art Galleries for permission to publish our frontispiece and Plates 1 and 2. We thank Mike Scarlett, Amanda Reid and Stuart Hastie for Plates 41, 47 and 103; we thank Jim Meads, who has been so helpful before, for Plates 43 and 75, and David Hancock for certain selective enlargements. We are also grateful to the other photographers named in the text for permission to publish photographs taken by them.

Finally, our thanks to Ian Lowe, who kindly negotiated the use of the frontispiece and plates 1 and 2, and supplied the inconographical details in Appendix 6; and to Anne Boyes who has, once again, worked her way through dyslexic typing to produce what we hope is a readable text.

Authors' Introduction to The Second Edition

In this second edition we have brought the Show Champions and Stud Dog records up to date.

Our views on Whippet Origins, Ownership, the Kennel Club, the Whippet Breed Clubs, the Breed Standard, Showing, Coursing, Hunting, Racing, Breeding, Rearing and Looking after Whippets remain as they were when we wrote *The English Whippet* in 1983.

It is not possible to cover every aspect of the whippet, nor is it possible to try and answer every question that might be asked about whippets by beginners, or even by hardened veterans, without writing an encyclopaedia. We hope that we have steered a middle course between the too simple and the too complicated; we hope that we have given novices some idea of the breadth of interests there are in the whippet world and some hints on how to join in these activities; and that we have given some entertainment to those who know all about whippets.

Neither of us could have written this book, which we hope is of wide coverage, on our own, hence the dual authorship; but the opinions expressed are those of us both.

Ted Walsh
Akeley
Buckingham

Mary Lowe
Newton Reigny
Cumbria

November, 1989

1. *'The Earl of Northampton', by Pompeo Batoni, (1708-1787). Fitzwilliam Museum, Cambridge; see Appendix 6.*

Chapter 1

Origins and Ownership

According to the Oxford English Dictionary the first use of the word 'whippet' in print was in 1610, though it is merely a mention of the word and no description is given. A method of trying to find out the origins of the whippet is to look at what was written by contemporaries, on the supposition that they wrote of what they had actually seen. In 1577, Harrison had described the 'whappet, or prick'eared cur' but the dog he wrote about must have been the terrier of the day. 'Certes, it is impossible to describe these curs because they have not any one kind proper unto themselves but a confused company mixed of all the rest.' It is a description that could be applied to some working terrier shows today.

Whippets are not mentioned in the dog books written by Daniel (1801), Taplin (1803), Youatt (1845), 'Stonehenge' (Dr Walsh, 1860), or 'Idstone' (The Revd Thomas Pearce, 1872) and a clue to this lack of mention of a dog that, from the evidence of art, undoubtedly existed at the time and much earlier, may be found in Vero Shaw's *Illustrated Book of the Dog,* (1879), where he says, 'The whippet, or snap dog as it is termed in several of the Northern Districts of the country, may scarcely be said to lay claim to be considered a sporting dog except in those parts where it is most appreciated. The whippet is essentially a local dog and the breed is little valued beyond the limits of the Northern counties. In these, however, the dog is held in high respect and its merits as the provider of sport are highly esteemed.

'Unfortunately for the dog, the uses to which he is often placed have, naturally enough, done much to injure his reputation in the sight of many who would otherwise have regarded him with a favourable eye. So many scandals have arisen from time to time in connection with the quasi-sport of rabbit coursing that many who would have felt disposed to do their best to elevate the breed in popular estimation have reluctantly been compelled to discontinue their efforts on its behalf, on account of the unpleasant treatment they have received from other admirers of the dog.'

Twenty years later, W. D. Drury, in *British Dogs* (1901), wrote, 'Though it is not until recent years that the Whippet, or snap dog, has come into such prominence as to warrant its recognition by the Kennel Club as a variety, yet for many decades the animal has been known to the miners and other workers in the North of England. More than 30 years ago at least, the name whippet was bestowed upon a dog built very much on the lines that today find favour. It is, however, only some 12 or 13 years since the effort to popularise the dog in the South of England was attempted.

There are two kinds of whippet, distinguished respectively by a rough and a smooth coat, the latter being the favourite and the one usually seen. These dogs may be called the poor man's greyhound, being similar in form and having to undergo the same preparation for work. The smooth-coated form an immense majority in Lancashire, Yorkshire and the Midlands; but amongst the pitmen of Durham and Northumberland are found a great many rough-haired ones, many of which are the result of crossing with the Bedlington terrier and these are naturally hardier.'

These authors are, no doubt, quite correct in what they say but they are only writing about cross-breeding for specific sporting purposes, just as small lurchers are still being bred today. What they do not mention is the fact, easily verified by reference to art, whether painting or sculpture, that there had been dogs of whippet *type* and *shape* for many hundreds of years. It is possible that they were called whippets but it is more likely that they were just called small greyhounds. The writer in the oldest work in the English language on the chase, Edward, Duke of York, in *The Master of Game,* (1413), wrote, 'The good greyhound should be of middle size, neither too big nor too little, and then he is good for all beasts. If he were too big he is nought for small beasts, and if he were too little he were nought for the great beasts. Nevertheless whoso can maintain both, it is good that he hath both of the great and of the small, and of the middle size.'

What could be more 'whippety' than Misse and Turlu in Oudry's picture (Frontispiece), painted in 1725? A clue to scale is given by the rose showing between the two dogs. In 1758 Batoni painted the Earl of Northampton, showing the Earl (Plate 1) with a whippet standing on the chair beside him; it is not a greyhound either in size or type. The little dogs were there all the time but they may have been few in number, if common locally. To make them more acceptable as house dogs there may well have been infusions of Italian greyhound blood though the Italian greyhound of the Continent is a larger and more sporting dog than that seen in England today.

Sometime in the early or middle 19th century, possibly co-existent with the growing popularity of public coursing with greyhounds and the rising number of public coursing clubs — a sport which, for various reasons, was then more or less confined to the 'nobility and gentry', — the sport of rabbit coursing gained popularity in the northwest, north and north Midlands.

One cannot course rabbits in the accepted sense of the word. Rabbits cannot be driven across country by beaters as hares can be driven and, in daylight, they do not sit far enough out from their holes to be walked up; a 30 or 40 yard dash for cover is the longest chance that most dogs get at a wild rabbit. The rabbit coursing for which dogs were specially bred, 100 or 150 years ago, took place in enclosures and the rabbits had been netted previously.

Vero Shaw (1879), gives a good description of the dogs used for rabbit coursing: 'Rabbit coursing, once so popular a sport, has gradually waned. Some ten or twenty years ago it was all the rage with that class with which the whippet is so closely associated. The dogs then used were of an entirely different stamp to the dogs of the present day; in fact they were *terriers proper.* The predominating colours were red and wheaten, many too were blue with tan markings. With the gradual decay of rabbit coursing and the introduction of straight-out running has disappeared the type of terrier formerly used. Now speed is the main object sought for; the main consideration is to get the greatest amount of speed into the least possible size. Hence, to obtain speed, those interested in the breed have resorted to Italian and English greyhound crosses; many are so finely bred that they strike the observant eye as little else than diminutive greyhounds. Not only in outline are they alike but most of the smooth specimens are of the same colour as the greyhound — we have whites, blacks, reds, fawns, brindles and compounds from each; there are now many rough-haired whippets.'

Finally, to quote from W. D. Drury (1901) again, who would have seen the whippet both at rabbit coursing and at racing: 'These dogs which are kept in large numbers by the working classes of the Northern counties of England, may be called the poor man's greyhound. The breed is kept for the sport of straight running and also for rabbit coursing. The fastest dogs have been produced by a first cross from the greyhound, but those used for rabbit coursing have, generally, an infusion from the Bull-terrier or some other game blood, to give them staying powers; for to run 31 courses in a day is not only a trying test of condition but also a severe test of gameness.'

The '31 courses', or however many were run in a match between two dogs, were short. The starter put a rabbit on a spot about 60 yards in front of the two dogs which were held by the slipper. As the starter, who was also the judge, let the rabbit go the slipper let the two dogs go and the dog which first caught the rabbit was the winner of that 'course'. A rabbit in a strange place, surrounded by shouting, cheering spectators, would not know where to run to and would not go far before it was caught. It may be that the dogs were not running more than 80 or 90 yards at a time but to do this for the 'best of 31 rabbits' needed not only speed but tremendous stamina and gameness.

So, in the evolution of the whippet, we have the 'little running dog' whose existence is proved by writers, painters and sculptors. His type carries on like a river into which flow side streams from English greyhound, Italian greyhound and terriers of various sorts. But one is forced to the conclusion that whippets share the dominent genetic purity of greyhounds or they would not have survived the many infusions of cross-breeding over so many years for so many purposes. It cannot be coincidental that the same size, type,

2. *'A Nymph taking a thorn out of a Greyhound's foot', by Richard James Wyatt, (1795-1850). City of Leeds Art Galleries; see Appendix 6.*

and quality, exists in the modern whippet as can be seen in so many examples in art, painting, sculpture, and bronzes. Prior to the date when the term 'whippet' was commonly used for the dog as we know it, the dog was probably known as an English greyhound, a small greyhound or even an Italian greyhound. There is a reference in the latter half of the last century to them being called 'H'Italians'. Size, after all, is a relative quality. Coomassie, a greyhound bitch of 24 inches at the shoulder, won the Waterloo Cup in 1877 and 1878; a whippet of 22 inches is acceptable in America today and there are specimens not far off that height appearing in the English show-ring despite the fact that the 'ideal' height, according to the Standard, is 18½ inches for a whippet dog and 17½ inches for a bitch. On the Continent, Italian greyhounds are larger and more strongly boned than those in this country and they are included in the Hound Group, not the Toy Group as in England; Maria Luisa Incontri, in her book, *'Il Piccolo Levriero'* shows photographs of modern Italian greyhounds with hares they have caught, the scale of which shows the dogs to be much nearer the size of small whippets than Italian greyhounds as we see them here.

We believe that with selective breeding from the same genetic pool one could, in a few generations, produce an Italian greyhound and a greyhound from original whippet stock. It is a fact that as whippets get larger they begin to look more like small greyhounds, and, what is more revealing, they begin to gallop like greyhounds rather than like whippets. Similarly, the smaller, finer whippets tend to have the more rounded skull, protruding eyes and finer bone of the Italian. We do not believe that any amount of selective breeding would produce any sort of terrier, Stafford, Bedlington, Old English or Black and Tan. Our conclusion, like Lewis Renwick before us, is that, far from being any sort of cross the whippet is essentially a small greyhound, sharing the same dominant genetic purity of the breed.

Recognition as a pure breed

Whilst whippets had been around for many centuries, had appeared in various guises as 'Rabbit Dogs' at shows in the north of the country and had slowly got classes to themselves, it was not until 1890 that they were officially recognized as a breed by the Kennel Club. Challenge Certificates were first granted in 1896 and in 1899 the Whippet Club, the oldest and most prestigious of the Breed Clubs, was formed. The early efforts of a small number of devoted fanciers laid the solid foundations of the breed for which we must be grateful today. Such names as Mr H. Bottomley (Shirley) and Mr Albert Lamotte (Manorley), whose prefixes lie behind almost all current whippet pedigrees, are synonymous with the breed when any study of its history is made. It is impossible to list all the breeders who

3. *Black-and-Tan, or Manchester terriers were crossed with small greyhounds to produce dogs for rabbit coursing and racing. (Walsh)*

have contributed to the whippet from 1890 to the present day and, since the early history of the breed has been fully documented by authors such as Lewis Renwick, B.S. Fitter, Fitch Daglish and C.H. Douglas Todd, we propose to deal in detail with whippet history for the last twenty years, from 1962 to 1982. Obviously the events of the last twenty years have their roots in the past, in the importance of the foundation strains building up the breed structure; it is to the dedication of those early breeders that we owe the legacy we have received of a medium sized gazehound, fast and functional and very little altered in purpose or result from its forebears. Since those early days the whippet has gone from strength to strength in popularity, as a show dog, as a pedigree racing dog, as a small coursing and hunting dog and as a pet; at the time of writing whippets generally achieve the second highest entry in the Hound Group at Championship Shows and are widely admitted to be one of the most competitive breeds on the show scene.

Whippets are also one of the relatively few breeds which are still capable of doing that for which they were originally intended and what they have done for 1,000 years or more: coursing and catching their dinner.

4. *A Bedlington terrier of 60 years ago, Mrs M. Williamson's Worton Demon. They probably originated some 200 years ago as the Rothbury terrier and one theory is that they were a whippet-Dandie cross. They have certainly been crossed with whippets for 150 years or more to produce a very game little dog.*

Buying a Whippet

The decision to own a dog is one which far too many people take too lightly. This is why stray and unwanted dogs are always in the news, be it a picture of Battersea Dogs Home, a sob story in a local paper or messes on the pavement. They cause traffic accidents, not only in their own towns but also on motorways where unwanted dogs are pushed out of cars to fend for themselves; they foul public places, they terrorise children and, at times, adults and they are unloaded in their thousands on charitable bodies such

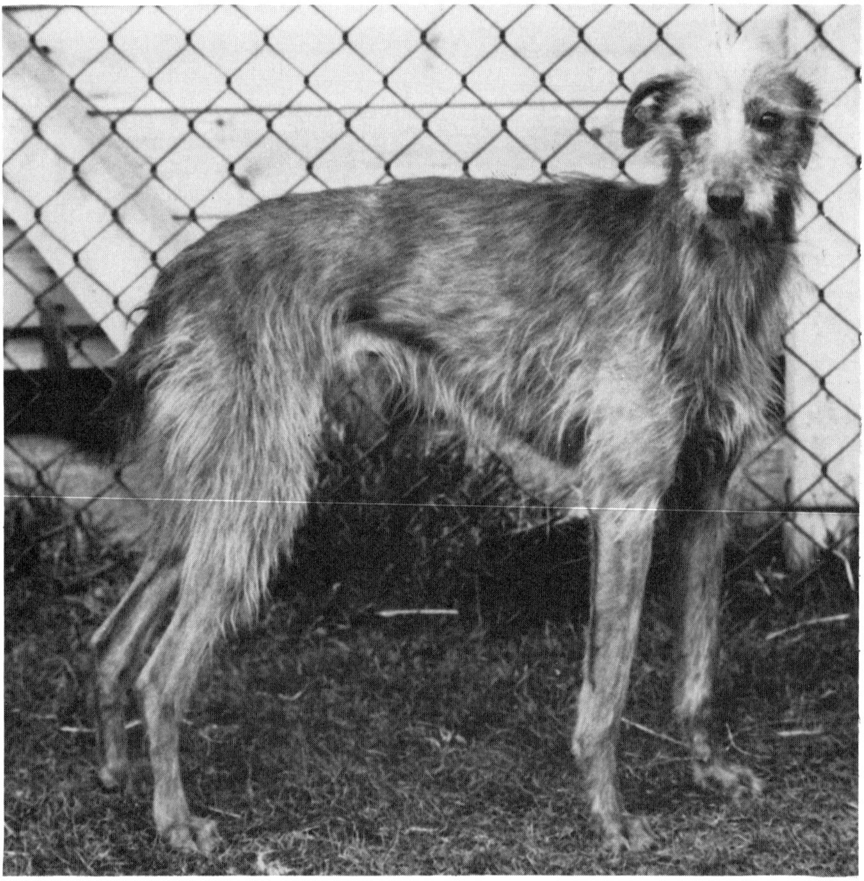

5. *Before the whippet was recognised by the Kennel Club in 1890, 'rabbit dogs', both rough and smooth, had their own classes at North country shows such as Preston and Bishop Aukland. This modern version of the rough whippet is a Bedlington-whippet cross, standing 19½ inches. (Walsh)*

as the R.S.P.C.A., animal sanctuaries and the many breed rescue societies all over the country. Many thousands are destroyed every year, many thousands more are found homes, often having been rescued from unbelievable conditions. The reason for all this suffering, and agonised effort on the part of many responsible individuals, could be avoided in the first place if the facts of dog ownership were thought out more carefully — or even thought out at all — by buyers who buy irresponsibly and by breeders who are often too keen to offload surplus puppies onto new owners without finding out whether they can offer suitable homes. The truth is that there are far too many dogs in the country and there are very large numbers of people who should never own a dog.

So, first of all, if you are thinking of buying, ask yourself some hard questions. Why do you want a dog? Have you the time and money and domestic circumstances for you to give a dog a happy and healthy life for twelve years or so? and, most important, what sort of dog will best suit your circumstances if the answers to these questions are all Yes? Much of the trouble with dog ownership arises from new owners not properly understanding the characteristics of the breed they have decided to buy. Breeds of dogs vary very widely in their habits and requirements, some needing very much more exercise, grooming and attention than others; if you don't like grooming or think you have no time for it do not buy a long-haired breed such as a Pekinese or an Afghan Hound which need hours of attention every day. On the face of it, whippets appear to be a breed which is easily adaptable to a variety of domestic circumstances. They are easy to feed, exercise and groom, they are clean and of medium size; they have good temperaments and few genetic faults. Nevertheless they have some peculiarities which make them unsuitable for certain kinds of owners. Firstly, they do not, on the whole, do well as kennel dogs, i.e., kept outside in kennels. They are very loving by nature and need to establish a close relationship with an owner or owners. They do not adapt well to being left alone all day while the owner is out at work and if they are neglected in this way they will quickly become claustrophobic and destructive. I have often heard owners complaining that their whippet chewed furniture or doors or carpets, but if one enquires more closely one finds that boredom and frustration are usually the roots of the trouble. Whippets do tend to be chewers, even quite elderly whippets sometimes when, for instance, they are shut up, being in season, and it is often the most expensive items in reach that are chewed. I once had a puppy returned to me for destroying a Cartier watch; my instinct was to tell the owners that they should not have left the watch within tempting reach. That puppy settled down happily with a family who were more loving and less affluent!

The advantages and disadvantages of whippet ownership can be outlined as follows. Whippets are medium-sized gazehounds with short coats and are endearing and loving companions. They can be obedient up to a point and they are intelligent, but in the way that a hound is intelligent rather than the intelligence of a working dog. It is pointless thinking that a whippet will come when called if it is chasing something — the deep-rooted instinct to chase and hunt is far stronger than any instinct to obey; in full flight there is no chance of getting a whippet back until it has lost whatever it was after and many whippets who learn to hunt when young are adepts at disappearing up the far side of a hedge if they think your attention is distracted for a moment. For this reason they can be difficult to control in areas where they may be at risk from cars, farm stock or game and why it is absolutely imperative that a whippet is trained not to look at sheep

6. *An 'English' Italian greyhound, Mrs Garrish's Ch. Fleeting Flavius. They are classified in the Toy Group in England.*

before it is let loose in the country; but more about this later. If you live in the country, surrounded by large estates where shooting is important, the area will be well-keepered, since shooting nowadays usually means expensive syndicates; poaching dogs are often shot on sight and their bodies disposed of in the nearest ditch and a whippet that has been allowed to hunt will, in the end, disappear, probably without trace. That is not to say that you cannot keep a whippet under such circumstances but certain precautions do have to be taken, for instance, making certain that there is some part of the garden which can be fenced securely or, alternatively that the whippet is never off a lead or out of your sight. Whippets adapt very well to London life provided that one realises that they do not have the quickly-learnt traffic sense of, say, a gundog; they can be trained perfectly well to walk to heel down the street to the pub or shop but they

7. *A 'Continental' Italian greyhound, Mrs Garrish's Ch. Odin Springinsfeld. They are classified in the Hound Group on the continent and are still used for hunting hares and rabbits.*

do not become natural town dogs as so many other breeds do. However, we do remember a whippet who, let out of a car by a garage attendant near the Stock Exchange, found his way home, safe and well, to South Kensington through the midday traffic; he was lucky. Whippets will exercise themselves very well in London parks provided that it is one that is secure from busy roads. Because a whippet is an 'explosive' dog, capable of taking a lot of exercise in a short time and able to run rings round you — and round most other dogs — it is quite possible to give a whippet its ration of morning and evening exercise without walking too far yourself. When not running at forty miles an hour a whippet will curl up happily in its basket or in the car, quite content in knowing that it is part of your life.

Whippets do tend to be thieves and scavengers. They can easily jump onto a table or dresser and must be taught not to do this at an early age; they can also, given the chance, lay out the contents of your dustbin for inspection in a way that can be embarrassing. They have excellent stomachs and can digest most things they find to eat; they are remarkably free from disease, either hereditary or contracted. Perhaps the most persuasive reason

8. *A show greyhound, Mrs Wilton-Clark's Ch. Shalfleet Stormlight. (Diane Pearce)*

for having a whippet is the many fields of activity it can lead you into. A whippet makes an excellent family pet, it is fun to take for walks whether you are interested in its sporting proclivities or not, but there are three quite separate but overlapping spheres of activity with whippets which can provide a great deal of fun and amusement for the whole family. Many close friendships quite outside the world of dogs have been made between people whose whippets introduced them to each other. All through the year there are shows, race meetings or, in the winter, coursing meetings almost every weekend. There is no need for the whippet owner ever to feel lonely or bored — there is always some form of whippet activity taking place, many of them in the happy atmosphere of family picnic; and for the lucky whippet owner who has access to farmland or estates there is a wide range of hunting with whippets which we deal with in Chapter 5. Few other breeds offer such a wealth of choice of activity and few other breeds have such a wide range of people from so many walks of life drawn together by love of the whippet.

If, by now, you have reached the point of deciding that a whippet is the dog for you, how do you set about getting one? Here again, you must ask yourself what you want a whippet for: to course, to race, to show or just as a pet? Most owners start off by buying a whippet and then discovering all the things they can do with it; by that time they love it dearly and the fact that it may, by temperament or ability, be unsuitable for their chosen activity will not matter. But it is generally a mistake if your original whippet is unsuitable for showing or breeding to think that you can mate it and

9. *A coursing greyhound, Mr R. W. Ennals' No Worry. Provided that it has no physical weakness the coursing greyhound's looks are immaterial and it is judged by its performance in the field. (Walsh)*

produce an offspring that can achieve what Mum could not do; it is more sensible to start again with good foundation stock, and there are certain basic rules which apply to buying a whippet, or any sort of dog. Decide what you want the whippet for; decide on the colour and type that you prefer. Do this by trying to see as many whippets as possible and ask the owners of whippets you like where they got theirs from. *Always* go to a reputable breeder, never to a pet shop or dealer; try to see both parents and other relations and decide whether they are to your liking because they will be a good indication of what a puppy will be when it grows up. Always choose a puppy from a litter that is friendly and forthcoming and beware the breeder who is prepared to sell you, a beginner, a puppy under 8 weeks old. The breeder should show concern about your circumstances if he does not know you and should ask you questions about your house, garden and family. Do not be offended by this because it will be a sign that you are dealing with a responsible breeder who cares where his stock goes.

10. *A 'standard' sized whippet at speed. (Walsh)*

11. *As the whippet is bred larger and larger it loses whippet type, looks more like a greyhound and even begins to gallop like a greyhound. (Walsh)*

12. *The modern English whippet. (Diane Pearce)*

If you want to show, breed from, race or course your puppy, tell the breeder this; it is not fair to ask a breeder for a pet puppy, pay a pet price and turn up in the show ring later on, saying, 'Look what Mrs So-and-so sold me; I can't seem to win a prize with it anywhere'. For showing, racing or coursing a great deal more time and attention must go into choosing your foundation stock than if you simply want a pet and companion. In theory, all whippets should be able to excel in all these activities — and there are some who do — but in general there can be wide discrepancies in the type of dog required; so take your time, go to as many shows, race meetings or coursing meetings as you can, whichever it is that you are interested in, talk to people and find out which kennels or bloodlines regularly produce the top winners. Then visit the breeders concerned and talk to them; when they find that you are really interested and have taken some trouble to do your homework they will go all out to help you if they can.

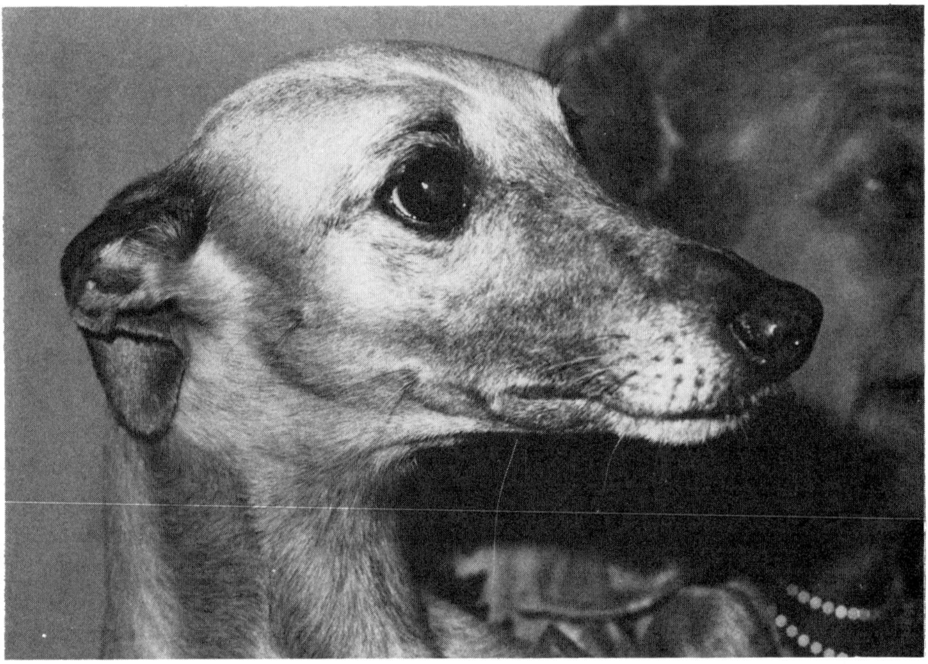

13. *'They are very loving by nature and need to establish a close relationship with an owner.' Mrs Anne Argyle with Ch. Harque the Lark. (Whimpanny)*

CHAPTER 2

The Pure-bred Whippet

As we have seen in Chapter 1, on Origins, whippets have existed over a period of many centuries in much the same form as we know them today; that is, a medium sized gazehound, short coated, elegant, graceful and functional. However, it was not until 1890, seventeen years after its own inception in 1873, that the Kennel Club officially recognised 'Whippets'. Nine years later saw the foundation of the Whippet Club in 1899, one of the earliest Breed Specialist Clubs in the world. The history of any pedigree breed of dogs is inevitably bound up with the Kennel Club since they are the official governing body, they keep the Stud Books, they issue the registrations, make the awards, officially record them, and license the shows at which such awards may be made. To understand the world of pedigree dogs one must first examine the role played by the Kennel club.

The Kennel Club

The ordinary dog owner may not come in contact with the Kennel Club at all, or only in so far as he or she wishes to register or transfer a pedigree dog, but since the Kennel Club rules are fairly complicated, and are also subject to change from time to time, most people find the ways and means of the Kennel Club somewhat difficult to understand.

The Kennel Club is responsible for licensing all shows that are run under Kennel Club Rules. Any person entering a dog, or officiating at any show which is not licensed by the Kennel Club, is liable to be warned off if they subsequently wish to participate in Kennel Club licensed events. The Kennel Club lays down what types of shows may be held, how they must be run, what classes they may schedule and how dogs must be entered for them. Details of all shows and show regulations are published in the Kennel Club Year Book which may be purchased from the Kennel Club and which is issued free to Members and to Show Secretaries. Anyone who is really interested in the pedigree dog show scene should acquire a copy as it details all regulations which apply to Judges, Stewards and Exhibitors at all types of shows. Since the Kennel Club is a complete monopoly, anyone interested in showing in this country — and in other countries which have reciprocal arrangements — must conform to Kennel Club Rules.

Registration

All dogs which are exhibited at shows run by the Kennel Club must be registered and officially transferred to the name of the owner, if other than the breeder. Registration of dogs with the Kennel Club is also required by the Whippet Club Racing Association (the governing body which controls pedigree whippet racing) and the National Whippet Coursing Club which fulfils the same function for whippet coursing. These two bodies also require five generations of registered breeding, acceptable to their committees, for reasons which will be explained later.

Registration with the Kennel Club is, fundamentally, a simple transaction. Most serious breeders have their kennel name registered. This kennel name is known as the breeder's *affix* and it may only be used by that breeder or if both parents of a puppy were bred by the affix holder. Registered affixes are important to a breed as, through them, it is possible to trace bloodlines through pedigrees for many generations. Once a puppy has been registered with the breeder's affix the only way in which its name may be changed is by the addition, as a *suffix,* of the new owner's affix. For instance, a puppy bred by Mrs Jones (Allways) can be registered as Allways Beautiful. If it was bred by Mrs Smith (Sarsden), but the sire was Allways Brilliant and the dam was Allways Pretty, it could still be registered by Mrs Jones as Allways Beautiful. But if Mrs Jones was the breeder and the puppy was purchased by Mrs Smith it would be renamed as Allways Beautiful *of Sarsden*. If Mrs Smith was the breeder, and registered it herself, the puppy would be registered as Sarsden Beautiful.

Under Rules currently in force a breeder will register a litter (called Litter Registration) which will be automatic provided that both parents are already registered. The registration form is made out and signed by the breeder and also by the owner of the sire. The breeder will then name each puppy individually, giving it its affix and a chosen name. In a few cases the breeder may prefer simply to register the litter, leaving the new owners to name individual puppies; in which case the new owner will apply for a name in the same way as the breeder would have done, except that their affix will be used as a suffix since they did not breed the puppy. In the case where the breeder names the puppy (and most breeders prefer to do this, the prestige of the affix revealing the puppy's breeding for the rest of its life) the new owner will be given, at the time of purchase, a Transfer Form which the breeder will have signed and made out in the name of the new owner. This form must be sent to the Kennel Club, together with the current fee, in order that the puppy, having already been registered in the breeder's name, may be transferred to the name of the new owner. The 'Breeder of a Litter' is the owner of the dam at the time of whelping.

By payment of an additional fee, breeders can register puppies so that their names may not be changed in new ownership. Registration cards may also be endorsed, at the breeder's request, 'Not Eligible for Exhibition', and/or 'Progeny not Eligible for Registration', also 'Not Eligible for Export'; these three endorsements are a service supplied by the Kennel Club free of charge and can be of great use to breeders who wish to be sure that their stock will not be used in any way of which they do not approve.

The registration system of the Kennel Club has often been criticised for being unwieldy and slow but it has been much improved and tightened up in recent years. For instance, it used not to be necessary for the owner of the sire to sign the litter registration form, and the whole system has now been computerised, which has made processing much faster and has ironed out many human errors. However, as a system it depends on the probity of breeders; in general, this trust is respected since the great majority of breeders have nothing but the good of their breed and the correctness of its records at heart. In this respect whippets are in a somewhat different position from any other breed. So-called 'whippet' racing has been established for well over a century and as almost all the dogs concerned are (greyhound) cross-breeds, or lurchers, the sport should more properly be called 'dog racing'. It gives much pleasure to a great many people and the dogs are mostly of 'whippet type' but because a greyhound-cross, or three-quarter-bred, will usually be faster than the equivalent pure-bred, there is always a temptation to register such dogs as pure-bred in order to compete in racing or coursing under pedigree rules. Until the Kennel Club adopts the system used by the National Coursing Club and the National Greyhound Racing Association, in which every litter has to be inspected by a veterinary surgeon and the forms signed by him showing the number and colours of whelps, it will always be easy for the unscrupulous to infiltrate cross-breeds into the breed and this is done on a much larger scale than either the Kennel Club or the general public are aware of. For this reason the Whippet Club Racing Association and the National Whippet Coursing Club insist that all dogs not only have a Kennel Club Certificate of Registration but also a five-generation pedigree acceptable to their committees. Thus it may come about that a dog may be registered with the Kennel Club yet be refused a passport to run under W.C.R.A. or N.W.C.C. Rules. It is of the first importance, when buying a puppy to take part in any pedigree whippet activity, to buy from a breeder whose integrity is beyond question.

The Breed Clubs

In 1890 the Kennel Club officially recognised whippets as a breed, and nine years later, in 1899, 'The Whippet Club' registered its title with the Kennel Club, one of the earliest Breed Clubs to do so.

In any breed of dog, whether long established or of recent importation or development, the first breed club lays down the foundation for the breed on which succeeding generations are able to build. Whippets are fortunate in that, from its inception, the Whippet Club has numbered amongst its serving officers and members some of the most knowledgeable and experienced names in the breed. The first two Rules in the Whippet Club Statute Book are:

1. The Club shall be called 'The Whippet Club'.
2. Its object shall be to promote the breeding of whippets by endeavouring to make the qualities and type of the breed, as defined by the Kennel Club Standard, better known; to define precisely and publish a description of the same; to urge the adoption of such type upon breeders, Judges and Dog Show Committees as the only recognised and unvarying standards by which whippets are to be judged and which should, in future, be uniformly accepted as the sole standards of excellence in breeding and awarding prizes of merit to whippets.

A Breed Club is the guardian of the breed. It is due to the care and knowledge of the Committee of such a Club that the breed can be safeguarded in all its important aspects. It could be said that the attitudes and standards within a breed are as good as those of the officers of its breed club. By drawing up lists of judges who can be relied on to judge to the standard of the breed, by appointing such judges to officiate at their own shows, by encouraging the younger generation of fanciers and by ensuring that they get the help and guidance they need, a breed club can and should play a significant part in the development of a breed. A breed club is also in a position to make representations to the Kennel Club, the supreme arbiter in canine matters, as and when necessary. The Whippet Club, during its first 84 years, can claim to have fully achieved its objects, as defined in the Club Statutes. In the early years the Whippet Club owed much to such names as Mr Sobey, Mr Fitter, Mr Bottomley and Mr Lewis Renwick; more recently the Club has benefited from two Secretaries of exceptional breed knowledge and expertise, in the then Mrs Bobby Jones (Allways) and, up to the present time, Mrs Dorrit MacKay (Laguna). In the last 20 years such affixes as Poppy, Selbrook, Ballagan, Shalfleet, Nimrodel, Macfield and Martinsell have at one time or another been represented on the Committee.

At present the Whippet Club runs three shows a year, a Championship, an Open and a Members Limited Show; it also runs, through a sub-committee, the Whippet Club Racing Association, the governing body of pedigree whippet racing. Under the editorship of Mrs Caroline Brown a quarterly publication, *The Whippet,* is produced which lists show and racing results and carries articles and advertisements about, and for, the breed.

Besides the Whippet Club there are now seven other breed specialist clubs operating in different parts of the country, demonstrating the growth in popularity and interest in whippets. The second club to be formed was the National Whippet Association (1936), followed by the Midland Whippet Club (1948), the Northern Counties Whippet Club (1955) and subsequently the Whippet Clubs of Scotland, Wales, East Anglia and South Yorkshire, the latter having been accorded championship status in 1983.

Each of these separate Breed Clubs operates more or less in the area designated by its title, the National Whippet Association catering traditionally for the London area and southern counties and the Whippet Club, while retaining its national flavour as senior club, operating in the South Midlands, with shows held at Bicester, Oxford, and Cricklade in Gloucestershire. Each club provides some special feature or facility for its members. The National Whippet Association produces a three-generation pedigree for every entry at their Championship Show, making their catalogues collectors items of great interest to the breed enthusiast. The Midlands Whippet Club has recently produced a Breeders 'Code of Conduct' which should be of use to novices and could, with advantage, be studied by some who are no longer novices. The Northern Counties Whippet Club for many years published a really excellent Year Book with photographs, advertisements and lists of CC and RCC winners. This function has now been taken over by an independent committee under the skilled editorship of Miss Ussher, and a Biennial is produced which has the support of all the Breed Clubs and is much appreciated both in this country and abroad. The South Yorkshire Club, most recent of the Breed Clubs, has a very go-ahead committee and a complete list of all placings at Championship shows was produced last year which will prove an invaluable asset to all record keepers in the breed.

Responsibilities of the Breed Clubs

By far the most important business conducted by the Breed Clubs is the appointing of judges for their own shows, the drawing up of the official club lists of approved judges at all levels — Championship, Open and Limited — and the tendering of advice on this subject to the Kennel Club Judges Committee when asked to do so. It is a pity that the Kennel Club seldom appears to pay attention to the Breed Clubs' wishes in the matter of judges' appointments.

The appointment of judges is vital to the overall well-being of the breed to a degree that may not be fully appreciated. It is easy to think that a judge who does an incompetent or dishonest job may be soon forgotten but, in fact, the effects of his decisions on one particular day may spread far and wide. When a dog with serious breed faults is awarded a Challenge Certificate, for whatever reason, the damage does not stop there. Others seeing such an award made may, when their turn comes to officiate, emulate it. Others, again, may assume that because such a dog has won such an award it is a suitable choice for stud or brood, thus perpetuating its faults into the next generation. Again, novices at the ringside seeing such an award take place may take years to lose the wrong impression of excellence formed on that occasion.

It is very important that the committee of a breed club should adhere rigidly to the principle of appointing judges of known probity, who are capable of judging to the Kennel Club Standard for the breed. The swapping of judges, or the putting up of judges for personal or political reasons should play no part at breed club level. Breed clubs operating on correct principles will find that their shows attract large, high quality entries; there is no better place to study the breed, especially the 'young entry', than at a breed club Championship show where the classification is generous, the entry fee reasonable and the judge is a true breed specialist. Add to this the warmth of comradeship, and the club shows with their many trophies and special prizes of different kinds are the real red-letter days in the whippet show calendar.

THE STANDARD

The Kennel Club 'standard' for any pedigree breed, by which that breed is judged in the United Kingdom, is written by the breed club or, if there are more than one, the senior club in consultation with the others. It is put to the Kennel Club and, when approved, is published and remains the guide by which that breed must be judged until it is amended or altered.

The Working Dog and the Standard

The Whippet Standard lays down *what* a whippet should look like but unless one has a knowledge of *why* a whippet should look like the Standard one has no basis for judgement of one's own or other people's dogs.

We have seen that the modern whippet is the descendant of the little 'running dog' or little greyhound which has been in existence for many hundreds of years. As the smaller cousin of the greyhound its work it similar, and the experience of many generations has shown that a certain shape, be it in the horse or the dog, will produce certain results. What does the running dog need? It needs the eyesight to spot its prey at a distance, the speed, combined with balance, to gallop and turn and twist, the stamina for a long chase, the ability to snatch its prey at speed and the strength of jaw to hold and kill it once it is caught; and it must be sound, the lame dog can catch nothing.

So, the running dog needs a bright, prominent eye though the colour of the eye is immaterial. It needs a long jaw and sufficient breadth of skull for anchorage of strong jaw muscles; the 'bite' must be level, neither over- nor under-shot, to give a firm grip. It needs a long, strong neck, not only for snatching at its prey at speed but also because the top of the neck forms the anchorage for the long muscles which pull the front legs forward.

Speed in the running dog depends on the length of its stride and the rapidity of that stride. Length of stride depends on the ability to reach out as far as possible with the fore-legs. How far the dog can reach out depends on the angle of the *scapular* — the shoulder blade. As in many joints, there is a limited amount of extension in the joint between the *scapular* and the *humerus,* the joint at the point of the shoulder. If the *scapular* is upright the *humerus* will slope backwards, forward movement is restricted and the stride will be short. If the *scapular* slopes backwards, the *humerus* will be more upright and the stride will be longer since the fore-legs will be thrown further forward. To complete the long stride the hind legs must be brought well forward under the body. For this to be done the measurement from hip to hock must be long since length here allows for the long muscles needed for leverage. The third component of the long stride is the back. Of two whippets, the one with a long back and shorter legs will have a longer stride than the one which is higher off the ground with a shorter back. The rapidity of the stride depends not only on the dog's fitness, the working of the heart, lungs and muscles, but also on courage, determination and the instinct to kill; attributes that are not easily judged in the show ring.

Balance, and the power to turn and twist after prey, depend on a strong back and loin — both are compatible with a long back — and a long, muscular tail; watch a coursing dog turning and stopping and see how it uses its tail as a rudder and balancing pole. Stamina depends not only on the stride being as smooth and easy as possible but also on there being enough room for heart and lungs. This room can be obtained by breadth of chest, depth of chest or the two combined. The very broad chest of the bull terrier — the fighting dog — gives the dog a rolling action since the shoulder blade and elbow, sliding back along barrel ribs, are pushed outwards. In the running dog, the action of the shoulder and elbow must be straight forward and backward, so the necessary room for heart and lungs must be obtained by *depth* of chest and the depth must be between the forelegs.

If the running dog cannot remain sound he cannot run, and soundness depends on good feet; feet that have to carry his weight over all sorts of going from smooth grass to rough, frozen plough, at speeds of between thirty and forty miles an hour. The foot must be compact and tight, not

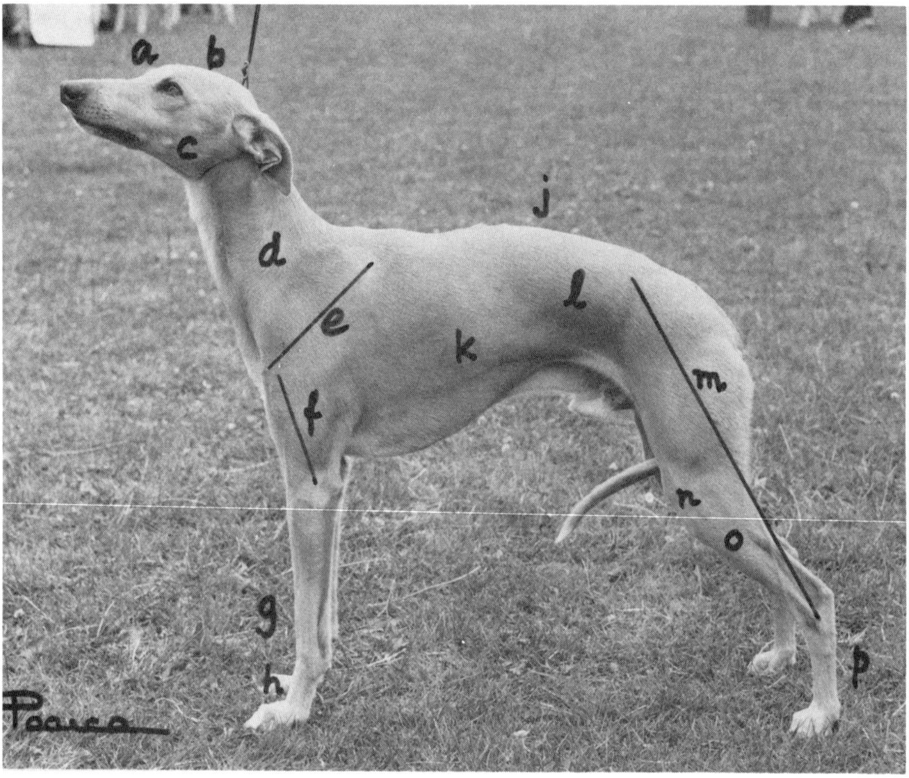

14. *The points of a good whippet: a. large bright eye; b. broad skull; c. strong jaw; d. muscular neck; e. sloping shoulder; f. upright humerus; g. good bone down to the foot; h. sloping pasterns; j. arched back; k. well-sprung ribs; l. powerful loin; m. long from hip to hock; n. bent stifle; o. well-developed second thigh; p. hock vertically above heel. (Diane Pearce)*

flat and loose; worst of all is the foot which looks like a hand placed on a table, palm down and the fingers spread out. Nor is the opposite wanted, the foot that is too bunched; this foot has no elasticity.

Having seen what is wanted in the running dog, of whatever size, let us look at the Standard for the whippet.

The Whippet Standard

General Appearance

Should convey an impression of beautifully balanced muscular power and strength, combined with great elegance and grace of outline. Symmetry of outline, muscular development and powerful gait are the main considerations; the dog being built for speed and work, all forms of exaggeration should be avoided. The dog should possess great freedom of action, the forelegs should be thrown forward and low over the ground like a thoroughbred horse, not in a Hackney-like action. Hind legs should come well

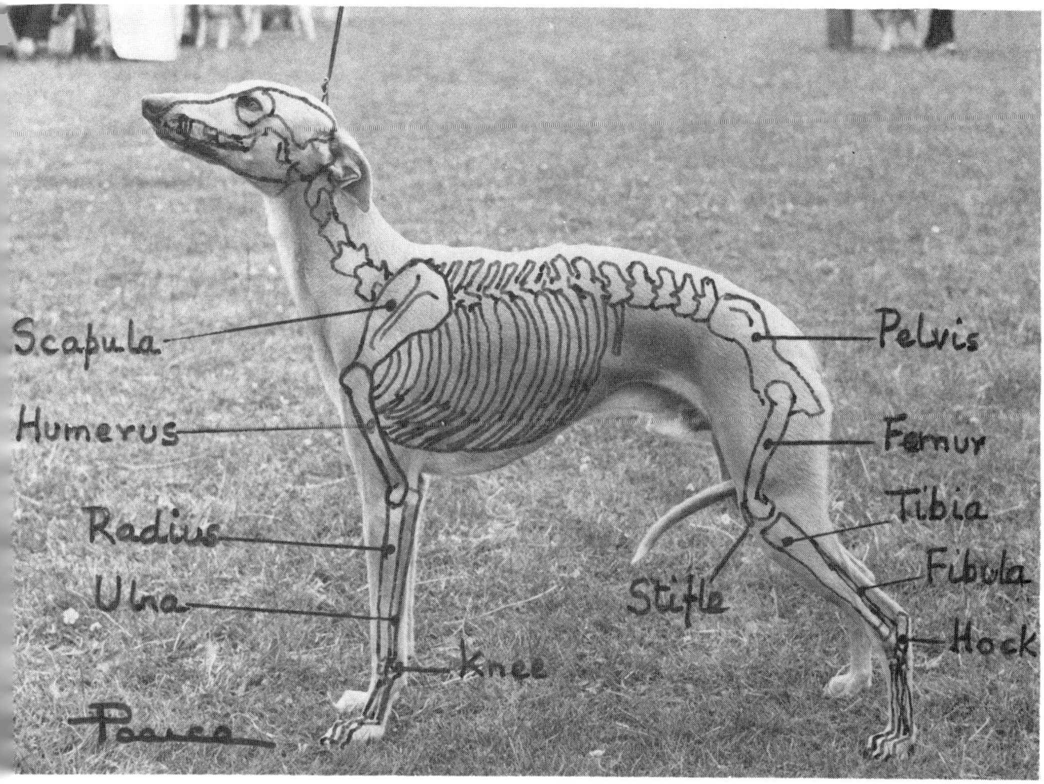

15. *The main bones of the whippet's skeleton. (Diane Pearce)*

under the body giving great propelling power, general movement not to look stilted, high-stepping or in a short mincing manner.

Note the words 'balanced muscular power and strength', then look at almost any whippet show and see how many dogs are hard and muscled up and how many are soft and flabby. Again, note the words 'movement not to look stilted, high-stepping or in a mincing manner', and watch how many whippets move in the ring. We can only assume that some whippet exhibitors never ask anyone else to lead their whippets about so that they can see for themselves how they move, because bad movement is one of the serious faults in show whippets today. If you are not certain what good movement is, watch an afternoon's racing on television from a course such as Ascot or Cheltenham where class horses are running. Listen to the commentator (usually an ex-champion jockey) describing the runners in the paddock and if he says 'doesn't he move well', watch that horse carefully. He will walk as described in the whippet Standard, 'the forelegs thrown well forward and low over the ground'. Then try and watch a driving class at a local horse show, or on television, where there are some Hackneys in action. They are very spectacular, lifting their knees almost up to their chins; as carriage horses who do their work at the trot their high-stepping action answers perfectly but they cannot gallop. So, the whippet Standard says, 'not a Hackney-like action'.

HEAD AND SKULL

Long and lean; flat on top tapering to the muzzle, rather wide between the eyes, the jaws powerful and clean-cut, the nose black. In blues, a bluish colour is permitted. In livers, a nose of the same colour, in whites or parti-colours a butterfly nose is permissible.

EYES

Bright; expression very alert.

EARS

Rose shaped; small and fine in texture.

MOUTH

Level, the teeth in the top jaw fitting closely over the teeth in the bottom jaw.

Greyhound people say that a dog does not run on its head, and we in England are accused by the Americans of not stressing head properties as much as they do. Certainly a handsome head does finish off the picture for a show dog. The nose is narrow since only an average sense of smell is needed but the jaw must be long, the jaw muscles strong and the teeth must meet correctly for a firm hold. There is one important qualification and that is that a dog's head must look masculine and a bitch's head should look feminine. There are few worse things than a whippet dog with a snipey, bitchy, narrow head; it must be masculine looking, relatively broad between the eyes and broadening at the back of the skull. A bitch's head should be finer but there is no objection to a bitch having a broad head.

There is no colour mentioned for the eyes and, whilst many people prefer a dark eye for aesthetic reasons, a light eye is not a fault. Many birds and animals that hunt by sight have light eyes and, certainly, some of the hardest and most determined dogs I have had had tawny eyes. Provided that the ears are not large, pricked or coarse they are not important compared with the other points of the whippet.

NECK

Long and muscular, elegantly arched.

Length and strength are needed for picking up prey and, since the top of the neck forms the anchorage for the long muscles which pull the front legs forward, the top line of the neck will — or should — look longer than

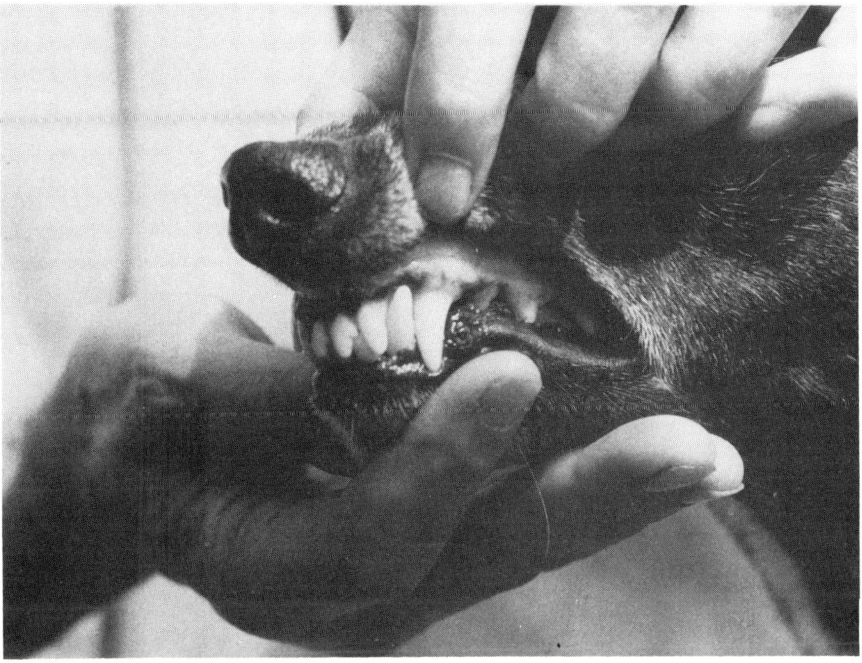

16. *'Mouth level, the teeth of the top jaw fitting closely over the teeth in the bottom jaw'. (Walsh)*

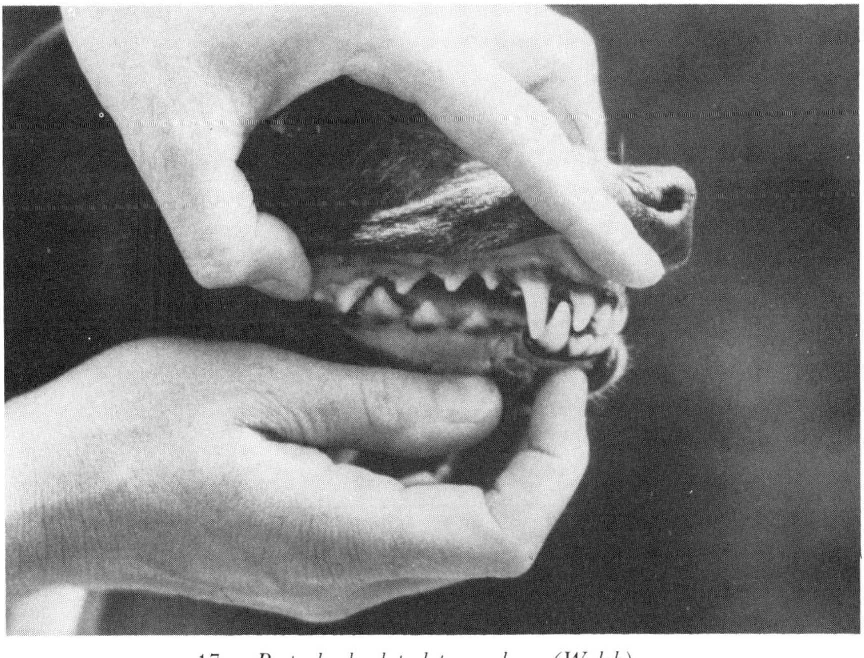

17. *Properly developed pre-molars. (Walsh)*

the bottom line. This is difficult to see if the dog's head is pulled up too high by the lead when being exhibited or photographed.

FOREQUARTERS

Shoulders oblique, the blades carried up to the spine, closely set together at the top. Forelegs straight and upright, front not too wide, pasterns strong with slight spring, elbows well set under body.

We have already explained the reason for a sloping shoulder blade. A chest that is too wide will push the elbows outwards but the chest must not be so narrow that both front legs look as if they come out of the same hole. Viewed from the front, the muscles above the elbow should appear to bulge out over the foreleg, the elbows must not turn out or in and the feet must point straight to the front. Spring of pastern is important as a dog which is running at speed, twisting and turning, often over rough ground, needs this spring to act as a shock-absorber. A straight pastern is often finished off by round, cat, feet which, again, are a fault; they do not enable a dog to grip the ground and retain its balance at speed. 'Tied elbows', set too closely into the body, with or without the front feet being turned outwards, are a serious fault as the dog cannot turn at speed if the elbows are so placed.

BODY

Chest very deep with plenty of heart room, brisket deep and well-defined, back broad, firm, somewhat long and showing definite arch over the loin but not humped; loin giving impression of great strength and power, ribs well sprung. Well muscled on back.

However good the forequarters and hind quarters, they are joined together by the back and if the back is weak the dog cannot gallop. The back of a galloping dog bends and stretches like a very pliable bow (see Plate 22). Much of this movement is carried out by the great dorsal muscles on either side of the spine and it is these muscles that should give the back an arch. A roach back — a skeletal malformation where the hump starts behind the shoulder — or a flat back, are weaknesses.

HINDQUARTERS

Strong and broad across thighs, stifles well bent, hocks well let down, second thigh strong, the dog being able to stand over a lot of ground and show great driving power.

The hindquarters are where the thrust comes from. Since they propel the dog forward at every stride, weak quarters with lack of muscular development mean that the dog cannot gallop. Viewed from behind, the upper thigh muscles should be large, well formed and hard, and the second

18. *a. and b. 'Ears rose shaped when alert, small and fine in texture'. The correct ear carriage is as shown and ears should not be pricked. (Walsh)*

thighs — between stifle and hock — should be well developed. The stifle must not be straight; there must be sufficient angulation for the upper thigh to appear vertical and for the second thigh — the tibia — to slope at about 140 degrees from the vertical. When the dog is standing naturally the hock should be vertically above the heel. From behind, the hocks should be parallel to the centre line of the dog. In the case of a very powerful dog the stifle may turn outwards and the hock turn inwards as the dog moves off, particularly at the trot. What the hocks must not do is turn outwards.

FEET

Very neat, well split up between the toes, knuckles arched, pads thick and strong.

The ideal foot is the foot that is strongest and most resistant to injury. The bad, splayed, weak foot will never produce a sound dog. Bad feet are a serious hereditary fault but even good feet can deteriorate in adverse rearing conditions.

TAIL

No feathering, long, tapering; when in action carried in a delicate upward curve but not over the back.

There is a rule-of-thumb amongst coursing people that a long tail means a fast dog. In greyhounds and lurchers one should be able to pull the tail through the hind legs and up over the spine. In the whippet it should at least reach to the hip bone.

COAT

Fine, short, as close as possible in texture.

A coarse coat and skin, whilst it may not stop the dog from working well, does detract from the overall quality which the breed should present. The whippet is, pre-eminently, a thoroughbred and the quality of the coat and skin should bear witness to this.

COLOUR

Any colour or mixture of colour.

Since the Standard permits any colour or combination of colours, including the recessive colours of blue and cream, it would be quite illogical to forbid the eye colouring which goes with those colours, i.e., in blues a slatey grey, in creams and golds pale gold or light hazel to tone with the coat colour.

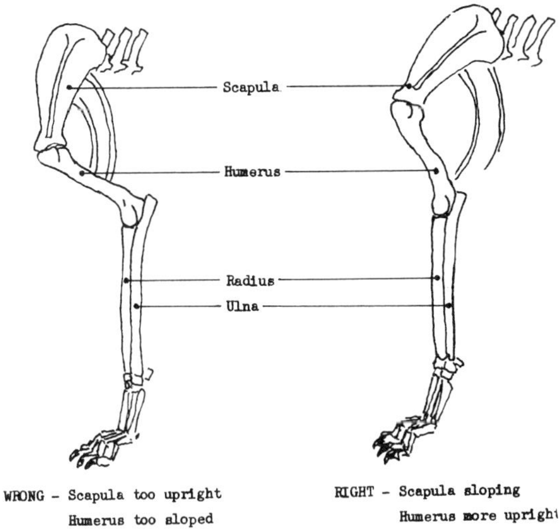

19. *The bones of the whippet's foreleg. (Walsh)*

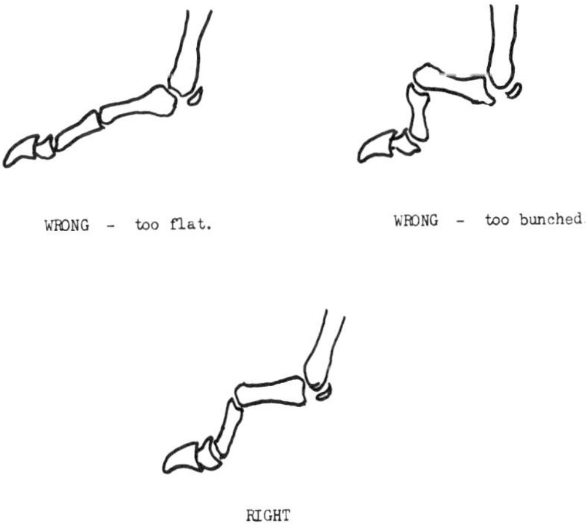

20. *The bones of the whippet's foot. (Walsh)*

WEIGHT AND SIZE

The ideal height for dogs is 18½ inches and for bitches 17½ inches. Judges should use their discretion and not unduly penalise an otherwise good specimen.

This is the part of the Standard which is most confusing to the novice since a quick glance at any show ring reveals that whippets of 18½ inches and 17½ inches are rarely exhibited today. The average dog is between

21. *Whippet movement at the trot: the front foot is thrown forward low over the ground, demonstrating full extension from a well-laid shoulder. Powerful drive comes from the stifle and hock. Note the amount of ground covered whilst retaining a good top-line and correct tail carriage. (Walsh)*

19½ and 20½ inches and the bitches between 18½ and 19½ inches. The Whippet Coursing Club has a height limit of 20 inches and the W.C.R.A. has a height limit of 21 inches. The ultimate criterion must be a balanced dog of average size. Over 20 inches, whippets begin to lose their breed characteristics and both look, and gallop, like greyhounds (see Plate 11).

Weight depends very much on the amount of bone a whippet carries; finely boned dogs without sufficient body will weigh lighter than smaller more solidly made dogs. Average weight for a 19½ inch dog would be about 24 to 26 lbs and for an 18½ inch bitch about 20 to 21 lbs.

22. *a. and b. When galloping, a whippet's spine bends and stretches like a bow. (Walsh)*

Faults

FRONT AND SHOULDERS
Weak, sloping or too straight pasterns, pigeon toes, tied elbows, loaded or bossy shoulders, wide on top and straight shoulder blades, flat sides. An exaggerated narrow front should not be encouraged.

HEAD AND SKULL
Apple head, short foreface or down face.

MOUTH
Over- or under-shot.

NECK
Throatiness at the join of neck and jaw or at base of neck.

BODY AND HINDQUARTERS
Short-coupled or cramped stance, an exaggerated arch, a camel or humped back (the arch starting behind the shoulder blades), a too short or over-long loin, straight stifles; poor muscular development of thighs and second thighs.

FEET
Splayed, flat or open.

TAIL
Gay, ringed, short or docked.

COAT
Wire or broken coat, a coarse or woolly coat, coarse, thick skin.

Perhaps the most prevalent faults in the breed today are those which result from breeders and exhibitors not requiring their dogs to fulfil any function in the field. Many show dogs are never let off the lead and never allowed to gallop, let alone chase anything. Hence the number of whippets which have stilted, Hackney action in front, wide, straddling movement behind, slab sides, narrow fronts, poor bone, straight pasterns and splayed feet. On the credit side almost all have good heads, necks, eyes, ears, fine coats and glamorous markings but what good are these points if the functional qualities are lost?

CHAPTER 3

The Show Whippet

TYPES OF SHOWS

Dog showing has become a great English pastime and English show stock is justly famous all over the world. All through the summer there are shows of every sort, size and description, up and down the country, and to a certain extent this activity continues through the winter as well. English dog shows for pedigree dogs fall into five categories and if you intend to compete in this field it is important to understand the different types of shows and the kind of award and prestige each will give you and your dog.

Exemption Shows

These are so-called because they are 'exempted' from Kennel Club rules in some respects, although licensed by the Kennel Club and held under their auspices. They are usually held in conjunction with some local fete, flower show, or gymkhana, and they are permitted to schedule only four classes for pedigree dogs. The other classes are at the discretion of the show committee and are likely to be classes such as 'Dog with the waggiest tail' or 'Dog the Judge would most like to take home', etc. They are generally judged by an All-rounder (that is, a Judge who is passed by the Kennel Club to judge a number of breeds, as opposed to what is called a 'Breed Specialist' who has great experience of one breed only.) These exemption shows are happy occasions for all the family and the competition, even in the pedigree classes, is chiefly confined to family pets, or dogs who happen to find themselves at the event. Entries are taken by the Secretary on the field and proceedings are much more informal than at other types of shows. It is generally considered rather poor form to show a dog which is regularly exhibited at the higher levels since this spoils the happy day out for local people who like to enter their pets for this type of show.

23. *Best Dog and Bitch, and finally BOB. Mrs 'Poppy' Martin judging at Three Counties Championship Show, 1958. Mr F. Jones with Ch. Robmaywin Stargazer of Allways (BOB and BIS overall), and Mrs F. Jones with Ch. Robmaywin Quicksilver of Allways. Best Dog and Best Bitch should, if possible, be the masculine and feminine editions of each other, perfectly demonstrated here. (Cooke)*

Sanction Shows

These are run by Canine Societies and, more rarely, by Breed Clubs. No dog is eligible for exhibition which has won a Challenge Certificate or any award which counts towards the title of Champion under the rules of any governing body recognized by the Kennel Club. No classes higher than Post Graduate may be scheduled at Sanction shows. These little shows are quite often held in the evening and can be an enjoyable social event, affording pleasure and experience to local members and providing excellent training ground for novice exhibitors and young stock. They are not as frequently held nowadays as they used to be, perhaps since the classification available does restrict the entry.

Limited Shows

These are limited in two senses, (1) as in Sanction shows, no dog which has won a Challenge Certificate or any award which counts towards the title of Champion may enter and (2) entries are limited to members of the Breed Club or Society which is holding the show. Most Breed Clubs run one Limited show yearly and despite the fact that Challenge Certificate winners are debarred, Breed Club Limited shows can present quite a wide choice of the breed for inspection. Limited shows need not be 'benched' thus the dogs do not have to spend the time at the show sitting on officially numbered benches but can lie at the ring-side, or indeed, sit on their owner's lap throughout the proceedings which can be quite an advantage to a young puppy attending its first show. To the aspiring judge of the breed an invitation to judge a Limited show for a Breed Club affords the best possible preparation for eventually judging at a higher level, since the classification approximates to that of a Championship show, and, numerically, the entry received will be of similar proportions. There is all the difference in the world in judging an entry of 100 or so in 16 classes and in judging 6 classes of mixed sex at an Open Show.

Open Shows

These can be run by Agricultural Societies in conjunction with their main agricultural show or by Canine Societies, or by the Breed Clubs. They are, as the title denotes, open to all, and Champions may enter. With the exception of the Breed Club Open shows they do not generally have a very large classification; anything from 4 to 12 classes, chiefly for both sexes, are usual. They also schedule what are called 'Variety' classes, judged again by an All-rounder, in which all breeds may compete against each other after the breed judging is completed. Wins at Open shows do not count towards the title of Champion since Challenge Certificates (known as CCs) are not on offer, nor do wins at Open shows qualify for Crufts, but each class win at an Open show contributes one point towards gaining a Junior Warrant. It is often a slightly different type of dog which does most of the winning at Open shows. Classes at these shows are frequently judged by All-rounders who may be judging other breeds as well or by Novice judges of the breed who are gaining experience; placings, where there is an entry of mixed sex and age at this type of show, are not of great significance in comparison to placings under a breed specialist judge at Championship shows, or at Open or Limited shows for the breed. It is more important to win a Junior class against a good entry of other juniors in the breed

24. *Another case of brother and sister emerging on top. Ch. Allgarth Envoy with his breeder, Mr F. Moore, and Ch. Allgarth Eidelweiss with Mrs Patsy Nicholas. Both gained their first CCs under the Author at the Whippet Club of Scotland Show, 1975. Envoy was BIS. (Vavasour)*

than to win a class at Open show level. On the other hand, many exhibitors are not especially interested in gaining the top awards, nor, with all the effort and expense involved, in campaigning a dog to the top; for this type of exhibitor the Open shows provide a good day out, a chance to visit some interesting places and to see friends, and all at considerably less cost than is involved in entering a Championship show. But should you be lucky enough to have a dog which is of championship class then its chances may easily be spoilt by over-entering at Open shows where it will suffer the knocks and tedium that will do its final career no good. Open shows are usually benched with the exception of Breed Club Open shows, which are exempt from this regulation.

Championship Shows

These are the most important events in the exhibitor's diary. Championship shows are those at which the Kennel Club Challenge Certificates are on offer for the breed; in brief, shows where there is a chance of making up a Champion. All awards at Championship shows are important in that

25. *Ch. Dondelayo Reinette, handled to her Group and BIS wins at Three Counties Show and the Welsh Kennel Club Show by owner/breeder, Mrs Anne Knight. (Whimpanny)*

certain class wins qualify for Crufts and each class win gains 3 points towards a Junior Warrant. Placings in the two top classes (the Limit and Open classes) qualify for entry into the Kennel Club Stud Book, which is published yearly and is a record of all wins at this level plus all Challenge Certificate and Reserve Certificate winners, thus being the official record of awards made under Kennel Club rules to pedigree dogs.

The Challenge Certificate is the most important award a dog or bitch can win. They are the property of the Kennel Club and may only be awarded by Judges of whom the Kennel Club has officially approved. This approval is not automatic, even in the case of judges who have previously issued Challenge Certificates. For every Championship show (including the Breed Club Championship shows) the Committee must submit to the Kennel Club the names of those whom they have invited to judge the breeds with Challenge Certificates on offer for Kennel Club approval and publication in the official Kennel Club Gazette. It is also the Kennel Club prerogative, based on the strength of the different breeds as reflected by numbers of Kennel Club Registrations and show entries to allocate sets of Challenge Certificates to the various shows which apply to them under

26. *Mrs D. Cleeve with Ch. Dragonhill Silver Ripple, and Mr C. H. Douglas Todd with Ch. Wingedfoot Wild Goose, at the Whippet Club Championship Show, 1956. The Judge was Mr Burrows. (Goater)*

licence. Different breeds have varying numbers of Challenge Certificates available each year depending on breed strength. Whippets were allocated 35 sets of certificates in 1982, comprising certificates at every general Championship show, two Group Championship shows, and 7 Breed Club Championship shows. In order to gain the title of Champion a dog must win three Challenge Certificates under three different judges, one of which must be won over the age of 12 months. On the Challenge certificate the Judge states that it is his opinion that the dog in question 'is of such outstanding merit as to be clearly worthy of the title of Champion'. The Reserve Challenge Certificate states that, in the event of the winner of the Challenge Certificate winner being disqualified, the same criterion shall apply to the winner of the Reserve Certificate. It is the duty of the judge to withhold the award of the Challenge Certificate if in his opinion there is no dog of such merit present on the day. Championship shows fall into several categories:-

General Championship Shows

These are often run in conjunction with the large Agricultural or Municipal shows. They will cater for all recognized breeds of pedigree dogs and each

27. *Leicester Championship Show, 1967. Mrs D. U. McKay with Int. Ch. Laguna Leisure and Mrs D. Cleeve with Ch. Dragonhill Tawny Owl. The Judge was Mr Norman Odell. (Cooke)*

breed will have 12 to 16 classes scheduled and Challenge Certificates will be on offer for those breeds to whom the Kennel Club have allocated them, which will be most of the breeds scheduled. Breeds for which Challenge Certificates are not available will compete in Variety classes under the heading 'Not Separately Classified' and a Best of Breed will be declared who will compete in the final stages against the other Best of Breeds.

Breed Club Championship Shows

These are run by the individual Breed Clubs for the breed alone, and they very often attract the cream of the entry since they schedule a more generous classification (ie, more classes) than the General Championship shows, and are usually very careful in their selection of experienced breed experts as judges.

Group Championship Shows

These are run on the same general lines as the General Championship shows but cater only for the breeds within a group, for instance the Hound Group. There are two Hound Group Championship shows, the Hound Association and the Border Counties Hound Club. Group shows fall somewhat between the previous two categories since they are much smaller than the General shows although larger than the Breed shows and they offer many advantages

28. *Ch. Beseeka Knight Errant of Silkstone, Hound Group Winner at Crufts. (Diane Pearce)*

to members of their group, including generous classification and prize money, and also interesting variety classes for Brace, Team, Progeny, Veteran and Champion Parades, all of which are of great interest to Hound enthusiasts.

The Awards System

At all shows in this country, of whatever level, the procedure for judging and the system of awards is exactly the same. Classes are scheduled according to the level of show and the sort of entry likely to be received, but the procedure will be the same, whatever the difference in classification. Classes must be judged in the order in which they appear in the schedule, starting from the Minor Puppy class, Puppy, Junior, Novice, etc, through to the Open class. In each show schedule it will be explained which classes, restricted by previous wins, are open to your dog. Those classes which are restricted by age, i.e. Minor Puppy, Puppy, Junior and Special Yearling, are exactly what they state — open to all dogs of that age regardless of any previous wins. The classes which are restricted by previous wins are Maiden, Novice, Tyro, Debutant, Undergraduate, Graduate, Post Graduate, Minor Limit, Mid Limit, Limit and Open, the last being the only class which Champions may enter. Consequently you must check the schedule carefully before entering because Limit, Open and Championship shows differ in the restrictions at different levels. Wins at Open or Limited show level do not necessarily prevent a dog competing in certain classes

29. *Knight Errant's daughter, Ch. Jubilant Lady of Tygreen and Lowerdon. Amongst her many wins was the Hound Group at Crufts, under Mrs Garrish (Garwood)*

at Championship shows but wins at Championship level may make a dog ineligible for smaller shows. Special classes are those which are restricted by height, or colour, or age such as Veteran, or in the case of classes for Special Beginners, by whether the dog and/or the handler have ever won a Challenge certificate, or in some cases, a first prize. The classes will be marked in the Judge's Book in the same order in which they appear in the schedule and they will be judged in that order. Once the dog classes have been judged the Steward will call into the ring all the 'unbeaten' dogs (that is, dogs which have won their class and not been beaten in any subsequent class) and these will be judged against each other to find a Best Dog, and then a Best Bitch, and finally a Best of Breed. At Championship shows (and at many Club Limited and Open shows provided there are no mixed special classes at the end) the Best Dog will be judged after the dog classes and before the judge starts the bitch classes. In each case the pattern will be the same. The judge will first look at the class all together in the ring. The whole class will then be moved round the ring. The judge will then examine each dog individually, either on a table or on the ground, and then move each dog separately. He will finally take another look at the whole class, possibly move some or all of them again and then place his winners, First, Second, Third, Reserve and Very Highly Commended, in order, in the centre of the ring. If the judge does not consider that there are any dogs present worthy of a first prize (or indeed any award) he can, and indeed should, withhold the prizes, or any such prize, explaining to

30. *'Judging to type'. Mr C. H. Douglas Todd judging at Bournemouth, 1953. Ch. Fieldspring Bartsia of Allways with Mrs M. R. Jones, and Ch. Dragonhill Silver Ripple with Mrs D. Cleeve. (Cooke)*

the exhibitors that he has done so and marking his Judging Book accordingly.

Once a judge has decided which is the Best Whippet, depending on the level of show, that dog or bitch will be Best in Show or Best of Breed. At a Breed Club show the award will be BIS as there is no further competition. At an Open show the BOB will then compete either in the Hound Group (if the show is judged on the 'Group' system and nowadays most are) or simply for BIS with all other BOBs. To win a Group at an Open show, and even more important, at a Championship show, is a prestigious win. Opinions vary as to how important Group wins are. Many breeders feel that to reach the top of the breed under a breed specialist judge is the most important thing and that to be judged against other breeds in a Group, possibly by a judge whose knowledge of the breed may be minimal, means very little. What a Group win does demonstrate, however, is that the dog or bitch in question is not only a fair specimen of the breed but capable of standing out in general competition against other breeds. In general this

31 *'What a lovely line-up'. Chs Dragonhill Silver Ripple, En for Nonsense and Silver Sprite of Allways in 1953.*

is not an easy feat for a whippet since they are not particularly impressive seen against some of the larger and more coated breeds, nor are they expected to demonstrate a great deal of fire or personality in the process of exhibition. All a whippet need do in the show ring is to stand in a balanced, graceful position and to move freely and willingly when asked to do so. Perhaps this is why a whippet has yet to achieve the distinction of going Best in Show at Crufts, although a number of whippets have beaten all opposition at other Championship shows.

Junior Warrant

The award of a Junior Warrant is rather a curious one. It is a Kennel Club award and Junior Warrant winners are published in the Breed Record Supplement of the Kennel Gazette, though not, oddly enough, any longer in the Stud Book as was previously the case. Unlike the title of Champion the letters JW are not used after or before a dog's name. A Junior Warrant is awarded when a dog or bitch has won 25 or more points before the age of 18 months. The points are made up of 3 points for each class win at a Championship show and 1 point for each class win at an Open show. When the dog has achieved the necessary 25 points the owner must write to the Kennel Club who will issue a Junior Warrant form on which the details of all wins must be entered. Once the form is completed and returned to the Kennel Club the Junior Warrant will be forwarded. While it is pleasing to have gained a Junior Warrant it cannot be said to be a very important award. If the points are gained at Championship shows in the normal course of events one can congratulate oneself and the dog; if, on the other hand, it is necessary to rush from show to show to attempt to amass the requisite points the damage to a young show prospect may far outweigh the honour of the award. Gaining a Junior Warrant could simply mean that a puppy was born at the right time of year, or that there was

32. *The Author judging at the Richmond Championship Dog Show; looking at an entry from a distance. (Walsh)*

very little opposition in the early classes, or that the owner attended one show a week for a year, or that the puppy was too mature too early. Whilst many dogs whose show careers have subsequently proved to be spectacular have gained their Junior Warrants it is certainly also true that the vast majority of Junior Warrant holders are never heard of again once they leave their Puppy and Junior classes behind them.

The making of a Champion

This is surely what showing dogs is all about. The very word 'Champion' has a mystique all its own. In Britain, a Champion is a dog which has won three Challenge Certificates under three different judges, one certificate of which must have been won over the age of one year; not a problem which generally besets whippets, since they are not an early maturing breed. It may sound an easy thing to win three Challenge Certificates, but in fact, in whippets where competition is almost always extremely hot, to achieve

33. *Examining the dog on the table. (Walsh)*

three Challenge Certificates is no mean feat. It is generally admitted that it is more difficult to attain Champion status in England than elsewhere in the world, not simply because of the generally large entries, or the high quality of the opposition, but because the system of awards in England permit full-Champions to be exhibited once they have gained their titles. This means that an up-and-coming youngster has to beat all the established winners as well as those of his peers whom he might naturally meet. In most other countries in the world Champions compete for the Best of Breed only, and non-Champions, below that level, gain awards towards their titles by their wins at the lower level. While our system may be out of line with many other countries there can be no doubt that it tends to a higher overall standard if youngsters have to beat the best of the generation before them whilst on the way up. It also means that if a breed is falling down in overall excellence it only needs comparison with one or two of the best dogs of preceding years to point out the discrepancy.

34. *Watching movement. (Walsh)*

Campaigning a Champion to the title can be an exacting and expensive business. While novices can and do make up Champions in our breed, they are more likely to fall by the wayside than the experienced breeder and exhibitor, not because their dog is less worthy, and not, as is very often imagined, because their face is unknown, but simply because, since they are novices, they do not have the experience to seize the opportunity when it arises. There is a good deal of skill in knowing just when and where to present a dog, let alone in knowing how to present it at the very peak of fitness and form. Even the simple business of which classes to enter at specific shows involves skill and experience. Novices are inclined to go to a show and when they see a seasoned exhibitor winning the top award say 'Of course she was bound to win because...'. She was indeed bound to win, but not for the reasons the novice imagined. She won because she had the right dog for that judge on that day, in the right condition and

35. *Competitors 'stack' their dogs. (Walsh)*

performing to perfection, the achieving of which is something experience alone can teach.

So, how do you set about it? Our purpose is to try and give to newcomers to our breed the help and support in each aspect of breed activity which we have ourselves received from breeders in the past, and in no field is this more important than in the campaigning of a champion. Firstly, let us suppose that you have acquired or bred a puppy which is of sufficiently high standard to gain its title. The prerequisite is of some importance since a great deal of time and money can be wasted campaigning stock which may well be typical and up to winning at Open show level but which is not of Championship standard. But let us suppose that your puppy has the potential to go to the top. Secondly, you must realise that there are no short cuts in this or any other competitive field. Dogs mature slowly and every stage contributes to the whole. It is probable that your potentially

36. *'Bring in yours, please'. (Walsh)*

top winner will not be spectacular at six months or nine months or even 15 months. All you should expect in the early stages is that your puppy is sufficiently correct in all essentials to gain a place in Puppy classes. You will probably be beaten by puppies, which, while they look more rounded and finished at nine months, will be of no trouble to you at all in the higher classes later on. At this stage you want to select your judges carefully, since it is vital not to over-show or over-expose a promising youngster. A Club Limited or Open show would be a good place to gain the first experience. After that, pick half-a-dozen carefully selected Championship shows with judges who are knowledgeable breed specialists. Avoid like the plague any judge who has the reputation of handling puppies roughly since this experience can set your puppy back. At this point you should be quite happy with the occasional win and second or third placings in your classes. At the first few shows, entry in only one class will be quite sufficient since every class takes something out of a puppy.

At nine months you can start entering two classes, Puppy and Maiden, or Puppy and Novice, which will be useful Junior Warrant points should you manage to win. Try and avoid winning a first out of Puppy classes at an Open show so as to be eligible for a Maiden class at a Championship Show, and observe the same tactics over Novice. A good puppy will be ineligible for the Novice class very quickly and there is then a large jump at most Championship shows to Junior and Post Graduate. It is easy to tell if you are overdoing the shows; a puppy which is overshown, too many classes, too many shows, too many long journeys, begins to look tight in its coat, and condition and muscle fall away; it gets a leggy, scraggy look, and ceases to show with the sort of friendly pleasure of the early days. A real rest is indicated should this happen; no shows for at least a month or six weeks and it is a good idea to let a puppy rest, eat and put on some surplus weight. Rather like a race-horse which has been trained over the top, a whippet puppy which has been overshown needs to be let right down, allowed to get fat and soft, and then gradually brought back up into condition again.

None of this will be necessary if you are sensible in the first place. By the time your puppy is out of Puppy classes and into Junior you may have a moment of depression. There is a great deal of difference in development in a whippet of 17 months and one of just 12 months. Junior can be a very competitive class, and indeed, can include dogs with CCs or RCCs, so it is probable that your puppy, who should now be in what is known as the 'legs and wings' stage, will look very babyish in this class. It is quite a good moment to have a rest from shows at this point and to allow a little development to continue unhindered. Remember that throughout this testing time your puppy will have needed plenty of the best; lots of free exercise, lots of fresh air and good food, but nothing too taxing. No road

37. *The Judge stands back to compare each dog. (Walsh)*

walking, no coursing or racing, just the amount of exercise a young dog which is still growing would naturally give itself.

Now your serious business will really begin. If development has gone according to plan at 16/18 months you should have a dog who is beginning to fill out and to give you glimpses of what the final picture is likely to be. At this stage you should be able to win Junior Classes and to be capable of going BIS or Reserve BIS at a Breed Club Limited show. At this point BOB at Open shows are a waste of time and all energies should be concentrated in the field that really counts — the Championship shows. You are beginning to think about an RCC and to that end it will be a better policy to enter one class only at a Championship show rather than be beaten in a subsequent class by older exhibits. When a judge comes to look for an RCC winner a youngster from the Junior class may well stand a good chance in the challenge. With the first RCC you may feel that your paws are at last on the bottom rung of the ladder, but now comes the tricky bit. Your puppy is out of Junior and looking well, but many a good dog has never been heard of again once in the grave-yard of the huge Post Graduate classes; especially is this true of bitches. It takes a great deal of winning to get out of Post Graduate (5 first prizes at Championship

38. *The Ring Steward hands out rosettes while the Judge makes notes for her report. (Walsh)*

shows in Post Graduate Classes and upwards) and by the time you have achieved that your whippet might be eligible for the Veteran class. The guiding rule here must be the state of development of your dog or bitch. Take a good hard look at your future Champion, and if you feel that a little more time is needed to finish maturing, then enter Post Graduate. After a win or two you can move up the scale to Limit.

The object of exhibiting dogs is to attract the judge's attention in order to win, and to that end it can make a difference which class you enter. Clearly it is counterproductive to enter a high class for which your dog is not sufficiently mature but on the other hand a minor placing in a good class can often mean more than a win at a lower level. The decision whether to go up to the higher classes and when is a vital one in campaigning, and the word 'campaigning' is self-explanatory in this context. In theory you can move a dog up through the classes counting yourself out of each class as the wins mount up, but in practice, unless you spend every moment of your spare time at dog shows, you will almost certainly find that your dog is ready for Limit or Open before it has won its way out of Post Graduate, if only because you will in fact have won a CC. The other factor is that showing has become so expensive that one cannot afford to attend every Championship show, nor would it benefit the dog to do so; consequently you must use your judgement over this point. It is also now very important whether you win or lose; at this stage in a dog's career never waste time exhibiting under a speculative judge; wait for the moment when there is the prospect of a judge who is likely to appreciate your dog, make sure that you present it right at the top of its form, and hope for the best.

Once you have achieved the first CC the requisite further two do not automatically follow, but perhaps the largest fence is behind you. It is not quite true that judges are like sheep but some do prefer to add CCs to ones already obtained and are apt to lack the courage or discrimination to give top honours to a new one. This is where experience really counts. It is impossible for the novice who is new to the show scene to know which will be the judges most likely to appreciate their dog. Here you must take advice from someone with experience in the breed. One can, of course, always be wrong about what a certain judge is likely to put up but anyone who has been a consistent exhibitor over the years will be able to tell you the type of animal individual judges are likely to prefer, and those judges are the ones under whom you should enter. Never be afraid of being beaten by good ones; a second or third in a hot class under a knowledgeable judge will do your dog no harm and has no shame attached to it. A dog which is basically correct in all essentials should always be in the cards under discriminating judges but what you want to avoid, if possible, is the waste of time and effort, let alone money, of attending a show where your dog is simply not looked at. You must always remember that not even the best can win every time out, so you will have to learn to take the rough with the smooth even though you may know that your dog is of the standard to trouble those at the top.

If it is a bitch you are campaigning (always more difficult than a dog) you will have the further problem of whether and when to take her out of the ring to have a litter, which she may well need to fulfil her potential. There can be no hard and fast rule about this but general health and development must be the first consideration, and future good should always take precedence over short term gain. If your bitch is one who needs a litter (i.e., if she is the leggy, slow maturing type) her second season at about 22 months is an excellent time for her to absent herself from the ring. She will be out of the Junior class and too immature for the higher classes so that is a good moment for her to have time off to raise a family. In such a case she will be ready, after her litter, to return to the ring in the Limit class, looking magnificent, as bitches are apt to do after a litter, and she should then, with luck, have an uninterrupted run to her title. Another problem with bitches is that they very often look and show badly after they have been in season. There is nothing you can do about this. There can be no point in exhibiting them even under a favourable judge in this sort of condition, and I very strongly advise against any form of innoculation or hormone treatment to delay or prevent coming into season. Although many veterinary surgeons recommend such treatment there have been far too many instances of bitches who have been so treated proving difficult or impossible to get in whelp later on. No judge or prize on earth is worth the risking of your bitch's health — especially if you intend to breed from her later on. You will simply set yourself back years or generations if you find that you cannot carry on your planned line because of this factor.

Finally, if you are seriously campaigning towards a title, always advertise a good win. Many people do not plough through the small print of dog show reports and a good photograph combined with a carefully worded advertisement in the Dog Journals can alert future judges and people in general that you have a good dog which is doing well. As one breed authority has said, a win which is not advertised, didn't happen.

Cruft's Dog Show

The world's first 'officially recognized' dog show took place on June 28th/29th, 1859, in the Town Hall at Newcastle upon Tyne. Advertisements for this show appeared in The Field, May 28th, 1859. The Kennel Club itself was founded in 1873 and in 1886 Cruft's Show was promoted by Mr Charles Cruft. This first show was confined to terriers and attracted an entry of 570 dogs. Since those early days the show has become the official Kennel Club show, famous all the world over as being the most prestigious event for pedigree dogs. Crufts is run by a sub-committee of the Kennel Club and due to its official position, historical mystique and metropolitan venue, its position in the eyes of the general public is unlikely to be seriously challenged.

In recent years, in order to restrain an otherwise unwieldy entry to the limited confines of, first, Olympia and then Earls Court, the Crufts entry has been a restricted one. In 1934 Crufts' entry was 9,363. In 1982, with qualifications in force, the entry was 9,844. The qualifications take the form of only allowing entries at Crufts from dogs which have won a first prize during the preceding year at other Championship shows in certain specified classes. The system has changed slightly from year to year but at the time of writing only first prizes in Minor Puppy, Puppy, Junior, Post Graduate, Limit and Open are qualified to go to Crufts, with the addition, of course, of CC and RCC winners during the current year and full Champions of whatever date. This system has several obvious disadvantages. Firstly, a judge does not receive the entry that exhibitors might ordinarily make; that is to say, the entry is not composed of those dogs which the exhibitors consider the judge might appreciate, but of those dogs to whom some other judge has awarded a first prize. Secondly, that first prize might well have been won in a weak puppy class at a show with a numerically small entry where that particular puppy stood virtually alone in its class. This results in unworthy dogs being included in the entry. Thirdly, dogs entered in the two top classes who might well be CC or RCC winners from the previous year could be placed in the Limit or Open Class (which qualifies for entry for the Stud Book but not for Crufts) but would nonetheless be excluded from Crufts by not achieving a class win, thus denying spectators the satisfaction of viewing high-class representative stock which should be present at this show. Fourthly, the very high entry fees, lack of facilities for exhibitors, difficulties of travelling in early February, and absence of prize money all contribute to a certain lack of enthusiasm amongst exhibitors for Crufts. The result of all these factors is that, in recent years the whippet entry at Crufts has not been either particularly large or particularly representative of the breed; consequently, wins at Crufts, while they may signify great importance to the general public, may not be of great significance to exhibitors. To take the breed (BOB or the Group) or even a higher award at shows such as Windsor, Birmingham or Richmond may actually represent greater achievement than the same award at Crufts.

However, while these factors are all well-known to the seasoned campaigner, there is no doubt that the mystique of this show mentioned earlier leads the novice exhibitor and the general public to think that even a minor placing in an intermediate class at Crufts is the seal of success. The show does have an atmosphere and charm of its own quite separate from the activities in the breed rings. The sense of occasion, the trade stands, the Obedience and Agility classes, all add enormously to the rather special atmosphere of Crufts. Crufts is now held over three days rather than two, and this has added very considerably to the comfort of the exhibitors, although financially it would appear to have been a poor decision. But as long as dog shows continue so will Crufts, and whether it means a lot or very little indeed it will certainly continue to be the official premier show in the dog calendar.

Qualifying for Crufts

The need to qualify for Crufts becomes a sort of nightmare to some exhibitors. Rather like those who are determined to gain Junior Warrant points, some exhibitors will enter show after show attempting to qualify their dogs so that, regardless of the judge designate, or their dog's possible condition at the time, they will be able to exhibit at Crufts. A sense of proportion is essential in this respect. Any dog which is worth campaigning at Championship show level will qualify for Crufts many times over during the course of the year, but even so the same criteria for entering any other show should be applied to Crufts. Is it the right time to exhibit the dog in question, and is the appointed judge for Crufts likely to appreciate him? Qualifying for Crufts should not alter your plan of campaign at general Championship shows; enter the classes you would normally enter and if your dog is of Championship show standard it will qualify automatically. If it does not, you might ask yourself whether such a dog is really worth its entry fees at Championship shows, let alone at Crufts.

Whippets at Crufts

A whippet has never achieved the highest honour, that of going Best in Show at Crufts, but the last twenty years have seen some prestigious wins by whippets. Ch. Dondelayo Duette (Ch. Samarkand's Greenbrae Tarragon-Ch. Dondelayo Roulette) bred, owned and campaigned by Mrs Anne Knight, achieved the highest win ever at this show with a whippet, that of Reserve Best in Show. Her sire, Ch. Samarkand's Greenbrae Tarragon (Ch. Laguna Limelight-Ch. Greenbrae Laguna Lucia) bred by Mrs Alicia Yerburgh, owned and campaigned by Mr R.M. James, was twice runner-up in the Group. Ch. Robmaywin Stargazer of Allways (Ch. Evening Star of Allways-Ch. Mistral's Mrs Miniver) bred by Mr Robbins, owned and campaigned by Mr F. Jones, won the Hound Group. Only two others have achieved a Hound Group win at Crufts, namely Ch. Beseeka Knight Errant of Silkstone (Oakbark Moonduster-Newbold Madelina) bred by Mesdames Lumb and Hughes, owned and campaigned by Mrs Roma Wright, and his classic daughter, Ch. Jubilant Lady of Tygreen and Lowerdon (Ch. Beseeka Knight Errant of Silkstone-Oakbark Miniver) bred to all intents and purposes by Mrs Roma Wright and owned by Mrs Sandra Marshall.

It is possible that the larger indoor venues, with their sound echoes and artificial lighting do not favour whippets. Certainly whippets have taken their share of the top wins at other general Championship shows, most of which are held out of doors on grass, where the hound breeds tend to come into their own. Perhaps the next twenty years will produce a dog or bitch who can do one better than Duette, and achieve BIS at Crufts.

Training a Puppy for Show

Training plays a much smaller part in preparing a puppy for the ring than might be imagined. Half the art of preparing a whippet for the ring lies in its condition, the other half lies in the puppy's sense of willingness and pleasure. One of the most precious attributes a whippet can have in the ring is its ability to appear gay and willing. Whippets are basically hunting dogs and, in common with their larger cousins, deerhounds, greyhounds and salukis, they tend to look on shows with a kind of dead-pan boredom. So many potentially good dogs and bitches have never quite made the top because, when the moment came, they tended to hunch up, look bored and/or miserable and to move with the greatest reluctance, hanging back on their collars. One well-known winner would stand in the ring with his eyes shut, a look of speechless disgust written all over his face. He never did become a champion, although he won one CC and numerous RCCs and sired a champion daughter and many other winners. Perhaps it is just because a whippet is asked to do so little in the ring that it is of the first importance that what it does do should be done willingly. To this end the minimum of training is the best approach. If you start ring-craft classes at four months (as many novices do) and then go on to show your puppy from six months onwards, the chances of his still showing willingly are non-existent. At four months you should lead train a puppy in the normal way so that he goes willingly with you wherever you want him to. From twelve weeks you can stand a small puppy on the table just for a few moments, with pats and tit-bits, perhaps two or three times a week, BUT NOT MORE. When you actually start showing, your puppy may fool around a little, perhaps snatch at the lead or jump up — NEVER slap it down. A discerning judge will be able to assess its movement despite the playfulness and this will wear off very quickly, probably by the next show. Always treasure your puppy's sense of pleasure in what you are doing together; if you are too severe on a young puppy you will very quickly have a bored and miserable show dog and with whippets this can be fatal. There is no other breed that have such a capacity for looking miserable and downtrodden in the ring, and once you have allowed this syndrome to set in there is little you can do about it. This does not affect kennel dogs to the same extent as house-dogs, since to them any attention is welcome, but whippets who live in the house, as the vast majority do, have a very low boredom threshold, and one should never forget the fact.

General Information for Exhibitors

The best way to find out about dog shows is to become a regular subscriber to one of the two excellent Dog Journals, either 'Dog World' or 'Our Dogs'. These two papers are published weekly and are full of interesting comment, news, articles on every aspect of the dog-game, show results and critiques, as well as advertisements for forthcoming shows. Every advertisement will give the name of the Show Secretary with an address and telephone number for enquiries about schedules. When you receive a show schedule, be it for a Limited, Open or Championship show, study it in depth. Every schedule will include a list of the Kennel Club qualifications for class entries and this should be carefully noted as nothing is more disappointing or time wasting than to arrive at a show only to find that your dog is not eligible for the class for which you have entered. The qualifications for each class vary slightly at each level of competition so that, until you are familiar with them, it is essential to check them through before making entries. Entry forms should also be carefully read and filled in clearly and correctly, with attention paid to the provisos under which you make your signature. It is inexcusable to take an ill or vicious dog, or a bitch in season, to a show, and in the long run it is damaging not only to others but to your reputation as well.

Preparing for Competition

Whippets are a breed where almost all the preparation is done during the weeks or months before a show. Because the basic construction of a whippet is self-evident (i.e., not disguised by coat or trimming) not only is it necessary to have a good whippet to start with but it is essential that it should be in just the right sort of muscular condition and bloom. A whippet will show if it has slack muscle, surplus body-fat, dull coat or dirty skin at the first brief glance; after all, there is nothing else to distract the eye. Therefore the great art of putting a whippet into the ring in peak condition lies in judging to a nicety just how much weight and muscle, and their ratio to each other, is necessary for that particular dog to look its best. It is not always easy to ensure that a certain dog looks just right on a certain day and only experience will teach the whippet exhibitor just how to pull off this crucial feat. In general, the dog which is fit and healthy, with just enough flesh to give a smooth outline, with coat clean and shining, will be at its peak fitness and therefore looking its best. Many show dogs are in superficially good condition but are actually shown far too fat and soft and many judges do not seem to notice or object to this fact. However, in a breed whose proper function is a sporting one, good muscular condition and development are an essential part of the overall picture. Exhibitors who show fat, over-weight dogs, would be amazed at how much better their dogs would look if they were in harder condition. They need not be as hard or muscled-up as a dog in top racing or coursing form, this also looks inappropriate in the show ring, but there is a happy medium where dogs lead a normally active life which is reflected in their condition.

Added to the general health and bloom of your dog there are a few other simple preparations which can be made before a show, all of which should be routine to the owner of a pet dog just as to the exhibitor, since they contribute materially to the welfare of the dog. Teeth must be clean and toe nails neat and short. With a young puppy, possibly still in its woolly puppy coat, it may be necessary to trim away the few longer hairs along the underneath of the tail, but that is all the trimming necessary if your puppy has the correct, short, close whippet coat. In America, exhibitors trim, clip and chalk their dogs to a much greater degree than in this country where the use of chalk is now banned by the Kennel Club. Trimming for whippets should be neither necessary nor encouraged. Some English exhibitors shave their dogs haunches and up the side of the neck which produces a very ugly look quite out of keeping with the spirit of the breed, which, after all, is neither terrier nor toy, but hound. The removal of the whiskers is also a very unkind practice although some people seem to think that it makes a dog's head look finer. Whiskers are essential to a dog and act as sensors; it really is not kind to remove them, and it is most unlikely to persuade an experienced judge that your dog has a finer or racier head.

Frequent bathing is not a particularly good idea but with white, or mainly white dogs, this may be necessary a few days before a show. Bathing removes the natural oils from the coat and in the English climate there may be a real risk of a dog contracting a chill just when you want him to look his best. It is fatal to wash black or blue whippets since it is almost impossible to rinse out the soap and it also appears to activate a fine white scurf which will show up on coats of these colours for up to a week after a bath. The normal healthy dog who gets plenty of free exercise will naturally clean the coat by rolling in wet grass or being out in the rain from time to time. A good roll in long clean grass after a heavy dew is the best possible way to ensure a gleaming coat. The dog should be thoroughly dried with a rough towel and then strapped with a dry chamois leather. An old silk square is excellent for the final polish before going into the show ring. A useful tip for blacks and blues is to rinse them with an infusion of nettle water and then dry as above. Nettle water is an excellent treatment for scurf or dull coat but it must always be remembered that the superficial glamour of a show dog must be based on the fit, healthy animal. No amount of polishing and preparing will disguise the dog which is basically unfit or unwell. An alternative to bathing white dogs is to use baby powder all over the dog a day or two before the show, then brush it vigorously out. A great deal of dirt will be removed during this process.

Preparations for the show may well be more complicated for you than for your whippet. Having done your best to ensure that you have a sleek healthy dog to take to a show there are a good many other preparations which you will need to make to enable you and the dog to have a comfortable day out. It is practical to make all such preparations the day before because, depending on the distance which you may have to travel, the morning of a show is generally one in which last minute things tend to get forgotten in the rush. The regular exhibitor will have a show bag which is used specifically for that purpose. Many people use a bag of the type issued by airlines which can be slung over the shoulder on that (often lengthy) walk from the car park to the benches; remember that you will need a free hand to lead your dog or dogs, and another free hand to deal with your exhibitor's passes and catalogue at the entrance to the show ground. I personally advocate the kind of shopping trolley on wheels which will stand upright if you require both hands to deal with other things. These trolleys are very light and will tow along behind you containing all you need for your day at a show. A show bag should contain the following —

A thick clean rug for the dog to lie on when benched.

A chain for attaching the dog to the bench. (Your leather lead is not good enough; many whippets, especially when bored, will chew through a leather lead and you will return to your bench to find that you have no dog and that the end of a chewed lead is staring you in the face. It is very frightening to lose a whippet on a crowded show ground since they easily become alarmed and difficult to catch, and there is always the risk that they may escape from the show ground onto a busy road with tragic results.)

Several spare show leads, in case you lose or break one.

A rubber grooming glove and silk square.

A small towel for drying and cleaning feet in case the car park is wet and muddy.

A small light bowl for water, milk or any food you wish to give your dog.

A small bottle filled with a solution of TCP or Dettol for wiping nose and mouth on return to the car. This simple precaution has saved many a household from contracting a virus.

Plenty of Kleenex or paper towels (always useful).

A coat for your dog to wear on the bench if required.

Your own picnic lunch in a polythene container (which a dog cannot open).

At the Show

Always try to arrive at a show allowing enough time to walk your dog around, to allow him to relieve himself and have a scamper if this is possible in the car park. If you take a dog out of a car in which it has travelled for several hours and then expect him to sit on a bench for any length of time, you will find, when you come to enter the ring, that you have a stiff and reluctant dog. If it should be an indoor show make very certain that the dog has had a good chance to empty itself thoroughly before you enter the venue. Whippets are fundamentally very clean and they will often refuse to oblige their owners in a roped off area at indoor shows, so it really is important that they have a good run before they leave home and another on arrival at the show. Always take your dog straight to the bench when you arrive at a show and settle him down comfortably; dogs quickly learn that their bench is their 'base' when they are at a show and they will jump up and settle themselves on their own rug and in their own place where they feel secure. Never leave a new puppy for hours alone on a bench. It may easily panic and become tangled up in its chain with the effect that it may never again be happy on the bench. If you have other dogs in other classes arrange for a friend to sit or stand with a new puppy while you have to be away from the benches. On the whole whippets are very good about being benched and once you have established that the bench is their 'place' to which you always return they will soon settle and feel happy. It is very important if you are planning a show career for your puppy that he learns to look on it with pleasure. A dog which hates shows and showing will have the greatest difficulty in making his presence felt when the top moments come. Dog shows are tiring for dogs as well as for owners so if your dog can sleep comfortably on the bench in between his arrival and when he is wanted in the ring he will be in better form when being judged. Make sure that you take him off the bench in good time before the class in which he is entered to give him a chance to walk around, and if a puppy, to get used to the people, other dogs, noise and general atmosphere.

When you arrive at the benches check whether your ring numbers (which will correspond with your bench numbers) are lying on the bench waiting for you. It is easy to miss this point and to settle the dogs on their rugs on top of the numbers, and then to find, when you get to the ring, which may well be some distance from the benches, that you were supposed to have collected your number off the bench, thus involving yourself in a last minute rush which will unsettle both you and the dog. At most shows the ring numbers are distributed by the Ring Steward in the ring at the start of each class but some show societies either send out the ring numbers with the exhibitors' passes, or leave them on the benches, or in the case of Breed Club shows, have them available for collection at the entrance to the show. in order to save time in the ring. Always try and avoid being in the position where you need to rush in or out of the ring because you have forgoten something or are in the wrong place at the wrong time. This can unsettle a dog, especially a young puppy, so that it becomes more difficult to handle them or to get them to concentrate once they are being judged in the ring. Once you are actually in the ring being judged, concentrate on your dog and on the judge so that you can be sure that you are doing what the judge requires and that your dog is happy and relaxed throughout the class. There will be plenty of time to talk to friends after you have completed your classes. Equally, do not button-hole some other exhibitor asking for advice or expecting attention when they may be busy getting their dogs prepared. If you do so you may get a short answer, whereas if you approach them at the right time most breeders and exhibitors are only too willing to answer questions and to help a novice.

When your classes are completed, win or lose, remember to pat and praise your dog. Even if he has not been successful he will have done his best for you and if he feels he has pleased you he will enjoy himself and will make an effort for you on another occasion. It is always distressing to see those exhibitors who are themselves disappointed making their displeasure plain by jerking the lead or even speaking disparagingly to the dog. Remember that the dog you take into the ring is the same dog you leave the ring with, whatever placing you may have achieved on the day. Your love and affection for your dog should not be coloured by his placings in the show ring. Exhibitors who care for their breed and have the good of it at heart will have dogs at home, which for a variety of reasons have not reached the top or even half-way up the ladder but which are nonetheless much cherished members of the family. The owner who 'passes on' the dogs he has acquired and cannot win with is not a good home to which to sell a puppy, and as soon as an exhibitor becomes known as that type of person, responsible breeders will close their doors against him. If you have a dog whose show career is disappointing it is still an individual and entitled to your love and care for the rest of its life; it will not endear you to other breeders and exhibitors if you go from kennel to kennel trying to buy and then discarding show stock.

Buying your First Show Whippet

Many people start showing dogs by accident. They have a whippet or perhaps two, and a friend says, 'Why don't you show it?' You go along to your first show and you know nobody, your friend is not there, your dog turns out to be the wrong shape and behaves badly, or you feel that perhaps it is you that are wrong — you have always heard that all judging is crooked; obviously this particular judge doesn't know your face. In any case he or she does not appear to appreciate your dog with whom you can find no fault, since you love it and have always thought of it as rather particularly beautiful. You go home miserable and disappointed after a tiring and dreary day and you feel 'this is not for me'. You may even feel strongly enough to write to a dog paper and sign your name 'Disgusted'. All this can be avoided if you set about things in a more sensible way.

Having decided that you are interested in showing dogs, the first thing to do is to find out about it. Take out a subscription to a dog journal, buy a book on your chosen breed, and join a Breed Club. Let us suppose that your first whippet which has endeared the breed to you has come to you from some source other than a breeder/exhibitor, so that you do not have that particular mine of help and information. The first person who will be able and willing to help you will be the Secretary of your nearest Breed Club. Get in touch with him or her and join the Club so that you will get any publications available and schedules for their shows. Start attending the Breed Club shows as a spectator. Introduce yourself to the Secretary who will be only too pleased to advise and help you. From the Secretary you can obtain a list of breeders who might be able, in due course, to supply you with a puppy of show standard. But you should be in no hurry to buy a puppy. Many beginners rush off to see the first litter they hear of and buy a puppy which may be neither the type they prefer nor of the standard they require. It is most important to take your time to look about you at a few representative shows to decide what type of whippet you would like. You may not prefer the type which win at the first show you attend so trust your judgement and go to some more shows. You will begin to see a pattern in what the judges like and what you yourself prefer. Look up the names and addresses of the owners in the catalogue, check if any of them correspond to the list the Breed Club Secretary has given you. If you are interested in a certain line of breeding then introduce yourself to the breeder (choosing a good moment — not when they are just going into the ring) and tell them what you require and why. It may not even be a bad idea to write to one or two breeders, again setting out your requirements. Many breeders will have more time to consider a detailed letter at home than if you speak to them hurriedly at a show. Knowledgeable breeders are usually anxious to help novices coming into the breed since they may well represent the future, and will take time and care to fulfill their wants and endeavour to start them off in the right direction, but you may well have to be prepared to wait anything from six months to a year to get the sort of puppy you want. You must remember also that, with the best will in the world, it is very possible to be mistaken about a young puppy. The most amusing and best age to have a whippet puppy is between eight and twelve weeks old, but it is quite difficult to be absolutely certain that a twelve week old puppy will mature into a show specimen. It may well be safer to buy a young dog or bitch of six to twelve months old which has been to a few shows and whose potential is therefore more guaranteed, but there are also some drawbacks to this course of action. Few breeders will sell a really promising young winner and only a large kennel will have this sort of stock for sale. This means that you are immediately limited in choice since there are very few large whippet kennels, most whippet breeders being of the sort that keep relatively few adult dogs and will therefore be reluctant to part with a young adult of which they had become fond. Possibly the best solution is to find a breeder who has a promising litter of show stock puppies and to trust them to pick the best they can for you at twelve weeks, telling yourself meanwhile that if the puppy should not turn out as successful as you and the breeder hope, you will still have a well-bred, well reared and typical specimen of the breed, and you can, at a later date move on from there. It is most unlikely that you will be able to campaign your first whippet to the top simply because there is so much to learn that you are almost certain to make mistakes and find out the answers as you go along.

Choosing the kennel from which you buy your foundation stock is a critical decision. It is not only a question of buying a good dog or bitch in the first place but the whole future of any breeding plan must be based on the bloodlines which you originally acquire. If you buy a bitch of a certain type but eventually prefer a different type it may take you generations to correct your original mistake. Similarly, it is of the greatest help to have the advice and expertise of a clever breeder behind you at every stage of your new activity. A good breeder can advise you which judges to exhibit her stock under, which stud dogs to patronise, which puppies to keep, and all these factors will be of the greatest help to you as you start out until you have gained the experience to make you own decisions in such areas.

Having chosen your breeder, booked, paid for, and finally collected your puppy you must still be prepared to ask advice at every stage. Breeders who care about their stock will never grudge the time and trouble involved in back-up care, but it is disheartening to sell a puppy with complete instructions on diet and care and to find later on that such instructions have been totally or partially ignored. The growing stages of a whippet from twelve weeks to one year old are terribly important and the wrong food, exercise or treatment can completely ruin a promising puppy long before it ever gets into the ring. It is surprising what very stupid things a new owner can do to a puppy however much they may love it. Too much exercise at an early stage can be quite as bad as too little. Muscle formed over unfinished bone growth can actually deform a puppy if it is road-walked too soon or allowed too much galloping over unsuitable terrain or with adult dogs. Too much or too little food, or food of the wrong sort can again hinder growth. A puppy needs a lot of sleep and in a household where there are several young children for instance, a puppy can have too much attention and playing with, so that again, its growth may be hindered or impeded or its temperament spoilt. Kind, sensible treatment, combined with loving care are the best preparation a show dog can have for the stress and strains of its future life; and make no mistake, the life of a show dog is extremely taxing. A good, steady, outgoing temperament is vital in a show dog and anything less will be immediately shown up when it gets into the ring. For that reason it is an excellent policy to see the parents of your puppy before you decide to buy and if they appear to you to excel in this respect, the chances are that your puppy will also have all the right instincts.

Judges and Judging

Judges fall into two categories; those who have been passed by the Kennel Club to award Challenge Certificates in the breed and those who are still gaining experience towards that end. For Championship shows all judges must be passed by the Judges Sub-Committee of the Kennel Club to award Challenge Certificates. For all other types of shows a judge needs only to be invited to officiate by the committee of the show concerned. Breed Clubs whose committees are familiar with all those involved with the breed will select people to judge, who in their opinion, will give a knowledgeable verdict on the entry. Open show committees seem apt to select their breed judges in a more haphazard way. If there is someone on their committee familiar with the breed they may appoint aspiring whippet judges (or indeed even ones already passed and experienced at Championship level) but quite frequently the breed will be judged by an all-rounder or perhaps an expert in some other hound breed who will agree to take on whippets as well as other breeds. This is a financial saving to the Society concerned since they will not have to pay two (or more) lots of expenses and it also gives up and coming all-rounders another breed in the Hound Group which will be to their credit when they come to be considered for further appointments.

Sooner or later most people closely involved in showing a breed will be asked or will wish to try their hand at judging their own breed. In the natural course of events a person will be invited to judge once they have some years of experience of exhibiting and breeding good stock. Some Breed Clubs stipulate a certain number of years in the breed before they will consider including a judge's name on their Breed Club judging list. Five years involvement at an active level would be a minimum before an individual would have sufficient knowledge to enable them to give an authoritative opinion about other exhibitors' dogs. Many novices seem to consider that judging appointments should come before they gain the knowledge and some have even been guilty of touting for appointments. As a general guideline one should have had at least five years experience in the breed and have bred a number of animals entered in the Kennel Club Stud Book before even considering accepting an appointment to judge at Limited or Open show level. The exception to this rule are people who have reached the top in other breeds since one should assume that their knowledge in their other breeds, especially other breeds within the same Group, will have given them a depth of general experience. Even so, they should have had experience at Breed Club level before awarding Challenge Certificates. The award of a Challenge Certificate is a serious one since the dog or bitch gaining such an award has an influence on the breed in the eyes of many people to a greater extent than if it had not won such an award. Consequently a dog which gains the title of Champion unworthily, i.e., under judges who are either ignorant or unscrupulous, can do a great deal of damage in the breed in quite a short space of time.

For the serious exhibitor or breeder the path to judging appointments is quite straightforward. After acquiring your first good puppy from a reputable kennel, you join a Breed Club and attend their shows regularly, gaining experience all the time. When you have handled several good dogs and subsequently bred one or two of your own, a Breed Club committee may invite you to judge or put your name on their list of judges of whom they approve to officiate at Limited or Open shows. It is essential to have the support of one or more of the Breed Clubs because not only are they the guardians and arbiters of the breed but when eventually a general Championship show offers you an appointment to award Challenge certificates your name will be submitted to the Kennel Club who in turn will write to the Breed Clubs asking whether they approve the appointment. It is an honour to serve on a Breed Club Committee if asked to do so and a great deal of general experience can be gained in this way; it is also a chance to put back into the breed some of the work required to repay the debt which you will owe the breed for the pleasure you get out of it.

There is an aspect of judging which should be very carefully considered before appointments are accepted. Judging requires certain abilities over and beyond knowledge. A judge must be patient, courteous, and above all absolutely honest in judging to the official standard for the breed. If you find it difficult to make decisions, or that other people's opinions are liable to influence you unduly, judging is not for you. There is no shame involved in this, nor will it hamper your progress as an exhibitor. There have been several exhibitors at the very top of our breed who have steadfastly refused to judge and their names are held in very great respect wherever whippets are known and loved.

A great deal has been written and said about the honesty of judges, and at almost every show exhibitors are to be seen coming out of the ring saying what a crook the judge was. The few cases that have actually been brought against the honesty of judges have been extremely difficult to prove and it is my opinion that there is far less dishonest judging than people like to think. On the other hand there is a good deal of ignorance and 'kennel blindness' (a term used for breeders and exhibitors who, while they may be quick to criticize others' dogs can never see any fault in any dog owned or bred by themselves) to be seen. For instance, it is not a good idea to encourage your own stock to be shown under you since once it becomes known that you tend to favour your own breeding other exhibitors will not give you an entry and you are left in a position of having to give all the top awards to your own breeding as there is no alternative. A judge who is also a large breeder and perhaps has several good dogs at stud will obviously have some of their progeny entered and it is essential to judge such progeny scrupulously against the standard and against the rest of the entry. There are a number of breed judges who fall into this category and you can see the results of their judging by the sort of entry they attract. If they draw a good overall entry which includes some of their own stock you may be sure they will judge the dogs fairly on the day. If, on the other hand, many of the current top winners stay away and the classes are filled with entries bred by them or sired by their dogs you will know that there can be little point in exhibiting anything of different breeding under them.

There are certain simple rules which should apply to judges at all level of shows. A judge should always honour a judging engagement which he has accepted unless actually prevented by ill-health or Act of God. He should make sure he is in good time and report to the show Secretary at least half an hour before the advertised time for commencement of judging. He should be neatly and somewhat more formally dressed than if he were exhibiting. This is a courtesy to the exhibitors and as a judge on the day is the most important official he or she should look the part. A judge should allow ten minutes or so in the ring with the Steward before zero hour so as to be able to have a good look at the ring and the position of the table. It is as well to take these factors into consideration and to decide with the Steward how to position the dogs, where to stand those which have been seen and those which are awaiting their turn, and in which direction dogs should be asked to move individually. The moving dogs must not be impeded by those waiting to be examined. It is a good idea for the whole class to be moved round the ring once or twice at the beginning of each class as this settles the dogs and handlers and gives the judge an overall idea of the quality of the class. When the winners are pulled into the centre they should be lined up facing the spectators; this is a Kennel Club rule and a good one, since a line of dogs facing a blank ring-side can lead to misinterpretations. The same procedure should be followed in each class thus leaving both the ring-side and the exhibitors in no doubt as to what is happening. The winner of each class should be in the same position at the end of the judging. Novice dogs and exhibitors should always be dealt with patiently, every opportunity being allowed to give them a chance to settle and fulfil the requirements even if it is immediately obvious that such an exhibit has no chance of winning or being placed. The judge should always remember that every single exhibitor has paid an entry fee for his opinion. Every entry made is a compliment to the judge, and each exhibit deserves the judge's full attention for the period of its individual examination. The judge should not talk to the exhibitors however well they may be known, nor should he call them into the middle of the ring by name, but a pleasant smile and a 'thank you' after the dog has moved can make a great deal of difference to the atmosphere in the ring. A judge should always be quite clear in his directions to the exhibitors so that they know exactly what it is that they are to do. When judging is finished it is always appreciated if the judge either visits the benches or waits for a time in the ring to give exhibitors a chance to question or thank him.

To be asked to judge a show at any level is an honour and a compliment. A judge has two prime obligations; to do his duty by the Society which has invited him, and to do his duty by the exhibitors who have paid him the compliment of entering their dogs for his opinion. A judge may make errors of judgement but they should be honest ones, and he should try to officiate in a competent and polite manner while in the centre of the ring. The ring-side will forgive almost any error which is made in good faith, but rudeness, sloppiness and bias are very obvious to exhibitors, and it should never be forgotten that whilst the judge is judging the dogs the ring-side is busy judging the judge. On what a judge does in the centre of the ring will depend his future invitations to judge and the entry he will receive. A large entry of top quality dogs is the greatest compliment a judge can expect and it is a most exciting experience to judge such an entry.

Having looked at the exhibitor from the Judge's point of view let us examine the situation from the other side. How do you decide where and under whom to enter your dogs? Making out the show entries at the beginning of a busy summer is quite as complicated and skilled a business as that of a racehorse trainer deciding where to run his horses. Nowadays, it is also such an expensive business that one cannot afford to travel all over the country making mistakes. Of course one cannot be sure that one's dog is going to win even if one knows that the judge in question likes everything about him, since every dog looks different on different days and in different company. But there are a few guiding rules which can help you choose your judges before you become sufficiently experienced to know what different judges prefer. Firstly, think about what a judge breeds and shows himself. If they are of a consistent type and quality it is likely that such a judge will have a good eye and be able to stick to the type they like. If the judge in question has never bred or owned a good dog or has bought in dogs of differing types and bloodlines none of which resemble each other, it is unlikely that he will have a firm picture in his mind's eye of what he does like, let alone what is correct. If it is a judge who has judged before or who judges regularly you can quite easily find out what he likes by comparing the various winners he has put up at previous shows. If you think that your dog is of similar type or similarly bred to previous winners you may stand a good chance. If you discover that the judge in question always gives the top awards to dogs which are his own breeding or sired by his stud dogs there will be no point in entering unless your dog is bred in the same way. Then there are judges who have perhaps not judged before and about whom no information is available. If they have owned good dogs themselves, even in another breed, it is well worth giving them an entry to see how they interpret the breed standard. If they are honest and intelligent you will be able to see a pattern to their judging and even if it does not include your dog on the day you may well do better under such a judge next time with a different dog. It is never a crime to be left out of the cards by a judge who found five good ones of the type he preferred. What is a scandal is if you are rejected with a good dog and indifferent ones which belong to the judge's friends and relations are placed. It is quite easy to see when this is happening since the line-up in each class and of the unbeaten dogs at the end for the challenge will have a very uneven look. This can, of course, occur when a judge has a very small or uneven entry but in the kind of entry seen at most Championship shows it should be possible for a discerning judge to produce a level result. There is only one answer if you feel that the judge falls into the category which I have described — do not enter under them in the future.

Having decided to enter your dog, the exhibitor no less than the judge has certain obligations. It is up to the exhibitor to arrive in the ring with the dog properly exercised, groomed and ring-trained. With the best will in the world it is hard for a judge to look at a dog seriously when it won't walk in a straight line or stand still to be examined. The dog should be clean and shining and well-behaved. The exhibitor should be practically and tidily dressed. Sloppy clothes, too much jewellery or revealing garments are quite out of place in the show ring. Lady exhibitors should remember that they will have to bend and stretch when handling their dogs and should do so at home in front of a mirror in order to make sure that they do not look in any way spectacular. Once in the ring exhibitors should not laugh or talk loudly; they should pay attention to what the judge requires of other exhibitors so that they are ready to conform. It is advisable always to do exactly what the judge requires because an exhibitor who persists in being different from everyone else will only succeed in breaking the judge's concentration and very probably irritating him. An eye should always be kept on the judge because it is impossible to keep a dog stacked throughout a large class and an exhibitor must be alert as to when he can let his dog relax and when it must be on its toes for the judge to look at. The final placings should be accepted with good grace and it is courteous to congratulate those who have beaten you, as you hope they will congratulate you when it is your turn to go to the top of the class. It is unforgivable to leave the ring looking disgruntled and casting slurs on the judge — if that is how you feel then it should be kept to yourself and a mental note made not to exhibit under that judge again, but one should never be guilty of making such a grievance public. At the end of the show, win or lose, it is polite to thank the judge, the stewards, and to congratulate the chief winners. It is little things like this which make showing a pleasure to us all and make us come away from a show feeling that whether we have won or lost we have had a good day out with our dogs and our friends. And there is always another day, and another opinion!

39. *Mrs D. U. McKay, with four Lagunas, at a coursing meeting. (Sport and General)*

Chapter 4

The Coursing Whippet

Before discussing coursing with whippets it is necessary to give some of the background of coursing in general.

Coursing means hunting by sight; it has been the hunting method of many predators for millions of years and it was probably what man used dogs for when dogs were first domesticated, 10,000 or more years ago. Unorganised coursing in Britain, the chasing of hares with dogs that hunt by sight, goes on today as it has done through many centuries; its reasons vary from exercise for man and dog to deliberate poaching, but the object is to kill the hare for food (and very good food it can be when properly cooked); there is little or no formality about unorganised coursing and the dogs are usually cross-bred, or lurchers. Organised coursing, on the other hand, has a different object: that of testing one dog against another. Killing the hare can be incidental and plays a minor part in the test. Coursing has been defined as 'a competitive test of the merits of coursing dogs — two dogs only in each course — under formalised conditions regulated by a strict and detailed code of rules.'

Throughout the recorded history of hunting there have been three sizes of coursing dogs listed: the large dog for the large beasts, that became today's Scottish Deerhound, the middle-sized dog for medium beasts, that became the greyhound, and the small dog for the smaller beasts which became the whippet as we know it today. The greyhound was the dog of kings, barons, bishops and landowners and from running hares privately on their own land there arose, through the spirit of competition, challenges against neighbours' dogs. For some this was not enough; the wonderful dog at home often turns out to be useless when tried in public and the desire for wider competition led, in the middle part of the 18th century, to the formation of coursing clubs where greyhounds could be tried against strangers. The first club to be so formed was the Swaffham Coursing Club, established in 1776 and still running coursing meetings in 1983. By the middle of the 19th century there were some 380 coursing clubs and in 1858

40. *Miss S. Baird's Ch. Sound Barrier, a show champion who has won the Whippet Coursing Club 'Moonlake' Cup two years running. (Whimpanny)*

the National Coursing Club was formed to regulate and control coursing. The 1880 Ground Game Act, which gave occupiers of land the inalienable right to kill ground game on their land as a form of crop protection, led to a swift reduction in the number of hares, so much so that 12 years later Parliament, with hindsight, had to pass the Hares Preservation Act, limiting the *sale* of hares to the period from August to February (though there is still no *close season* for hares). It is not surprising that the number of coursing clubs dropped to about 130 by the turn of the century.

Despite fluctuations in the number of hares, changes in farming practices, loss of countryside to urban development and repeated attacks from those who would stop country sports, coursing continues; there are some 20 greyhound clubs actively running coursing meetings in Britain today. The necessity for a working dog to carry out the work for which it is bred is seen all too clearly in the difference between the coursing greyhound and

41. *Secretary and Judge. The Author and Mr Ralph 'Judge' Jefferies. (Mike Scarlett)*

the show greyhound. The coursing greyhound is purely functional; it is the fastest dog in the world and it has tremendous agility, strength and guts. Its looks are immaterial; handsome is as handsome does. I remember a very respected greyhound trainer once saying to me about a young dog, 'He's too... good looking to be any good'; the proof of selection and breeding is seen on the coursing field. On the other hand the show greyhound branched off from the coursing greyhound early in the 20th century; it has since been bred for its looks and is judged solely on its looks; one need say no more.

We have seen that the whippet type, the small running dog, has been in existence for hundreds of years and that the whippet of today evolved from the racing whippet of the latter half of the 19th century. Thus, when whippets were first registered and shown they were very close to the finely-honed little dog that was doing its 200 yards in 11 or 12 seconds. Because whippets are small, easily managed and trained and will hunt anything from mice upwards, they are popular dogs for casual sport and many whippet owners have so used them since they were first registered. Despite the temptations of the show ring, the *type* is so strong that the working whippet and the show whippet have not yet split into two breeds. They can be, and often are, the same dog.

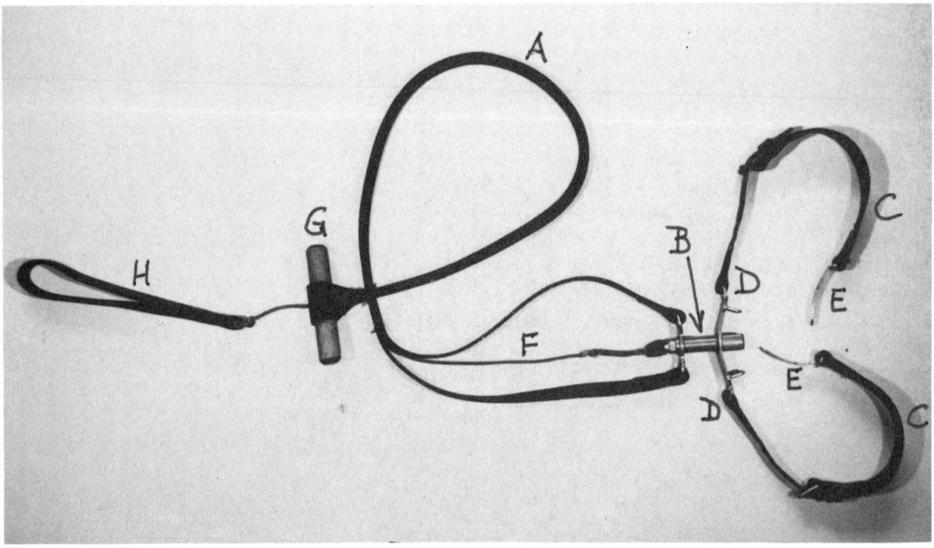

42. Slips. For explanation see text pages 88 and 89. (Walsh)

Organised coursing with whippets — and the start of the Whippet Coursing Club — began in 1962. Two whippet owners, then unknown to each other, met by chance at a hotel in Burford with their dogs. They talked, as whippet owners will, and with the suggestion that some whippet coursing might be possible they went their ways. That autumn a meeting was held, and the five people present — Miss Carpenter, Mrs McKay (Laguna), Mr Riviere, Mr Scrimgeour and Mrs Ticehurst (Porthurst) — decided to form the Whippet Coursing Club. It was agreed that the Club should have no affiliation to or connection with any breed club or society; this condition still holds good though many of those who course with whippets are members of both breed clubs and coursing clubs. Other whippet owners were canvassed, amongst them being Lady Selway (Ballagan), The Hon Mrs Richardson (Hungry Hall), the then Mrs Odell, now Mrs Wilton-Clarke (Shalfleet) and Mr and Mrs Francis (Franciscan). After trying out their dogs in an invitation stake at a Deerhound Coursing Club meeting in Norfolk the Whippet Coursing Club's first meeting was held on the 1st December, at Fawler, in Oxfordshire. Five of the dogs that ran at that meeting were able to parade, fit and well, and to loud applause, at the Club's tenth anniversary dinner in 1972.

Frost and snow stopped any more coursing that winter but meetings started again with the 1963-64 season (the coursing season runs from the 14th September to the 11th March, inclusive). Early members of the Club included Mrs Cleeve (Dragonhill), Mrs Coller (Linknumstar), Mr Craig, Mrs Derby (Nipalong), Mr Mathews (Karryanup), Brigadier and Miss Nicholl, Mr and Mrs Ryan (Twiggen), Commander and Mrs Stubbs (Taimo), Mrs Webb (Padneyhill), Group Captain and Mrs Whittingham

43. The start of a walked meeting on autumn stubbles. (Jim Meads)

(Culverstreet) and the authors, Mrs Lowe (Nimrodel) and Colonel Walsh; the latter look over as Secretary from Mr Riviere in 1967 and Mr Scrimgeour remained as Chairman until 1978, handing over to Mrs McKay. Other early members of the Club included Mesdames Russell and Brown (Martinsell), Lady Horsbrugh-Porter, and Lady Anderson (Tweseldown); of these prefixes, Laguna, Ballagan, Hungry Hall, Taimo, Nipalong, Culverstreet, Nimrodel, Martinsell and Tweseldown still appear regularly on the meeting cards of this and other Clubs.

With the help and co-operation of many landowners and farmers the Club's activities expanded until some 10 or 12 meetings a year were being held in an area from Newbury and Stow-on-the-Wold in the west, to Kings Lynn and Braintree in the east. The two principal trophies, which are still competed for, were the Nicholl Cup for dogs (now the Moonlake Cup, Miss Robertson's Madishan Moonlake having won it three times in succession) and the Laguna Cup for bitches.

By 1970 applications for membership had reached the stage where it was becoming difficult to allow even one runner per member at meetings; to ease the pressure, and to lessen the amount of travelling that many members had to undertake, the Hon Mrs Richardson, and members living in East

44. *In slips; Bob Blatch with Laguna Black Lupina and Crawshaw Witch Queen. (Walsh)*

Anglia, formed a separate Club, the East of England Whippet Coursing Club; meetings were, and still are held in Essex and Suffolk.

In 1971, Mrs Gilpin (Wenonah), and Mrs Webb (Padneyhill), started the East Anglian Whippet Coursing Club, holding meetings in Norfolk, Cambridgeshire and Suffolk. With three Clubs in existence and the possibility of others being formed it was thought that some form of central control — and representation on such bodies as the British Field Sports Society's Coursing Committee — was desirable; so the National Whippet Coursing Club was set up in 1972 with a Chairman (Mr Scrimgeour), a Secretary (Col Walsh) and two representatives from each affiliated Club. In February, 1973, a very successful inter-Club coursing meeting was held near Huntingdon, a meeting that was repeated in 1982, near Hitchin. Also in 1973, the Woolley and District Whippet Coursing Club was formed by Mr 'Badge' Jarvis, running meetings to the west of Huntingdon. In 1975 Miss Baird took over as Secretary of the N.W.C.C.

Coursing Bloodlines and Winners

Since the foundation of the Whippet Coursing Club in 1962, most of the successful dogs and bitches have shared the same bloodlines which are also well known in the show ring. Coursing, to a far greater extent than racing, has retained the type and breeding which is shown successfully. A number of bench champions have run well and competitively and many coursing dogs have been sired by bench champions or have come from the same strains.

Probably the greatest influence on coursing breeding has been Mrs McKay's world famous Laguna kennel. Not only have there been many Laguna winners, both for Mrs McKay and for other owners, but some of the most successful coursing dogs have been sired by Ch. Laguna Light Lagoon, who never ran himself. Ch. Laguna Light Lagoon was bred by Miss Clay (Tantivvey), by Laguna Lightstep-Tantivvey Oriole, and was the sire of, amongst others, Madishan Moonlake, who won the Nicholl Cup, for dogs, three years in succession, thereby retaining it outright. Moonlake's half-brother, Lady Horsbrugh-Porter's Silver Whisper, was another impressive coursing dog; without Moonlake's top speed, he had great working ability and the sight of him turning a hare again and again is one that many whippet coursing enthusiasts will always remember. A very good coursing bitch was Miss Carpenter's Laguna Little Lucille (bred by Mrs McKay) who, at the standard height of 17½ inches, could hold her own on any terms. Laguna Lacquer, Laguna Lilywhite, Laguna Great Circle Marjorie and Laguna Lupina all ran well for Mrs McKay.

Mrs Whittingham's Laguna Lauraine was another very successful bitch, not only on her own account, but when mated to the Racing Ch. Chancerick Koh-i-Nor she produced Culverstreet Concubine — rarely beaten even as a veteran — and her two good sisters, Columbine and Chianti.

Mrs Cleeve's Dragonhills always gave a good account of themselves; her Ch. Dragonhill Woodpecker ran well and sired a number of very good winners amongst whom were Col Walsh's Nimrodel Ent Wife and her sister, Mr Hamilton's Nimrodel Windwraith, Mrs Coller's Linknumstar Ben, Mrs Matthews' Hungry Hall Hannah and the Hon Mrs Richardson's Hungry Hall Harriet. Nimrodel Bilberry of Allways, a grandson of Int. Ch. Playmate of Allways, always ran courageously and sired Easter Wedding, Black Mischief and Nimrodel Belladonna, the latter being the dam (by Koh-i-Nor) of Mr Hamilton's Nimrodel Bezique, a Laguna Cup and Breeze of Ladiesfield Trophy winner. Perhaps one of the most impressive dogs and one of the most consistent winners in the early days of the Club was Miss Nicholl's Apbrenin Piquet (Int. Ch. Playmate of Allways-Brekin Terra Cotta) whose progeny not only performed well but whose breeding is behind Ch. Nimrodel Ruff, another sire of coursing

45. *Slipping; the release cord can be seen above the collars. (Walsh)*

winners, and also behind Mrs Mather's well known kennel in France. Another consistent early winner was Col. Walsh's Parvenu Picture Girl (Wingedfoot Dent de Lion-Blue Haze of Test).

In more recent years Mrs Rawlings' Maximilian of Chyton won the Moonlake Cup (the original Nicholl Cup) twice as did Miss Baird's Ch. Sound Barrier, the first, and to date the only show champion to have won either that or the Laguna Cup. However, a number of show champions have competed successfully including Ch. Carina Mia, Chs Dragonhill Woodpecker and Tawny Owl, Chs Nimrodel Ruff and Willow Daughter and Ch. Laguna Linkway. A glance through the cards of Clubs affiliated to the National Whippet Coursing Club will show a number of CC or Reserve CC winners competing and, certainly, a number of dogs who are regularly exhibited, Crufts qualified or otherwise successful in the ring. Coursing has played a definite part in retaining the breed standard since the height limit for coursing dogs is 20 inches, a limit which is certainly

46. *'They're running'. (Walsh)*

not conformed to in the show ring. The kennels which regularly course their dogs are those who have supported the breed standard in respect of size and who are willing to test their dogs, in public, in respect of working ability as well. Laguna, Martinsell, Tweseldown, Ballagan and Nimrodel are prefixes which are as common in the one sphere as in the other.

Suitability of the Whippet for Coursing

Some have said that the whippet is over-matched by the hare; and a well-known show-ring whippet owner, judge and author wrote that whippets were inefficient killers, that a hare was too big a quarry for a whippet and that whippets sustained injuries, even to the extent of broken necks, through the hare turning short when snatched at by a whippet. We do not know what practical knowledge the writer had of *working* dogs but his remarks can be shown to be nonsense at any whippet coursing meeting. Of course whippets will be damaged by barbed wire and sharp stones as will any other

47. *An even slip but white collar looks as if he is unsighted. (Amanda Reid)*

running dog at times; but the whippet and hare are well matched for speed and stamina. Relative to its size a whippet has a deeper chest and more heart room than a greyhound just as, relatively, a hare has a larger heart and lungs than a rabbit; we have known small whippets that would turn at full gallop, sharper and quicker than the hare, and so long as the slip is kept to about the laid-down distance some wonderful work can be seen with whippets. Because of its size and lighter weight the whippet cannot produce the storming rush of the greyhound that often kills the hare in a straight gallop — on the run-up — but when it catches a hare an experienced whippet will usually shift its grip to the neck and the hare is soon dead.

The Rules of Coursing

When the Whippet Coursing Club was started it was obvious that the Rules should be based on the Rules of the National Coursing Club. These Rules had stood the test of time since first laid down by the 4th Duke of Norfolk for Queen Elizabeth the First; there have been changes of detail but the

48. *The relative size of whippet and hare shows clearly. (Walsh)*

spirit of the Rules has remained the same for 400 years. On setting up the National Whippet Coursing Club the Whippet Coursing Club Rule Book was adopted by affiliated Clubs.

There were certain necessary alterations to be made to the rules governing greyhound coursing; greyhounds have their own Stud Book whereas whippets are registered with the Kennel Club. Registration is required for all whippets running under N.W.C.C. Rules and proof of registration can be demanded at a meeting if so required by the Stewards. In order to maintain the true whippet type, all whippets running under N.W.C.C. Rules must measure 20 inches, *or under,* at the shoulder; and the length of slip is laid down as being 'not less than 35 yards'.

The only other main change in the Rules is in the scoring of points for the run-up, i.e., from being let out of slips until the first dog reaches the hare. With greyhounds, whose speed is so obviously shown in the run-up, the Judge can award one, two or three points, according to the degree of superiority shown; with whippets the run-up is not such a feature of the course and the points laid down are ½, 1 and 1½.

49. *A driven meeting, with flankers visible in the background. Mrs Smith-Maxwell's Nimrodel Blackmail (red collar) and Mrs Derby's Nipalong Nocodemus are slipped. . . (Walsh)*

Duty to despatch the hare

One of the most important rules in the N.W.C.C. Rule book — as it is in that of the N.C.C. — is Rule 17, 'Duty to Despatch the Hare'; this rule says that when a hare is brought down by one or both dogs it is the duty of the nearest person to make sure that the hare is dead as quickly as possible. The importance of this rule is obvious from humanitarian reasons; less obvious to many people is how to kill a hare once they have picked it up. It is a job that needs knack, practice and a strong wrist; the way not to do it is to try and hit the hare on the back of the head with a stick or the side of the hand. A hare held by the back legs is not an easy target and few are killed outright at the first blow by this method. The

50. . . . *and run-up to the hare. (Walsh)*

quickest and therefore the most humane, method of killing a hare — or a rabbit — for a right-handed person is to hold the hind legs in the left hand, put the right hand over the back of the hare's head, fingers under the left side of the jaw and thumb under the right side; a pull upwards with the left hand, a quick pull downwards and a backwards twist with the right hand, the neck is broken and the hare dies instantly.

An introduction to coursing

What will you see at your first coursing meeting with whippets? Members of the Club concerned will have had their entry forms three or four weeks beforehand. These forms will have shown the place and date of the meeting and will have given details of the stakes to be run; in almost every case they will be 8-dog stakes, with varying conditions. There may be challenge

51. *'Live hare'. The hare has outrun the whippets and is going for home at her own speed. The dogs are merely following her and will score no more points in this course. (Walsh)*

trophies; or it may be a non-trophy meeting with, perhaps, a stake for '8 mixed all-ages (dogs and bitches of any age) that have not won more than three courses', a stake for '8 mixed puppies' (in coursing, dogs run as 'puppies' in the *season* — September to March — following the *calendar year* in which they were born, but may not run under the age of 12 months), a stake for '8 bitches under 18½ inches' and a stake for '8 bitches over 18½ inches'. So the card will contain the names of 32 dogs in all. Entries will have been sent in, the draw for each stake made and cards printed.

The meeting place may be a private house, a farm, a pub, a cross-roads or a bridle way and the time will be fairly early; 9 am for 9.30 is a usual start. This means that members are expected to arrive by 9 and the first two dogs go into slips, ready to run, at 9.30. Winter days are all too short, no one can forecast how the day will go and an early start is essential.

52. *The Judge signals red collar as the winner. (Walsh)*

At the rendez-vous you will find 20 or 30 cars and vans unloading people in a motley of outdoor winter dress and a joyous collection of whippets in coats of many colours; we say 'joyous collection' because that is just what whippets are at the start of a coursing meeting. There is absolutely no doubt that they recognise other whippets as kin and it is certain that those who have been at it before know that there will be hares to be chased.

You must buy a card since that is the condition of your attending — it is your admission ticket. On the cover of the card you will find the name of the Club, the date, the place and, most important, the words 'By kind permission of. . .'; these will be the landowners and farmers over whose land the meeting is taking place. Next you will see the names of the Stewards of the meeting, always an odd number in case a vote has to be taken on any matter; the Stewards are responsible for seeing that the Rules of Coursing are carried out and for adjudicating on any controversy or difficulty. Next will be shown the names of the Judge and Slipper; at greyhound meetings these two are always paid professionals, licensed by the National Coursing Club, but at a whippet meeting this is not always the case. There will be a Slip Steward, responsible for seeing that dogs go to slips in their proper turn, and one or more Field Stewards, responsible for crowd control. At a big meeting there may be a Flag Steward, responsible for repeating the Judge's signals by holding up different coloured flags; these are RED for the dog wearing the red collar, WHITE for the dog wearing the white collar, both RED and WHITE held up for an 'undecided', when the Judge has not been able to decide between the work of the two dogs (a YELLOW flag is held up when a course is to be re-run). In addition, a BLUE flag signifies a bye, when one dog has been withdrawn and the other has to run its course either on its own or with a spare, 'bye', dog; and a GREEN flag held up means that a Stewards' meeting is needed. At the bottom of the page, on the front of the card, will be found the name of the Secretary responsible for running the meeting (which may be different from the Club Secretary), and there will be a reminder of Rule 17.

Inside the card will be printed the stakes set out in order of running. In each stake the runners are numbered from 1 to 8 (or 1 to 16 or 1 to 32 or however many entries there are); this will be the order in which entries were drawn. Each stake is run on the knock-out principle; in the first round numbers 1 and 2, 3 and 4, 5 and 6, 7 and 8 run against each other; in the second round the winners of the first round courses run against the winning opponent next below on the card, say, 2 against 3 and 5 against 8. In the final, the winners of *these* two courses run against each other. For each dog, details of ownership, colour, sex, name and breeding will be given. The recognized abbreviations for colour are:

f. for fawn (fawns of all colours except red are entered as 'f')
r. for red (i.e., r.f. = red fawn)
be. for blue
bk. for black
bd. for brindle
w. for white

and combinations of these letters for parti-colours, i.e., bk.w. for a black and white dog, or be.bd. for a blue brindle. The letters d. and b. signify dog and bitch and the letter p., added, shows that the runner is a puppy running in an all-age stake.

The meeting starts with the first pair of dogs on the card being buckled into quick-release slips. It has been found that the only way of ensuring that both dogs start off as nearly as possible together is to use these slips, and a short-lead type, preferred for walked meetings, is shown in Plate 42. Although differing in detail, the basic action is the same for all patterns; the dogs are held in the leather collars, the collars are kept closed by a spring-loaded pin passing through holes in metal tags until the Slipper lets go of the leather lead and takes the weight of the two dogs on the release cord. In the example which is shown, a leather lead in the form of a tube (A) is fastened by a swivel to a metal tube (B), through the centre of which is a metal pin held down by a spring. The collars (C) are sewn at one end to a 'D' (D) on a bracket and at the other end of each is a metal tag (E) with a hole drilled through it; the pin inside the metal tube fits through this hole and holds the collar closed. A cord (F) passes down the leather tube lead at the top of which is a wooden toggle (G); the cord passes through this toggle and is sewn into a leather wrist strap (H) and the bottom end of the cord is fastened to a ring at the top of the spring-loaded pin. The dogs are buckled into the collars and the Slipper passes one hand through the leather wrist strap, holding the wooden toggle with that hand; he either lets the dogs pull to the full length of the lead or, more usually, holds the lead with his other hand. On seeing a hare the two dogs strain forward, putting their weight on the collars and thus on the leather lead; the Slipper lets go of the toggle, taking the weight of the dogs on the wrist strap and the cord. The pull of the two dogs lifts the spring-loaded pin out of the holes in the metal tags, the two collars open and the dogs are released together, (see Plates 45 and 46).

A great many whippets are of a similar colour, or colours, and are difficult to distinguish at a distance; for this reason dogs wear knitted collars, the top dog of each pair on the card running in a red collar and the bottom dog of each pair running in a white collar. In every course, the 'red' dog goes into slips on the left and the 'white' dog goes into slips on the right. At the end of each course the Judge indicates his decision by holding up a red or white handkerchief to show the winner (see Plate 52); if there is a Flag Steward he will repeat these signals for the spectators, since the Judge may be some distance away from them. In fact, the clue is that the white handkerchief is tucked between the top two buttons of the Judge's coat and he holds it out with his right hand; the red handkerchief is kept in his left hand coat pocket and he holds it out with his left hand.

The meeting will be either *walked* or *driven.* A WALKED meeting means just that; there are no beaters and the members and spectators walk each field in line in search of hares. The line will be close, 30 to 35 yards long, if the cover is thick such as long stubble; in these conditions in the autumn hares will often sit tight and get up behind the line after it has passed over them and many hares are lost in this way. When the ground cover is thin or the ground is bare arable the line can be a bit longer but for whippets it should never be more than 60 to 70 yards; if it is, hares will be lost through getting up out of slipping distance on the flanks. Whatever the length of line, the Slipper will walk, with two dogs in slips, in the centre and some 20 yards ahead of the line. When a hare gets up, not too far away, the

Slipper must decide that the hare is sound and courseable — not lame and not a leveret — and must make certain that both dogs have seen it; he then runs a few yards in the direction of the hare to get the dogs balanced and moving together, he slips them after the hare, the line stands still and the Judge takes over.

The two whippets streak off after the hare and the Judge rides level with them on a flank, near enough to see what each dog does but not so close as to interfere with the hare or the dogs in any way. If the hare was too far off when the dogs were slipped they will probably not get right up to it and the course will merely be a procession until the hare is lost. In this case all the Judge can do is to award the course to the dog that showed most pace; if the dogs get nowhere near the hare the Judge will signal a 'no-course' by a wave of his arm and the dogs will go back into slips after the next two courses to try again. If the slipping distance is correct the whippets should reach the hare within 150 to 200 yards, depending on how fast the hare is going, and as they reach it the hare will turn left or right, or sometimes double back on its track, at full gallop. The whippets swing round after it, catch it up and again the hare will turn; this goes on until either one of the dogs catches the hare or the hare, through repeated turning and twisting, tires out the dogs and gradually gallops away from them; or, the hare may escape through going into a wood or other cover where the whippets lose sight of it. As he follows the course the Judge will award points to the dog which does most work until the hare either escapes or is killed. He then signals the winner of the course by holding up the coloured handkerchief corresponding to the dog's collar.

Whilst the course has been going on the next two dogs to run will have been put into slips while the line of spectators stands still, watching and waiting. As soon as the two coursing dogs have come back to their owners and have had their leads and collars put on again the line starts forward to look for the next hare. So the day goes on, each field being walked in strips, if possible up-wind, or across the wind, until either the card is finished, i.e., all the courses have been run and there is a winner for each Stake; or the meeting has to stop because of a lack of hares, no more ground available, or the approach of darkness.

For a DRIVEN meeting, beaters are required. The number will depend on the type of ground, the estimated number of hares and the people available but at least 25 beaters are necessary if hares are to be driven successfully. Twenty five to thirty beaters can take in some 75 acres at a time with a fair chance of not too many hares going back, or sideways, through the line of beaters and being lost. If more beaters can be got, so much the better but it does increase the costs of the meeting.

A running ground will have been selected, usually of grass or stubble, towards which the hares will be driven. The beaters go out, either walking or on a tractor and trailer, and surround the first drive. The Slipper, with the first two dogs in slips, walks the running ground in case there are any hares squatting there; once this field has been walked and, one hopes, some courses run, the Slipper goes to a position behind the hedge or wall towards which the hares are to be driven. The spectators will stand on one side of the field, out of the way, and the Judge — who is, of course, mounted — takes up his position 100 yards or so up the field. A signal is given and the beaters start to walk forward, slowly and quietly.

If there are hares in the beat they will be on the move sooner or later. When they move will depend on the time of year, recent disturbance or not, the weather last night and this morning and the ground on which they are sitting, whether it is bare or thick cover, or even rough plough which they prefer to sit in above all else; the trouble is that one seldom comes across rough plough in the winter nowadays. The hares may sit tight until prodded up by a beater's stick, or if they are wild they may get up as the beaters start forward, in which case most of them will be lost for coursing; but for a typical course we will assume that a hare gets up some 40 yards ahead of the line of beaters and moves down the field at half speed. After going some way she will very probably stop and sit up to see where the danger is. She can see the beaters behind her and can probably see some of the flankers but we devoutly hope that she can neither see nor hear danger to her front; a hope that is seldom granted. The beaters keep walking quietly forward and the hare starts off again, running to a point near the tree in the hedge behind which the Slipper is standing. The Slipper, who has seen the hare through the hedge and expects her to come through on his left, is crouching down with the two whippets and has turned their heads to the right so that they do not see the hare straight away and, by barking, turn her back through the hedge. There is a shout from the nearest flanker, 'Coming through, Slipper, on your left', the hare comes through and starts straight down the field at best pace. The Slipper turns the dogs towards the hare and walks forward to get them both sighted and balanced; all the time he is assessing the hare to make sure it is courseable. Satisfied that it is, he runs a yard or two with the dogs straining at the end of the lead, he lets go of the toggle, the collars open and away go the whippets. Now several things happen at once: a flanker holds up a flag to stop the beaters, the Judge starts off after the whippets, the Slip Steward shouts, 'Next pair in', and owners of the next two dogs to course, who have already taken the dogs' coats off, run across to the Slipper and their whippets are buckled into slips to await their turn.

Meanwhile the course continues until the Judge signals a winner, the owners run to pick up their dogs — since the next course cannot start until this is done — the flanker with the flag signals for the beaters to start again and the Slipper peers back through the hedge for the next hare. In due course the beaters will appear by the hedge having finished the beat, the two dogs in slips will be taken out and led by their owners until the next beat is ready and the Secretary walks across to have a word with the head 'keeper about where to go next.

Understanding Coursing

There is probably no other sport in which a knowledge of the customs and Rules is so necessary for an understanding of what is going on than coursing. The Rules were laid down some 400 years ago and though they have altered in detail the principles are the same and it is the Rules governing judging that everyone, whether participants or spectators, should know and understand.

The Judge decides all courses on the one uniform principle that the dog which scores the greater number of points during the continuance of the course is declared the winner. This principle is carried out by estimating the value of the work done by each dog, as seen by the Judge, on a balance of points according to a laid down scale. It is worth emphasising the words 'as seen by the Judge', because what the Judge sees is often not the same as what the spectators see. Spectators only watch from one viewpoint which, as the course goes away from them, may be straight behind the dogs and hare or at a very oblique angle; the Judge is riding alongside the dogs and watches from as near a right angle to the hare's line as he can. Many people who do not watch much coursing forget this and are quick to criticise a judgement which they have not been in a position to see properly.

The points of the course are:-

a. SPEED to the hare — which for whippets is estimated as ½, 1 or 1½ points according to the degree of superiority shown
b. the GO-BYE — two points, or if gained on the outer circle, three points
c. the TURN — one point
d. the WRENCH — half a point
e. the KILL — not more than one point in proportion to the degree of merit displayed in the kill which may be of no value
f. the TRIP — one point

Points are defined as:-

a. SPEED:-
In estimating the value of speed to the hare the Judge must take into account several forms in which it may be displayed:-

1. If in the run up to the hare from slips a clear lead is obtained by one of the dogs one or one and a half points may be given to the leading dog apart from the score for a turn or wrench when the hare is reached. In awarding these points the Judge must take into consideration the merit of a lead obtained by a dog which has lost ground at the start either from being unsighted (losing sight of the hare) or from a bad slip or which has had to run the outer circle (through the hare turning away from him).
2. Where one dog leads the other so long as the hare runs straight but loses the lead from her bending round decidedly in favour of the slower dog of her own accord, in which case the one dog scores one point for the speed shown and the other dog scores a point for the first turn, if he should make it.
3. Under no circumstances is speed without subsequent work allowed to decide a course except where great superiority is shown by one dog over another in a long lead to covert, i.e. the hare reaches cover before the leading dog gets to it and no work is done.

b. The GO-BYE is where a dog starts a clear length behind his opponent and yet passes him in a straight run and gets a clear length before him. This applies not only to the run up but also between turns of the hare. I do not know how many courses the great Captain Jack Chadwick judged in his career — it must have been many tens of thousands — but on the subject of go-byes he was apt to say that the spectators saw more of them than he did!

c. The TURN is where the hare is brought round at not less than a right angle from her previous line.

d. The WRENCH is where the hare is bent from her line at less than a right angle. The important point in the turn and the wrench is that the hare is 'brought round' or 'bent' from her line, i.e., the leading dog is so close that in order to avoid him the hare has to turn. Quite often a course is seen where the hare bends right and left on her way to the far end of the running ground but she is doing it of her own accord and not because the leading dog is close enough to make her turn. When this is happening no points are scored (see Plate 51).

e. The merit of the KILL must be estimated according to whether the dog kills the hare by his own superior dash and skill, whether he picks her up through any accidental circumstances favouring him or whether she is turned into his mouth by the other dog. In the first case the judge would award one point and the latter case the dog may or may not score anything for the kill. A dog can 'kill to lose'. This can happen when, say, red collar has scored five points; white collar then gets in and turns the hare well three times thus reducing red's score to two. White then kills handsomely, reducing red's score to one but the course is ended and red is the winner. Had white scored another two turns and then either killed the hare or lost her he would have been the winner but he killed too soon.

f. The TRIP, or unsuccessful effort to kill, is when the hare is thrown off her legs, or where a dog flecks her (gets a mouthful of fur) but cannot hold her and the course continues.

Allowance for accidents

The following allowances can be made for accidents during a course but the dog concerned does not gain a point; any alteration is made by a deduction from the other dog's score.

a. After a fair slip no allowance may be made for a dog being unsighted; the Judge may decide the course then and there, or may declare the course to be an 'undecided' or a 'no-course' as he thinks fit.
b. Where a hare bears very decidedly in favour of one dog after the first or subsequent turns in which case the next point is not scored by the dog unduly favoured, or only half his points allowed, according to circumstances.
c. It can happen that a dog makes a dive at the hare, just misses it and loses his footing; so although no dog can receive an allowance for a fall, if it happens when pressing the hare his opponent does not score the next point made.

Coursing penalties

a. Where a dog, from his own defect, refuses to follow the hare at which he is slipped, he loses the course.
b. When a dog wilfully stands still in a course or departs from following the hare he scores no further points; but when one or both dogs stop with the hare in view, through exhaustion, the course is decided according to the number of points gained by each dog during the whole course.
c. If a dog refuses to fence — to go through or over any hedge or fence where the hare has gone — any subsequent points made by him are not to be scored; but if he does his best to fence and is foiled 'by sticking in a meuse'*, the course shall end there (the Rules were originally written

*MEUSE: an opening or gap in a fence or hedge through which hares habitually pass and through which they run when chased.

for greyhounds; whippets are small enough to go where the hare has gone). When the points are equal the superior fencer shall win the course.

Second hare

If a second hare is started during a course and one of the dogs follows it the course shall end there. This Rule is the reason for walking a running ground to clear it of hares before the beat starts.

No-course

a. A no-course is when by accident, or the shortness of the course, the dogs are not tried together. The two dogs go straight back into slips if so ordered by the Judge; otherwise the course is re-run after the next two courses.
b. An undecided is where the Judge considers the merits of the two dogs to be equal and he cannot give a winner; in this case he takes off his hat as the signal for the undecided. The two dogs go back into slips after the next two courses.

So much for the theory of judging, taken from the Rule Book; now for the practice. During a course the Judge will be awarding points to one or other of the dogs according to the work that they do. He is riding alongside them watching them and the hare and like a Huntsman or a polo player he must be a good enough horseman to forget about horsemanship; the horse is merely the vehicle that keeps him close enough to see what the dogs are doing. One dog may dominate the course and score all the points to come out a clear winner; the two dogs may score points turn and turn about; there may be no score at all. What the Judge does is to score the leading dog until his opponent gets in and starts to work; the Judge then subtracts this score from that of the dog in the lead and in this way he only has to remember one figure.

The Slipper is waiting behind the hedge with two whippets in slips, red collar on the left and white collar on the right; the Judge is sitting on his horse some 100 yards or so up the field opposite the point where he estimates that the whippets will reach the hare. A hare comes through the hedge from the beat, the Slipper starts moving forward until she is about 40 yards up the field and he slips the two dogs. Off they go after the hare and the Judge starts to ride parallel with them. He watches the run-up and, with both dogs level until nearing the hare, red collar goes a length in front and scores the first turn, the hare having come back almost on her tracks as the whippet lunged at her; the Judge says to himself, 'Red, one for the run-up and one for the turn', so red's score is two points. When the hare came back, white collar turned the faster and is quickly on the hare's tail; he makes a dive at her, she turns sharp to the left and white scores a point; the Judge says, 'Red one', subtracting white's one point from red's two. Now to illustrate something that often happens with whippets; after this turn the hare puts on a spurt, the two dogs are not exceptionally good or absolutely fit and by the time they are on her track again the hare is five yards ahead. With eyes set high on either side of her head her forward vision is not good but she can see behind her by turning slightly from side to side. She seems to be making for the wood at the top of the running ground and as she goes she bends left and right, left and right, keeping an eye on the leading dog and just maintaining her safe distance. She is going directly away from the spectators and to them it appears as if white collar is working the hare well and building up a commanding lead over red. The Judge, however, is galloping along, watching at right-angles to the hare's line and he can see that she is bending of her own accord and not because she is being pressed by white collar. The hare eventually reaches the wood and disappears, followed by the two whippets; the Judge puts his hand in his left pocket and pulls out the red handkerchief. Red collar is the winner with a score of one point, neither dog having *scored* again after the second turn, (see Plate 51).

Behaviour

The success, or otherwise, of a day's coursing can depend as much on the spectators as on the officials of the meeting or the beaters; one stupid act can spoil a beat and everyone, whether dog owners or visitors, should help as much as they can.

Firstly, it is important to know the Rules since it is the Rules that govern the sport and ignorance of them can lead to the frustration and annoyance of others. Secondly, it is important to listen when instructions are being given. Time after time one has heard a meeting secretary or a field steward say something like, 'We're going to walk this field from side to side; the Slipper will then stand by that ash tree and I want the crowd by *that* hedge on the right'. No sooner has he said it than several people are saying, 'What are we meant to be doing?' They were too busy gossiping and didn't listen. On the other hand, anyone who is giving out instructions should wait until as many people as possible are present, or at least within earshot, before doing so.

Throughout the day you should try and think like a hare, to think what a hare might do; this may stop you from standing in a gap or a gateway through which the beaters are trying to drive the hares and it may stop you from looking back over the hedge or wall to see what is happening in the beat. Despite what a lot of people believe, the sight of red faces and coloured headscarves above a wall does not encourage hares to come forward. At a walked meeting, keep half an eye on the Slipper so that you keep in line, but watch the ground carefully, some four or five yards in front of your feet. Under certain conditions hares sit very tight indeed and it is remarkable how often one sees thirty or forty people and dogs apparently walking in a close line across a field and hares getting up after the line has passed and stealing quietly away.

Mark your card after each course and keep it marked up to date; if you are away for any reason, picking up a dog perhaps, make certain your card is marked up when you get back. Although there is a Slip Steward, it is your responsibility to get your dog into slips at the right time, in the right collar and on the correct side and if your dog is absent for more than ten minutes your opponent may be awarded the course. As soon as your dog has been buckled into its slip collar, get away from the Slipper. At a walked meeting you may walk alongside your dog if it is misbehaving *and if you have the Steward's permission to do so* but there should be no reason for it to misbehave in slips if you have trained it properly. At a driven meeting do *not* sit down in the ditch or against the hedge by the Slipper; your presence will probably upset your dog and sooner or later you will start talking to the Slipper and distracting his attention. The Rules say that you may walk up the running ground, on the same side as your dog is in slips, so do this. You will see much more of the course than if you went back to where the spectators are standing and you will probably be able to pick up your dog the quicker when the course is ended. The moment you get hold of your whippet and have got his collar and lead fastened, get off the running ground as quickly as possible as the next course cannot start until you are out of the way. Then look at your dog for any damage and put his coat on.

The following list of DO's and DON'Ts is the result of a great many years experience of coursing:-

DO get a copy of the Rule Book and make yourself familiar with it.

DO arrive early at the meet; your whippet may be first in slips.

DO report your arrival and entries to the Secretary and Slip Steward.

DO bring your own knitted collars — red and white. DON'T rely on borrowing.

DO remember that it is your responsibility to get your dog into slips at the right time and in the right collar; if there is an undue delay your opponent may claim the course.

DO get away from the Slipper as soon as your dog is fastened in slips. If your dog is in the red collar and on the left hand side at a driven meeting, go down the left side of the field; similarly for white collar, go down the right side of the field from where you will pick up your dog when the course is finished.

DO remember that except in an emergency you may not call to, handle or pick up your dog until the Judge has given his verdict; if you do your dog may be disqualified.
DO lead your dog off the field as soon as you have done up its collar; the next course cannot start until you are out of the way.
DO make certain that any hare brought down near you is dead.

DON'T ask the Judge to explain his decision; once given it cannot be altered and he may only be questioned by the Stewards.
DON'T gossip when coursing is taking place; there is plenty of time to talk when the meeting is ended.
DON'T grumble when your dog is beaten; you only see the course from one angle, the Judge sees it from many angles. To quote the late Captain Jack Chadwick again, 'I have seen very few unlucky dogs but I've seen an awful lot of slow ones.'

Running a Whippet Coursing Club

With only four whippet coursing clubs affiliated to the National Whippet Coursing Club this may seem to be gratuitous advice; but secretaries do change, newcomers to the job may have nowhere to look for advice and it is always possible that other clubs may be started in the future. My excuse is that even after a lifetime of coursing, 10 years of running the Whippet Coursing Club did teach me something about the job and I would have welcomed a *vade mecum* when I took it over.

Who runs a club usually depends on which member will, or can be persuaded to do the job. There is no doubt that it is time consuming, the endless telephone calls and exploratory journeys make it expensive and it is often bad for one's blood pressure. But a good meeting successfully run does give one an enormous amount of satisfaction and the 'helpers', the gamekeepers and beaters whom one 'employs' are, almost without exception, wonderful people to deal with.

There are no qualifications for running a club but in my opinion a knowledge of coursing is essential and a knowledge of whippets is a bonus. A person who has spent years attending greyhound coursing meetings is better equipped to run a club than the whippet owner who has never seen professional coursing — and that is what greyhound coursing is. Practical experience has to be acquired; more than enough canine advice will be passed on by members. When a new club is being formed, I would advise a small number of members to begin with; it is better that a few members can run their dogs at every meeting than a large number of members have to be disappointed. Unlike the National Coursing Club, the National Whippet Coursing Club does not hold a Club Secretaries' meeting in the Spring and does not issue a fixture list for the season. This would be a useful thing to be able to do but so far it has not been possible. Few whippet coursing grounds are traditional, as most greyhound coursing grounds are; not many landowners can give a firm date six months or more ahead, weather and crops will affect dates and new running grounds are sometimes found after the season has started. All the club secretary can do is to try and get regular meeting dates fixed by September and let members know about other meetings as soon as dates are firm.

Running grounds have never been easy to come by; now, due to various factors, most of which come under the heading of 'pressures on the countryside' they are harder to find than ever. Even a club's 'own' running grounds may be lost through a change of ownership, tenant or use; every effort must be made to keep on the right side of landowners and farmers for a ground once lost is unlikely to be recovered. Whether a meeting is walked or driven depends on the time of year, the ground, the size of the fields, availability of beaters, the numbers of courses to be run, the importance of the stakes on the card and, last but not least, the state of the club's finances. As a rule, meetings up to Christmas can be walked; in the autumn hares sit tight in their forms, the weather is usually good, the going is not too wet so most people can keep up with the walking line. After Christmas the hares are wilder and will get up out of slipping distance, they are beginning to congregate together and sometimes several are on the move at once, the ground is much wetter and difficult for elderly club members to walk over and the days are short; so meetings should be driven if possible. In detail, a walked meeting uses a lot of ground, hares are lost through getting up out of slipping distance, it is impossible to make conditions equal for every dog, strict crowd control is essential, but it is cheap, and in a fine autumn I do not know a better way of spending a day. A driven meeting uses far less ground, with a knowledgeable keeper and beaters few hares are lost, conditions are the same for every dog (or should be) and it is much better for spectators but it is expensive. Whichever type of meeting is arranged there will be payments to the judge, the slipper, and hire and transport of the judge's horse; but in my opinion less than 25 beaters are a waste of time and money and at 1982-83 prices 25 beaters would add £175 to the bill at least, not counting payment to the head keeper and underkeepers, and beaters' beer. Entry fees cannot be pitched too high without prize money to be won (no prize money is given under N.W.C.C. rules), but raffles at meetings, if well organised, can bring in a surprising amount of cash.

Sometimes the ground will dictate what sort of meeting can be held. Very open country, downland or East Anglian 'prairies' almost always have to be walked; the number of beaters required would be prohibitive for a whippet club. Small fields and a lot of hares mean a driven meeting; the best example I have known was Alderton (which many W.C.C.

members will remember with affection). There could be as many as 150 hares on the 300 acres of the farm; this made it impossible to 'walk' but the beats were easy to organise and as half of the hamlet, men, women and children, turned out to beat for us, we had some very memorable meetings there thanks to Mr Jim Fountain, the then tenant of the farm. Trying to drive hares from woodland is a waste of time and money, despite what the resident keeper may say.

Once a possible coursing ground has been found the secretary should get to know as much about the farm or estate as possible; time spent in reconnaissance is certainly not wasted as far as coursing is concerned. Though there may be local, resident, keepers or farm managers or farm tenants, a lack of local knowledge on the part of the secretary may make things difficult. 'Put the slipper by the double oak and we'll bring Starveall and the 40 acre to it', is no doubt clear to the head keeper and his beaters but if it is not just as clear to the secretary the slipper may be faced with hares coming across the running ground towards him, instead of through the hedge from behind.

Without traditional running grounds, where the locals know about coursing, whippet clubs often have to arrange meetings where coursing has not been seen before. Usually the first time is a walked meeting but if beaters are available the problem arises of a keeper who hasn't seen coursing. When driving hares for a hare shoot — or perhaps for netting hares — they are being driven on a fairly wide front; with ten or a dozen guns lining a hedge over a 'front' of some 400 yards it doesn't really matter how many hares go forward together nor does it matter, within wide boundaries, exactly where they go. But for coursing, hares must come through within slipping distance of where the Slipper is standing, otherwise the beat is a waste of time. When dealing with keepers and beaters who had not seen coursing before I used to liken it to driving hares to one man armed with a muzzle-loading gun which has a range of about 30 yards and which takes five minutes to re-load. If beaters walk too fast they will walk over hares and not put them up; if there are a lot of hares the beaters will put too many up at one time, several hares will come forward together and the Slipper will not be able to let the whippets go. It must be remembered that the object of coursing is a contest between two dogs, not between the dogs and a hare. The best way to organise beaters who have not seen coursing before is to divide the team into three equal gangs. The beat takes the shape of a horseshoe, the Slipper standing at the open end; one third of the available number makes up flankers on one side, one third beat down the middle of the horseshoe and the remaining third are flankers on the other side; flankers are just as important as beaters.

Take one or more dogs with you, on leads, when you look at a new and possible bit of ground; they will see hares much quicker than you will.

However, we remember going to see what sounded like a very promising estate but where we had heard that the landowner did a lot of shooting and was very dubious about the whole idea of coursing. He took a lot of persuading before giving a somewhat grudging consent and was obviously worried about whippets going into his coverts and disturbing his pheasants. We assured him that we certainly didn't intend that any whippet would go into any covert and, in any case, if they did they would be far too intent on hares to look at pheasants. In the end he agreed and we went off with the head keeper to look at the estate and work out a plan of campaign. We had three whippets with us and at one point the head keeper said we could let them off leads for a run as they could do no harm on that part of the estate. All went well and we were walking along a track between highish hedges when the whippets suddenly stood, 'marking' at a spot in the hedge some 30 yards ahead; we realised what was about to happen but before we could get to our dogs they dived into the hedge and emerged, carrying a cock pheasant between them. At that moment the landowner came round the corner in his Land Rover.

We got our meeting on that estate in the end but it was a near-run thing.

Getting a dog fit for coursing

Adair Dighton's words* on the principles of training are as true now as they were when they were written in 1921:

'In the training of anything, man, horse or dog, the whole secret depends on an intimate knowledge of the subject under training. What is one man's meat may be another's poison, and to be successful as a trainer it is absolutely necessary to know and understand each dog's eccentricities and whims. Some dogs do well on horse flesh; others do not. Some do better when kennelled with a companion; others are worse than the proverbial pig and must be restrained. All these and a thousand and one little things must be noticed, remembered and understood; otherwise the game is better left alone. The man who feeds and trains half-a-dozen greyhounds all on the same food and each the same amount of exercise may occasionally, by good luck, have one fit, but he is not a real trainer.'

Given some space, a garden or orchard, at least one good walk a day and sensible feeding, a whippet will keep itself reasonably fit without further trouble. Many whippets live by no set regime; they sleep up against the Aga, they are not above accepting titbits under the dining table and they come out at coursing meetings from September to March and give good accounts of themselves on all sorts of going and in all sorts of weather. But the dog that has been properly hardened by training at the beginning

---

* *'The Greyhound and Coursing'*, Adair Dighton (Grant Richards & Co, 1921)

of the season will run the better for it and will win a second or third course against dogs that have merely kept themselves fit.

Luckily for the whippet owner, a whippet takes less training than a greyhound. The whippet is much lighter and will suffer far less damage to his feet and legs. He has more natural stamina and will take less out of himself than a greyhound does. Run a whippet and a greyhound or big lurcher together after a hare: if it is a long course they will both be panting when they come back but, whereas the greyhound will go on panting for some time, depending on his fitness, the whippet will have his tongue in after a couple of minutes and will be looking about for more game.

With these natural advantages the whippet owner has an easier training job to do than those who course with greyhounds. A very few owners are so luckily placed that they can take their whippets out with horses, the best exercise of all for running dogs, but this can only be done where there is a network of bridle paths and 'green roads', and should never be attempted on public roads. Loose dogs and today's motor traffic can only mix to the detriment of both.

Living in a town is no bar to getting a dog fit. We know of many London-based whippets that have been stake winners under N.W.C.C. Rules; one of the best of the 1982-83 puppies was 'trained' on grey squirrels in Battersea Park. But the groundwork of training for fitness — whether it be for coursing or racing — is roadwork and there is no substitute for it. No amount of running on grass will give a dog the sound feet and joints that walking on hard surfaces will produce; and town pavements are no different from country roads in this respect.

First of all make sure the dog is clean inside and out. Give him a dose of 'Multispec' or other broad-based worm medicine. Then use an aerosol or rub insect powder into his coat and brush it out again to remove fleas and mites and their eggs. Depending on how soft the dog is the roadwork must be graduated. Two miles a day is probably enough for an unfit dog with soft feet but let it be a good walk, on a lead, and not a slow stroll. For a fitter dog, start with three miles which can be done in 70 minutes.

On return home look at the dog's feet and nails for any soreness or breaks and deal with these first. If there is any foot-soreness stand the dog in a tray of salt water — a dessert-spoonful to a pint — or if there is any sign of cut pads dab them with Friars Balsam. Broken nails must be trimmed with clippers or a file. Then spend ten minutes rubbing the dog down; bare hands are enough but a hound glove or towel glove gets up a better friction; it should be done systematically, starting with the neck, going on to the shoulders, back, ribs, loin, pelvis, quarters and second thighs. Remember that exercise will get a dog half-fit but massage produces the completely fit dog.

At the end of the first week increase the road work to four miles - or five if you have a convenient 'circuit' of that length — but it can still be taken at a reasonable pace; increase the hand massage to 20 minutes and keep it at 20 minutes for the rest of training. For the third and subsequent weeks the distance need not be increased but the pace must increase until you are walking as fast as you can for the full distance. Remember that you are getting yourself fit for the coursing season as well as the dog.

From the third week some galloping and agility exercises can be introduced. Greyhounds will gallop from an assistant to their trainer but this is not so easy with whippets though two or more can sometimes be made to gallop amongst themselves or chase a ball about a field. If you have any sort of dummy hare or lure they can be given two or three runs after it twice a week. The distance need not be far as the gallop can be repeated. A very good aid for strengthening a dog's back and loins is a lure on the end of a rope. An old, strong, fishing rod or an eight or ten foot bamboo pole with a similar length of line tied to the top; a piece of hare or rabbit skin is tied to the end of the line and the lure is swung round and round in a circle. Very few dogs can resist this and by changing direction, or swinging the lure across the circle the dog's every muscle is stretched and strengthened. It can be done on a small lawn and two whippets can be exercised at a time by this method. Do not overdo it or the dogs will become bored and you will have lost a good training aid.

As the dog's fitness increases, so the food should be adjusted. What adjustment is made will depend on what the dog's normal food is but as a general rule the meat should be increased and the biscuit or meal decreased to a proportion of ¾ to ¼. Fresh water must, as always, be freely available at all times.

Fast walking, four or five miles a day with your whippet, will get you fit too but to the halt and lame who are, maybe, advanced in years if not in wisdom, it may sound an impossibility. Do not despair; I ceased running years ago and can no longer walk four miles in the hour so I use a bicycle for road work just as Hunt Servants do when they start hound exercise in the summer. I have never understood why some authors say dogs should not be exercised from bicycles. Of course dogs must not run *loose* after a bicycle, or after a horse, on public roads, and of course one should avoid main roads. But it is surprising how little traffic there is on many side roads after the local commuters and school-run mothers have gone. I have no difficulty at all in exercising three whippets at a time, on leads, from a bicycle, though two large lurchers at a time are quite enough. The only thing to guard against is the occasional cat or rabbit. If you see it before the dogs do all is — probably — well; if they see it first you may be over the handlebars before you know what is happening. One warning: do not go too fast. So long as the dogs are slinging comfortably along the distance does not really matter; a mile an hour too fast and they will start pounding which jars their feet and joints and, if continued, will give them sore shins.

I find that, once the dogs are fit, a twice-weekly outing with a bicycle for four or five miles keeps them on their toes and they are ready to course at a day's notice.

Training to 'fur'

A whippet should not need any training to chase a hare — the instinct is there and is the result of hundreds of years of hunting. If a puppy attends a coursing meeting or two as a spectator it will very soon join in the general excitement and will probably be yelling with the best of them. What is important is that the whippet must follow the hare until it is either caught or disappears completely and must not stop just because the hare has gone through a hole in the hedge. For this reason, a whippet that is going to course competitively should not be used for rabbiting until it has had a season's coursing.

Rabbits seldom sit far from their holes; a 30 yard dash is all the chance a dog usually gets and down goes the rabbit out of sight. If this is repeated too many times with a puppy (and do not forget that for coursing purposes a 'puppy' may be anything from 12 to 25 months old) it will get the message that when fur disappears it has gone for good; so when the puppy starts coursing and a hare goes through a hole in a hedge the puppy stops from habit but its opponent, who has not hunted rabbits, goes on and wins the course. When a whippet has had some coursing experience then it can be started on rabbits.

There is one exception and that is the 'mixy' rabbit. At the start of its career a coursing dog should assume that it is going to catch what it chases and too many missed hares to begin with can put a puppy off. Whippets and hares are fairly evenly matched and it is difficult for a puppy to start off with consecutive kills unless you have lurchers or greyhounds as well. Then the puppy can be let loose the moment the bigger dogs kill a hare and it will get its teeth into warm fur. Not everyone has larger running dogs to help but if there happen to be mixy rabbits in the neighbourhood a run at two or three will convince the puppy that he *can* catch fur and he will try the harder after his first hare.

A Sense of Proportion

Coursing under Rules with whippets can be the greatest fun but the final results should not be taken too seriously; for certain reasons it cannot be the same as coursing with greyhounds.

With greyhounds the coursing is professional and a lot of time and money are involved. The greyhounds are bred only for coursing — though some do run at greyhound racing tracks; litters are expensive to breed and rear, as many as possible must be run on to their puppy season when the successful ones are kept and the unsuccessful ones are disposed of. Many owners who can afford to do so send their dogs to public, licensed, trainers; there are cash prizes as well as trophies for stakes. Almost all meetings are driven, despite the cost of beaters; meetings are usually held on traditional running grounds which will be grass or stubble. Slipping from one spot means that conditions are as nearly the same as possible for each pair of dogs throughout a stake. At a slipping distance of 100 yards the hare has had time to straighten out, the slipper has had time to get the dogs sighted and balanced; both being heavy dogs with little relative difference in height or weight they will come out of slips together. The greyhound's head is held higher than the whippet's so there is less chance of dogs being unsighted, though it can and does happen. Judging usually finishes when the hare goes through a fence or over a wall. Though luck plays a part in it — and some say a large part — the good dog makes its own luck and, in the end, the best dog usually wins the stake.

Coursing with whippets is an amateur sport. Very few litters are bred solely for coursing but even if they are, puppies can be sold for show, racing or as pets. There are no public trainers and no cash prizes. Running grounds can be of all sorts from grass to rough plough; most meetings are walked and if beaters are used there are often not enough of them to drive hares satisfactorily. Whether meetings are walked or driven the difference in ground and the shorter slip inevitably lead to uneven slipping. The slipper has about four seconds in which to make all the decisions that the greyhound slipper has to make in fifteen or twenty seconds. The greater relative difference between large and small whippets means that the heavier dog will unbalance the lighter one in slips, will break out of slips quicker and can mask the hare from the smaller dog. Though the whippet and hare are well matched for speed and agility the whippet has not got the stride of the greyhound and does not easily get up to the hare if the slip is a long one. Many courses are processions to a hedge or over the horizon and a whole meeting *can* take place with only one or two proper *working* courses being seen in the whole day. In the end the best dog may not necessarily win the stake; 'a swinging hare, a bye, and into the final' has been seen many times.

Nevertheless, whippets are exciting little dogs and tremendous courses can be seen, with both dogs tied to the hare's scut. Many of us wouldn't miss it for anything.

53. *Whippets should be the basis of every Bobbery pack. (Walsh)*

Chapter 5

The Hunting Whippet

In the last Chapter we described competitive coursing with whippets under a code of rules and we gave reasons why the results should not be taken too seriously. It is mainly for these reasons that, taking the season through, you will probably have just as much fun with your own 'pack' in hunting and coursing privately. With your own pack you are Master, huntsman, whipper-in (unless you can persuade some one to act as such for you), hunting correspondent, field, kennel-man and knacker, all in one. You go out when you please, you stay out as long as you want to. You must practise all the venerial arts; you draw up to your game, find it, start it, hunt it, perform the last rites — if you get there in time — and if it is edible you carry it home. Above all, you have the pleasure of watching your whippets do what they have been bred to do; to work.

The Bobbery Pack

Whippets ought to be the basis of every bobbery pack; whippets are very fast indeed not only in their reactions but also over the short distance that a rabbit usually travels for home. They have a wonderful built-in instinct for hunting and for devilment; they have tremendous stamina and powers of recuperation after a severe gallop. A whippet can do almost everything a terrier can do and often do it better; they have been known to go to ground after a fox or a badger but this is to be discouraged. They have useable noses; not as good as a proper 'smell' dog but quite enough to follow a fresh line, mark a rabbit or pheasant in a hedge or tell you if a hole is tenanted. They can follow rabbit runs through brambles or the middle of a hedge as fast as most terriers and, when coursing with a larger dog such as a lurcher, it is often the whippet that actually catches the hare.

Looking back over many years of sport it has often been the unexpected days that have been the best. Even on a blank day where game is concerned there is always something of interest to look at in a bit of country that one knows well. There may be nothing, there may be a brace of hares in the first field. The dogs may be in sight the whole day, they may disappear over the hill and return twenty minutes later covered in mud — and perhaps blood — and panting like steam engines. Have a quick look round for damage; tears and cuts on back or sides can be left to Green Oil and the dog's tongues but anything underneath will probably have to be stitched. Then start thinking about what they may have 'been and gone and done'. You may slip a whippet and a lurcher after a hare going down the field. A fold in the ground puts them unsighted but you can see the hare slow down, go through the hedge and away up the next field at half speed; she is not certain whether she is being chased or not. The dogs come up out of the dip and put their noses down to pick up the hare's line. The lurcher has it first and through the hedge they go, they pick up the scent again and they see the hare going over the top of the rise. We run up to the top of our field and looking over the fence we see the hare coming towards us. The dogs appear, closing on the hare rapidly and she starts dodging through and through the hedge; it is here that whippet scores for she can follow where the hare goes but the lurcher has to jump or wait on one side. The hare starts down the field in which she was found, the lurcher gains on her and turns her, the whippet, close behind, cuts the corner and catches the hare on the turn and she is dead by the time we reach them. One course is enough for the afternoon and we leave the hare at the farm house, with our thanks, on our way home.

'Lepus'

What a marvellous beast the Brown Hare is. She is born in the open, she lives all her life in the open, she has no natural refuge — though hares have been known to go to ground when hunted — she doesn't climb trees for safety and she doesn't fly. She is the dream supper of every predator in the countryside, she is hunted, shot, netted, poached, poisoned by farm sprays, and yet she survives. Her secret is constant alertness, instant reaction to danger, the ability to go from her form to full speed in a couple of strides, to turn and twist at a gallop and the stamina to outrun most pursuers if she is given a fair start.

As good a method as any of finding out where hares are is to hunt with your local pack of beagles. That is how I discovered Alderton where, as members of the Whippet Coursing Club will remember, Mr Fountain provided us with ten years of wonderful sport. It was in his last year as tenant of the farm that we played host at our Cup meeting not only to the House of Lords Select Committee on Coursing but also to some senior members of the 'cruel sports league' and we were able to see these animal lovers in action; we were not impressed.

If you are looking for hares with your whippets for private coursing it is worthwhile putting the dogs in slips, whether double or single. You will, of course, be walking, not beating and unless you are on long autumn stubble or on rape the hares will probably be getting up fairly far ahead. If dogs are running loose they will exhaust themselves chasing after impossible targets and when a hare does get up within reasonable distance they will not do themselves justice.

Ferreting with Whippets

If you intend ferreting seriously you will leave your dogs behind. A rabbit's senses — smell, hearing, and sight for a moving object — are acute. It is difficult enough for humans to remain downwind of a bury, to keep silence and move as little as possible till a rabbit is netted; a dog cannot understand the necessity for all this. Some will say that a dog will show them which holes are occupied but the sound of a dog snuffling and blowing down a hole is more likely to stop rabbits bolting. If a rabbit does appear at the mouth of a hole there is a chance of a man freezing, but a dog turning his head or cocking his ears will be seen and the rabbit will go down again. Whilst most dogs will chase a hare in silence a rabbit has a different effect and dogs will give tongue at the sight of that white scut bobbing along in front, a noise that will certainly stop more bolters. If it is a big bag of rabbits you are after, use nets in silence. If it is sport and a few rabbits then a lot of fun can be had with a ferret in your pocket and two or three dogs; more than this will get in each others' way. Two whippets and a terrier that know their job will do well but terriers are not essential and some would say positively unwanted.

The first and most important thing is to accustom the whippets to ferrets. This must be done when they are young. The adult whippet who is an experienced hunter may take no notice of the ferret on the lawn and round the house but in the heat of the moment the sudden appearence of a ferret from a hole, especially if it is a polecat ferret, may well be that ferret's last appearence alive. Secondly, dogs used with ferrets must be absolutely obedient; they must keep to heel or sit when ordered and if they can be taught to work the far side of a hedge to order so much the better. A problem often met with in whippets is running on. Most working whippets are jealous dogs and two or three together will go down a hedge, getting faster and faster until they get to the end, when they have to come back more slowly to try for the rabbits they have overrun. This is very difficult to stop and the answer is to let one loose at a time until it marks. The others will have spotted the 'mark' before you have done and will go straight to it as soon as they are loosed. Once a rabbit is on the move the dogs will keep in touch and let you know if it goes to ground. Then sit them out of the hedge and put your ferret in, provided that it is not a big burrow. If there is a big warren in the hedge, try and work away from it as a rabbit will not go down a strange hole if it can help it and by pushing them away from home you may get a nice run or two.

A modern problem is caused by mechanical hedge cutting. In the days when hedges were cut by hand the trimmings were burnt; nowadays with hedges 'cut' by flails mounted on tractors the cuttings and thorns choke up the bottom of the hedge and they are scattered for yards on either side where the dogs get them into their feet.

If you have a regular rabbiting circuit and you find that rabbits are escaping into drains under farm gates and similar places it is worthwhile leaving a 'rabbit extractor' in such drains. Cut a piece of stiffish wire a bit longer than the drain, twist a loop in each end of the wire, push it into the drain and leave it there. It will not block the drain but if a rabbit gets in there all you need do is to tie something to one end of the wire; a piece of furze or some sticks will do. Then pull the wire through the drain and if the rabbit is still at home he will be up your sleeve before you know what is happening. Another old country trick when the dogs have put a rabbit down a solitary hole that looks as if it is a stop — a short hole — is to cut a piece of bramble, trim a few prickles off one end as a handhold and push it down the hole. If the hole is short a rabbit can be extracted very easily this way.

Grey Squirrels

Grey squirrels were first introduced into England in about 1870 and from this and other introductions up to about 1929 have spread throughout most of the country and into the central Lowlands of Scotland. They are most numerous in hardwoods or mixed woodlands but are common in suburbs and Parks, where those who know no better feed them.

Whilst squirrels spend most of their time arboreally they do spend some time on the ground especially in Autumn, looking for and burying food; they often move from tree to tree on the ground. For the short distance usually involved, squirrels can move very fast and, with the help of a bushy tail almost as long as its body, the squirrel can turn quicker than a rabbit so it takes a good dog to catch one but it can be done. Whippets who know the game will run down a line of trees, along an avenue or through a wood hoping to find a squirrel on the ground. When alerted or chased at a distance a squirrel with often run 6 foot or so up a tree, round to the other side of the trunk, come down again and on to the next tree. A dog that hasn't been at it before will try and jump up the first tree and will bark at it but the experienced whippet will run on to the next tree and often catch the squirrel napping that thinks it has thrown off pursuit. Once up a tree a

54. *Rabbits sit close to home in daylight and sudden disappearance is usually the rule. Too much of this can sour a puppy for coursing. (Walsh)*

squirrel will lie tight to a branch on the opposite side to where a person is standing. This can be used to advantage with dogs as the squirrel does not know which to watch, man or dog, and the hunter can move round the tree until the squirrel is seen.

In a tree that is not too big a squirrel can often be moved on by the judicious use of a catapult but it is surprising what a near miss they will stand before shifting. When dreys are poked out in winter and squirrels are being shot, whippets will mark and follow from tree to tree as well as any gundog and will catch a squirrel that is wounded and jumps for it. The first time a whippet catches a squirrel it usually gets bitten; this is no bad thing as it will kill all the quicker in future. At one time when I was employed on an estate where squirrels were numerous in some 350 acres of woods, my young whippets were all started on squirrels; they did not catch large numbers — this cannot be done with dogs — but with what they did catch they became very quick killers which stood them in good stead when it came to rabbits and hares. Many London-based whippets get their exercise on squirrels in the Parks and good training it can be too;

the winner of the Whippet Coursing Club Puppy Cup for the season 1982-83 got much of her 'drive' from keeping the Battersea Park squirrels exercised.

As American cookery books show, squirrels are very good eating and undamaged carcases should not be wasted.

Rats

The Brown Rat is too well known to need any description. In most people's minds terriers are associated with rats but whippets can become good ratters, the only difference being when ratting is taking place amongst a clutter of machinery, stacked timber, etc, where whippets cannot crawl; all they can do there is to scratch and shout the odds.

Before the days of combine harvesters, when corn was stacked in the straw until threshing day, every farm had its colonies of rats. They lived in the corn stacks and runs could be found on the outside walls of the stack. Here they could be hunted at night; the stack was approached quietly, a torch was switched on and the pinpoints of light showed where a rat was on the move. A flick with a stick usually brought it to the ground for the dogs to deal with. Sometimes, if the runs were numerous, it was worthwhile jamming a board vertically against the side of the stack to stop the rats running on ahead and escaping.

If properly organised, threshing day was when the big execution was done. Each stack was ringed with wire netting, the sheaves were thrown up onto the machine and as the stack was lowered the rats began to run. Half a dozen dogs inside the wire fence ensured that few rats got away and with that number moving at once it was remarkable how quickly a whippet learned to kill and get the next one. No mouthing or worrying a dead rat; catch, bite, shake, drop and ready for the next was a knack that was soon acquired.

Nowadays colonies of rats are not so easy to find. Most corporation rubbish dumps are regularly poisoned by the pest man and, in any case, rubbish dumps are not good places to work whippets. There is too much broken glass around which, while it doesn't seem to bother terriers very much, can cut the back tendon of a whippet and almost always means a dropped toe. But pig farms and poultry farms can be good places for a bit of sport and even the domestic poultry house can have its colony of rats under the floor boards; if a ratting ferret is not available, one end of the house can often be lifted with a crowbar. Sometimes when the dogs are working a hedge they will mark something up off the ground; if it is a rat it may take a lot of catching.

There is one rule in ratting, be the dogs terriers or whippets; never enter a dog until it has got its full mouth of teeth and its neck is strong enough to shake a rat — for that is how rats are killed. Until a puppy leans to catch and shake quickly it will most certainly get bitten and a rat bite can be very nasty, opening up a lip or a cheek like a razor slash. A puppy that is badly bitten too early can be put off ratting for life. There are various methods of entering dogs. Sir Walter Scott puts it best in the often quoted advice given in *Guy Mannering* by Dandy Dinmont to Captain Brown: 'I had them a' regularly entered, first wi' rottens (rats) — then wi' stoats and weasels — and then wi' the tods and brocks (foxes and badgers) — and now they fear neathing that ever cam wi' a hairy skin on't.' In the past some writers advocated putting a dog into a barrel with a rat; the puppy that had never seen a rat before would try and climb out of the barrel and the rat would crouch still, waiting to see what would happen. If the puppy nudged or bumped against the rat it probably got bitten and put off rats for life. Keep your puppy on a lead until it is old enough to join in; then when it sees its mother, or another of the pack, kill a rat let it go for a worry. Until it is fully grown ensure that it is always one of a number when you take it ratting and by entering it quietly you should have no trouble.

If you are going to do any ratting with your dogs remember that rats are carriers of jaundice; make sure that all your dogs are inoculated at the right age and that their booster inoculations are up to date. Rats also carry Weils disease which can be fatal to humans, so don't get yourself bitten if you can help it.

Mink

Since feral mink live near water — rivers, streams, lakes — this section applies to those who have access to water.

Mink farming started in England in 1929 and mink have been escaping ever since; perhaps the early mink farms were not as escape-proof as they should have been; certainly the regulations are very strict now. But the English landscape and climate are favourable for mink and though their early spread was not quick and the first record of feral mink breeding was not made until 1956 in Devon, mink are now present in varying numbers almost throughout the British Isles. Although ranch-bred mink are found in a variety of colours, feral mink soon revert to the wild type which is dark brown, so dark as to appear black. A male can be up to 4lbs in weight and up to 24 inches long with the females about half this size. Mink swim as well as otters and can climb like cats; they live in tree trunks, clefts, and holes amongst tree roots and crevices amongst stones and boulders.

Some time will inevitably be spent in water so mink hunting is a summer sport. Whippets will mark an occupied mink burrow once they know what they are looking for but a 'smell' dog who knows the game is useful to start them off, and a beagle or a dachshound is useful for following a drag. Mink do not give a long hunt — even with proper mink hounds — but when bolted they will dodge fast from cover to cover if they do not dive and swim under water immediately and here the speed of the whippet comes in so long as the mink is in sight. To begin with, the whippets will not expect to see a two foot long black object, that moves like lightning and, if close enough, dives straight into the water. But they soon realise what they are after and will stand, quivering with excitement as a stick is rattled amongst tree roots where there has been a mark. A hiss like an angry cat shows that a mink is at home; keep your hands away from the hole as a mink can bite quicker than you will see him but rattle the stick about and get someone to jump on top of the tree roots. A move by the dogs means that they hear him on foot and unless they are ready a black streak will come out, down the bank and into the water without a splash. You won't see him again as he will swim under water for a distance but wade across and try the other bank; he must come up eventually and here a smell dog is useful. Mink move so fast over a short distance that you should try and keep the whippets between the burrow and the water; easier said than done. But they will catch the occasional one and, as mink are good fighters, three or four whippets are better than one.

I have had a whippet jump as the mink jumped off a bank, catch it in mid-air and the two of them disappeared into the river where, of course, the mink had the advantage; but a lurcher on the far bank picked him up as he surfaced and that was the end of the hunt. A mink is normally a clean feeder and its bites do not fester like those from a rat or a fox; but bites can be deep and should be washed out with Dettol or Savlon as soon as possible.

Fox

Most pure-bred, modern, whippets never see a fox face to face; this is probably a good thing when one looks at some of the whippets walking round the ring at a breed show. An average dog fox weighs about 15lbs (though the record stood for a long time at 24lbs and a 30lb fox was reported recently), as terrier men know it can 'fight like a chain saw', its canine teeth are longer and much sharper than a dog's as anyone who has been bitten by a fox can confirm, it is very agile and the fur round its neck gives some protection against bites. But whippets who do tangle with foxes become addicted to the sport and will find and fight a fox above ground with the best; they merely lack the ability to go to ground though there are small whippets who do this too. I have been asked how to prevent this habit and, at the time, could only advise the enquirer to move out of the country to London; now with the spread of urban foxes this is probably bad advice. Whilst a fox that is put up in a hedge or covert by large dogs will often escape by dodging through and through the hedge, or by running a deep overgrown ditch, a whippet will follow where the fox goes and often corner it and this is where the head-on fight takes place.

The majority of foxes that have been killed by my dogs over the past twenty years have been outliers, found in hedgerows. A few have been put up, hunted and killed in narrow shelter belts (a fox in a wood will usually escape from running dogs as they lose immediate sight of him). Two or three have been sighted in the early morning, 'going home'; one was once winded by the dogs in a great mattress of brambles some 40 foot across, a mattress so thick that four large lurchers were dancing about on top of it, unable to get at the fox underneath until the whippets managed to crawl in and bolt him. But the majority have been found in hedgerows.

A fox is a curious mixture; his sense of hearing and smell are amazingly acute and he is not often caught, literally, napping; but just occasionally a fox will sleep so soundly that one can almost stand over him and say 'Good morning' before he opens an eye. On such meetings I have found that the fox always had his brush curled tight round his nose. When this happens the dogs will probably have him out of the hedge before he knows what is happening. At other times I believe that the fox has sat tight until the last moment, thinking that he would not be noticed; it is this fox that will give a hunt with whippets though it is unlikely to be a long one. He is either caught in the first two fields, since foxes are not particularly fast, or he gets away since whippets cannot follow a scent fast enough once they have lost sight of him. I have always been interested in the fox's immediate reaction to danger if he has been asleep or resting. Being a predator himself — and the wolf who preyed on the fox having disappeared from England a long time ago — he seems to have no automatic escape reaction as the rabbit and hare have and if a fox is put up from a hedge, or perhaps out of a pollard willow, he will go away slowly and almost reluctantly, swinging his brush from side to side and looking as if he is uncertain whether he should have moved at all. It is different if he is driven out of covert or a crop such as kale; then he has had time to think and he goes off at best speed. Of course a fox has no need to be outstandingly fast; his food comes from opportunist hunting — he eats what is under his nose as he goes along, blackbird, slugs, earthworms, voles, fallen fruit; the rabbits and hares he catches are mostly chopped where they sit. But a fox is an adept at dodging, swinging his brush as he turns and using it as a balancing pole when galloping down a steep hill; I have seen a whippet that had not chased a fox before snatch at the brush instead of the fox's back.

The whippet 'Everywhichway', under bandages in Plate 55, met her first fox by chance at the age of six months when out on a quiet walk with her mother (if anything about mother, 'Nimrodel Ent Wife', was ever quiet). The older bitch hated foxes and she killed this one, the puppy joining in enthusiastically and, luckily, not being damaged. Aged eight at the time of writing she is known to have killed four foxes entirely on her own, one of which, dredged from a deep ditch, looked as if it had been drowned;

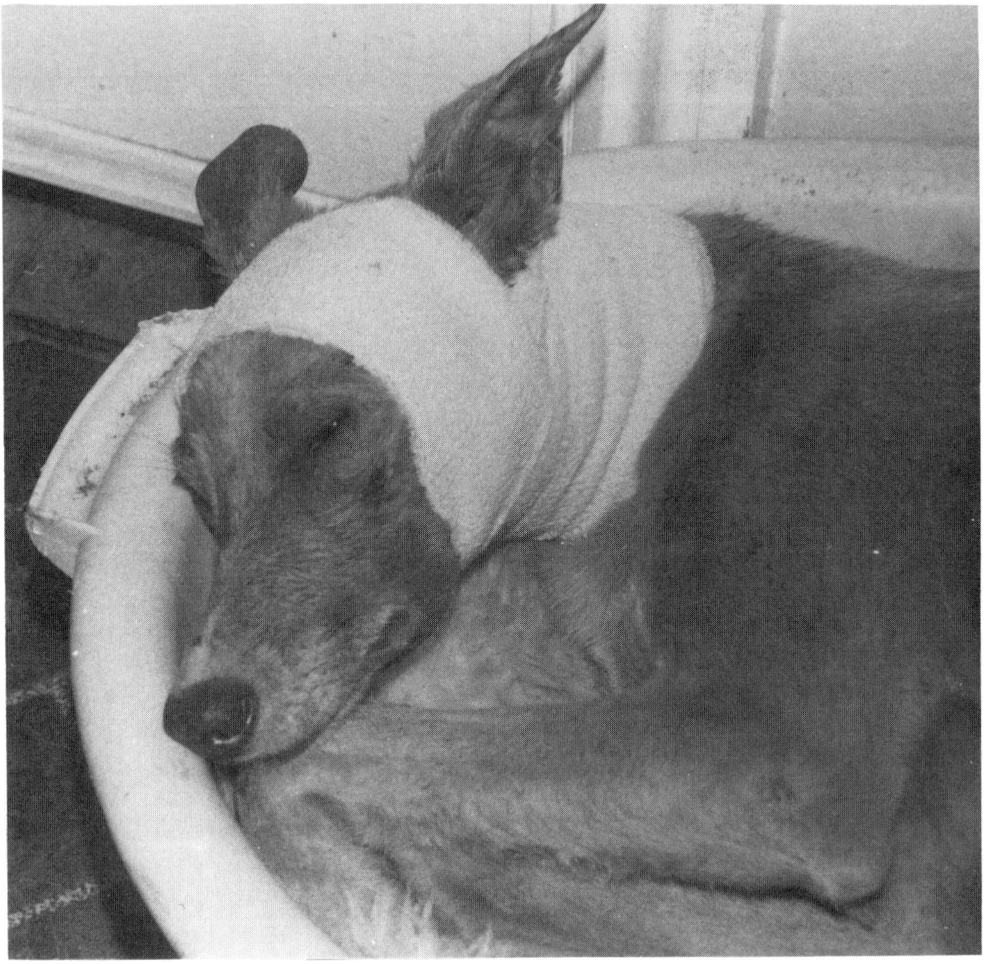

55. *Whippets who tackle foxes head-on usually get damaged. (Walsh)*

and she has assisted the other dogs in dealing with many others. Like all the whippets I have had she tackles foxes head-on and her nose has been punctured on many occasions; this probably accounts for her intermittent, chronic snuffles which, however, have not stopped her winning many courses, and some trophies, at organised coursing meetings.

Foxes are dirty feeders and will eat old, high-smelling carrion; for this reason their bites are often poisonous and fester badly if not treated straight away. Wash out wounds as soon as possible, preferably in hot Dettol or Savlon, and keep wounds open, particularly puncture wounds, until they have healed inside.

56. *So does the other fellow. (Walsh)*

Deer

There is one more category of 'game' — though oddly enough not game in the legal sense — and that is deer. Red deer and Fallow deer can be ignored by whippet owners; apart from being too big for whippets to look at they are normally not seen on a country walk. Roe deer, always wild and not kept in parks, can be a problem as their sudden appearance from a hedge or undergrowth, even in semi-built-up areas, can start a whippet moving but their size is usually enough to stop the movement becoming a chase.

It is the Muntjac, the Barking deer, that can present real problems now that it has spread far from Bedfordshire. Muntjac are natives of India and

South East Asia. A colony of them was kept at Woburn by the Duke of Bedford and from there they were liberated in the early years of this century and escaped during the 1914-1918 War. It was impossible to round them up or eliminate them and the population increased and spread slowly until by the 1940's they were established for many miles round Woburn. In the last 30 years there has been a faster spread and they are now found throughout East Anglia, the South Midlands, west to Wiltshire and beyond and southwards to Hampshire. They are small and secretive, they make their runs through brambles and briar and many estates and farms harbour them unknowingly; unless their feeding grounds are watched in the early morning they are usually only seen by chance. But that humped brown back and bobbing tail are irresistable to running dogs, not least to whippets, and a whippet that has once chased a Muntjac will chase again given half a chance.

Apart from the provisions of the various Deer Acts there is a practical reason why whippets should be deterred from chasing barking deer. An adult Muntjac weighs up to 35lbs, it is strong for its size, its skin is very thick on neck and shoulders and, whilst its horns are short and often curved over at the top, the buck carries two long and very sharp tushes, visible below the upper lip, and it is with these tushes that Muntjac fight. A greyhound or large lurcher can make short work of a barking deer — though I have seen foxhounds and gundogs cut about — but a whippet is not strong enough or heavy enough to hold a 'barker', nor can two or three kill one quickly. Apart from deep cuts, we have seen a whippet with blood pouring out from a jugular vein cut by a Muntjac, and only very prompt application of a pressure pad saved its life.

So, if you live in an area where barking deer are common, try and stop your whippet chasing them; it can only cause trouble in the end.

CHAPTER 6

The Racing Whippet

The subject of whippet racing in England today is a complicated one since it involves organised racing on two quite separate levels. Unlike other countries, where racing is an off-shoot or natural development of the Breed Clubs, whippet racing in England existed prior to recognition of the breed by the Kennel Club and prior to the foundation of the earliest Breed Club, the Whippet Club in 1899. Whippets were being raced to the 'rag' or lure in the middle of the 19th century, and although modern whippet racing takes a rather different form, the early days of 'ragging' as a popular Sunday sport in the Midlands and the North were undoubtedly the foundation of racing as we know it. In 1894 Freeman Lloyd wrote the 'Whippet & Race Dog' which gives a marvellous picture of the period. In those early days there was rabbit coursing with 'snap' dogs (nothing to do with Hare Coursing with whippets, run under Rules), whippet racing to the 'rag' or 'ragging' and whippet racing to the lure, probably with a good deal of 'ragging' involved at the same time. Judging from early photographs the dogs taking part in these early activities varied quite widely, some being so small as to weigh only 7lbs, and others weighing very much more. Dogs of whippet type ran alongside terriers and small lurchers. Any owner with a good dog could run it and owners bred their dogs to win races, mixing in a dash of terrier for 'spunk' and a dash of greyhound for 'pace'; the only criteria applied was the ability to cross the line in front.

Today non-pedigree whippet racing follows essentially the same pattern although most of the dogs, while neither pure-bred nor Kennel Club registered, are more or less of whippet-type and size, and few if any, are rough coated. In 1967 the British Whippet Racing Association (BWRA) was formed to provide some overall control of non-pedigree whippet racing. Member clubs are affiliated to the Association and dogs are issued with identity cards and registered with the Association. A year later, to counteract what the Committee of the Whippet Club felt presented a threat to the

57. *Rag racing at the beginning of the century; weighing.*

unity of the breed, the Whippet Club Racing Association (WCRA) was founded to provide the same control for pedigree whippet racing. This bold step, which was taken entirely with the long-term good of the breed at heart, was the first time that a breed club had become actively involved in racing. Thus a situation has arisen whereby there is non-pedigree whippet — or more properly, dog-racing — run under the auspices of the BWRA, and pedigree whippet racing, which concerns only pure-bred Kennel Club registered whippets, run by the WCRA.

At the end of the 19th century whippet racing was taken very seriously in those parts of the country where it was widely followed, chiefly the Midlands and the North. A day with the dogs was quite a social occasion, with book makers, large cash prizes, and more spectators than we are used to seeing today. A good dog was the pride of the family and often quite a source of income as well. Although the children might go to bed on bread and cabbage, the whippet was sure of his piece of steak. A dog which could possibly win more in an afternoon than its owner's weekly wage packet was well worth cherishing, so it was no wonder that, in an age of general callousness to animals, the racing whippet was usually very well-cared for. Up to this time the rules varied from club to club. Some required pedigrees, or that the dogs be of 'whippet-type', but at others whippets and terriers competed together, graded only by weight or performance. In the North, miners probably made up the majority of those involved and the Sunday morning activity acted as a tonic on members whose working week was spent chiefly underground.

Rag racing was the precurser of all other forms of racing. For a race, the runners were held at the starting line by handlers, one hand on the collar and the other hand holding the whippet by the root of the tail, whilst owners ran up the track to beyond the finishing line, each one waving a towel or rag, and calling to the dog. At the word to start, or the firing of a pistol, the handlers threw the whippets forward, to land galloping in full stride and the dogs raced up the track, each one to his owner and on reaching him, jumped for the towel which the owner would swing round and round thus stopping the dog in full flight. Needless to say, this took careful timing. The principle of calling and rattling the dinner dish, or waving the towel, can still be seen at Hound Trails at Patterdale and other Northern classics. Puppies were trained from an early age to tear and chew a rag and, by the time they were old enough to race, the sight of a towel would be enough to drive them wild with excitement. Training was severe, dogs often being 'broken down', that is, reduced until they carried no fat at all, the muscle then being carefully built up by special feeding, hand massage and hard exercise on the roads. For this a dog was encouraged to pull against the collar thus producing the terrific muscles on the back and quarters which are required by a dog which must sprint 200 yards straight. It was also, incidently, the method used to get fighting dogs fit, a sport which co-existed with early whippet racing. Modern training methods for racing whippets may not be quite as extreme, but they vary little in essentials, the job of walking the whippets frequently falling to the wives and children, contributing much to the fact that modern whippet racing, whether pedigree or non-pedigree, has become a great family sport, the whole family often taking off together every weekend through the summer, to compete at their own home-club, or elsewhere. The fact that bookmakers are no longer a feature, and that clubs no longer feel the need to keep the tracks railed off to prevent interference by owners and spectators, points to the much improved status that whippet racing has achieved. Before the first World War whippet racing was not a sport for women and children.

As time went by an artificial lure, a rag or rabbit skin, gradually took the place of the waved towel and starting boxes or 'traps' replaced the handlers. Whilst in the 1880s some efforts had been made to introduce whippet racing to the South and the London area, to make it respectable and to raise it above the 'cloth-cap' image, it was not until after the last war that its popularity all over the country began to take a real hold. With the increase of interest in the show whippet and the formation of the Breed

58. *The owners show their dogs the rag or towel before running up the track to the finishing line.*

Clubs various pedigree whippet racing clubs sprang into being and, when the WCRA was formed in 1969, clubs from as far afield as Scotland and the New Forest were anxious to affiliate to the Association.

Whippet racing today, whether non-pedigree or pure-bred, usually takes very much the same form. Dogs race over prescribed distances usually anything from 150 to 250 yards. The track can be straight or in a horse-shoe shape, comprising two bends, or an overall gentle curve. The track is not usually roped into individual lanes but has boundary ropes. The 'hare' will be electrically operated and in the case of bends, will be run on pulleys. The dogs start from manually or electrically operated traps, either in banks of four or six, or sometimes from individual traps which have the advantage that, for club racing they can be moved into different positions thus enabling handicap races to be run. Club racing varies enormously. Dogs can be run on a club handicapping system whereby each time a dog loses a race it gains a yard; or they can be handicapped on a time system which enables heats to be made up of dogs of equal prowess.

59. *'Pick up your dogs'. The race is about to be started by pistol. The whippets are held by the collar and root of the tail and are thrown forward, to land galloping.*

Equally, dogs may be weighed and handicapped on a yard per lb basis. Championships are run off 'scratch' (that is all the dogs in each heat start level) in weight groups. There are a number of ways in which a club can provide the fairest and most competitive sport for the members. Races are also run for puppies or veterans, or divided by sex, dogs and bitches. The age at which a puppy is permitted to run also varies with club rules. Puppies often compete with the BWRA as young as six months old whilst with the WCRA no puppy is issued with an official passport or permitted to run at any meeting run under WCRA rules until it is a year old. The reason for this rule is that whippets do not achieve maturity before at least 12 months old and a puppy which is put into training for racing is developing muscle on unfinished bone-growth which can cause long term structural damage and, ultimately, shorten life. All dogs are obliged to be muzzled and they also wear small coloured coats with their trap numbers on each side. The sight of four or five whippets parading in the paddock before

60. *'They're off'. (Sport and General)*

a race, being led around by their proud owners, dressed in their 'silks' and ready to go, is almost as exciting as seeing Derby runners in the paddock on the big day.

The WCRA and BWRA

The forming of the BWRA and subsequently the WCRA are two of the most significant developments, not only in the racing scene but in the overall development of the breed, during the last twenty years. To understand their importance it is necessary to take a look at their aims and objects and their mode of operation.

The British Whippet Racing Association (BWRA)

The BWRA, founded in 1967, came into being 'to promote greater friendship and understanding between whippet racing clubs; to give strength

61. *Over the line to snatch at the rag.*

to the advancement of the sport; to help clubs in dealing with local councils in negotiation for land, and to control and standardise whippet racing'. Ten regions make up the BWRA, each individual region being run by its own committee according to the rules of the Association. A member who wishes to join the BWRA does so via his club Secretary and in order to participate in Association events each dog must be registered with the National Registrar who issues an identity card and name which is exclusively the property of that individual dog for its racing life. The BWRA does not require dogs to be pure-bred whippets although a name for sire and dam is given on the passport. Greyhound three-quarter-breds are popular with the BWRA and provided they are 'of whippet-type' and do not exceed height and weight limits are fully entitled to run, which many of them do successfully. Many of the top dogs running with the BWRA have at least some greyhound blood three or four generations back and in some cases it might be difficult, as far as looks are concerned, to distinguish them from their pure-bred counterparts running with the WCRA. It is not difficult

62. *'Who won it?'*.

to understand why this should be so since, as we have explained in our chapter on origins, it seems probable that greyhounds and whippets share the same genetic pool, the differences in type depending largely on size. However, it must be remembered that while certain part-bred individuals may appear to conform very nearly to 'whippet-type' others of a litter may be very far from doing so and progeny, even from those of acceptable type, will certainly betray mixed ancestry in immediate and succeeding generations.

Most owners and breeders of BWRA dogs are perfectly honest and open about their dogs' breeding, and are indeed proud of it, and rightly so, since what they have produced is a top-class running dog. It is not uncommon to see Stud and sales advertisements in the Whippet News (the excellent journal devoted to all BWRA racing news) describing litters or studs as being by or out of a greyhound, or greyhound-cross. Problems resulting from such cross-breeding do not arise within the BWRA but rather within the WCRA, where a small minority of competitors who aspire to win 'at all costs' attempt to infiltrate such cross-breds into the pedigree racing scene. The damage which can be done to the purity of the whippet is considerable. No breed can hope to retain consistent breed type under constant pressure from the introduction of cross-breeding. Generally speaking it is members of the pedigree whippet racing fraternity who, through ignorance or competitiveness, endeavour to infiltrate cross-breds into pedigree whippet racing clubs.

A BWRA Pedigree

Wishy Was Reg. 7/70	Blue Star Peter 5/63	Joker UNR
		Jean UNR
	Blackie UNR	Unkown
		Unknown

(UNR = Unregistered)

A WCRA Pedigree

WCRA Ch. Madishan Moonlake Racing name Luke 9/70	Ch. Laguna Light Lagoon	Laguna Lightstep
		Tantivvey Oriole
	Madishan Moonflower	Ch. Telstar Moon
		Ch. Interflora

The Whippet Club Racing Association (WCRA)

The WCRA was formed as a direct consequence of the setting up of the BWRA. The Whippet Club, in 1968, mindful of that portion of its rules which states as an objective 'the promotion of the breeding of whippets. . . to the Kennel Club Standard of the Breed', formed a sub-committee to found and organise the WCRA. It was felt by the then permanent committee of the Whippet Club that the BWRA presented a threat to the breed as a whole, since it was possible that a situation might arise (as has happened in greyhounds) whereby the breed might become split into two distinct types, show whippets registered with the Kennel Club and racing whippets (strictly speaking, cross-bred whippets) registered with the BWRA. In order to prevent this divergence the WCRA came into being, to organise, standardise and promote pedigree whippet racing along the lines which are followed so successfully in the Netherlands, and elsewhere on the continent, under Breed Club control, and within the Kennel Club framework of the breed.

The WCRA is an association of racing clubs, the clubs being affiliated to the Association, rather than individual members. On affiliation, member clubs agree to abide by the rules of the Association, and the final arbiter in matters of racing procedure is the Committee of the WCRA. In matters pertaining to breed standards or involving any change in the Rules of the Association, the WCRA must seek a majority at the Annual General Meeting of the parent Club, the Whippet Club. A Registrar was appointed, as in the BWRA, who is responsible for issuing passports which are made out in the Kennel Club registered name of the dog, signed by the breeder, by the Registrar, and also by an authorised official of the WCRA (generally the Secretary of an affiliated club) as confirmation of identity. All identifying marks and details as to colour and markings, as well as a photograph, are included on the passport, an example of which is shown in Plate 71. Basic requirements for the issue of a WCRA passport are membership of an affiliated club, Kennel Club registration plus five generations of breeding acceptable to the Committee of the WCRA, of the dog or dogs in question. Problems have always arisen from the indefinite criteria for Kennel Club registration and for that reason we have included an example of a Kennel Club registration certificate for comparison with the WCRA passport. It will be seen that the details on the Kennel Club certificate are not sufficiently specific to describe any individual dog with any certainty. Whilst this fact is immaterial in relation to the vast majority of whippets, or indeed to all other breeds of dogs registered with the Kennel Club, since probity of breeders is the ground-rock on which the breeding of pedigree stock is founded, for the purpose of registering racing stock such slender identfication has not proved to be sufficient.

At the period when the WCRA was founded the Kennel Club were still accepting for registration dogs whose ancestors were unregistered or unknown. A whippet without papers could be submitted to a Championship judge of the breed and on the authority of his or her signature a Kennel Club registration card Class II would be issued. Resulting progeny were issued with Class I cards after two generations. In some cases such dogs were evidently pure-bred although their antecedants were unknown or for some reason unregistered. In other cases they were issued with cards although they were clearly not pure-bred. The issuing of cards was also sometimes problematical from an administrative point of view since cases have been known to arise where one half of a litter would receive Class I cards and others Class II cards, clearly an anomaly. Originally the WCRA accepted Class II cards provided that the Committee were satisfied that the dog or dogs in question matched the standard for the breed, but a time limit for accepting such dogs was set to allow owners and breeders to adjust their programmes accordingly. Shortly afterwards the Kennel Club also withdrew their facilities for Class II cards. As in the tightening up of civil laws such a step merely encouraged the unscrupulous to seek other ways of getting round the new regulations. As a result of concern on the part of the WCRA that only pure-bred whippets should compete under their rules a situation has arisen whereby the official WCRA passport, issued by the Registrar of the Association, might be a more authoritative document of origin than a Kennel Club registration certificate. Until the Kennel Club registration system is changed into line with that used by the Greyhound Stud Book, whereby each litter to be registered is inspected by an approved veterinary officer who testifies as to the number and colour of whelps, this anomaly is bound to remain with all the resulting confusion and complications.

Anyone buying a whippet puppy for the purpose of competing in pedigree whippet racing would be well-advised to seek confirmation from the Registrar of the WCRA that the puppy would be eligible for a WCRA passport before purchase. This equally applies to the use of stud dogs.

The WCRA has not only dealt with intricate problems arising from registration but the Rules of the Association also deal in some depth with the administration of racing. Track lay-out, arrangement of handicapping, and rules of behaviour of both dogs and owners are all dealt with at length and a copy of the Rules of the Association may be obtained from the Secretary of the WCRA or from individual club secretaries. Anyone who is interested in pedigree whippet racing should contact the Secretary of the WCRA for a list of member clubs which range from Scotland to Cornwall and cover most areas of the Midlands and the South of England. All such clubs run regular meetings through the summer under WCRA rules and the Association also run a number of Championship meetings

63. *Modern lure racing under W.C.R.A. rules; weighing. (Walsh)*

on neutral grounds, both for bends and straight tracks. Dogs which win two finals in their weight groups are awarded the title of WCRA Champion, an achievement to be proud of.

In all working breeds, there is a tendancy for divergence in breed type between the working and the show section. Ideally, the closer a dog is to the Breed Standard the better it should be capable of fulfilling the function of origin. Scrupulous breeders with the good of their breed at heart will always attempt, to a greater or lesser degree, to ensure that the stock they produce will be capable of fulfilling the original function. When a breed reaches the state that show quality has become paramount, to the extent that show specimens have neither the temperament nor the ability to perform the basic function, then that breed will have degenerated to an alarming degree. In the gundog group the title of Champion implies that a dog is exactly that, a full champion, having gained its title in the ring and a qualifying certificate in the field. Champions in the ring alone are designated Show Champion. Hounds are no less working dogs than gundogs and there are certainly a number of breeders who would like to see some kind of dual-title established for whippets. It is difficult to know, however, just what sort of qualification in addition to the show title would be acceptable or

64. *A bank of traps is used at a Championship meeting as all dogs run off scratch. (Walsh)*

practical to administer. In the meantime, as in deerhounds and salukis, there are a number of well-known show prefixes who consistently course or race their show stock in order to underline and demonstrate the principle of overall excellence.

It is a measure of the success of the WCRA that there are a number of individual dogs who have made their marks in two, if not three, of the possible fields of whippet activity. Further, an examination of the breeding behind many of the WCRA champions will show that the same bloodlines with which we are all familiar in the ring and on the coursing field are also responsible for winners on the track.

Despite this fact, however, individual dogs capable of such success are in a minority and great care needs to be taken if the overall type of racing dogs is not to diverge too sharply from the standard required elsewhere. Two factors are basically responsible for this falling off in breed type. First, almost all racing is organised in weight groups and it is an obvious advantage to have a dog which weighs as little as possible for its height. This encourages the breeding of dogs which lack body substance and have very little bone.

65. *A fairly level break. (Walsh)*

A 19½ inch dog with correct breed conformation and substance should weigh 24 to 26 lbs. A racing dog of that weight would be more likely to stand 20 to 21 inches at the shoulder. With overall lack of bone and substance other faults become prevalent which, while they would seriously impede a dog on the coursing field and be penalised by a judge in the show ring, are no barrier to being able to sprint over mown grass for 160 to 250 yards. When a whippet runs a course after a hare it brings every part of its body into use. To gallop fast over rough ground and to twist and turn at speed after a hare a dog must be properly constucted. Good feet are essential since thin flat feet quickly break down. Lay of shoulder and length of loin are also vital; a dog which is 'tied' in the elbows cannot turn satisfactorily. Substance is also important, since stamina plays a part in courses which may last three minutes or more, so a deep brisket and plenty of heart-room are needed. Just as show breeders must take care not to err on the opposite side by producing substance to the degree of breeding 'cloddy' or 'cobby' whippets, so should racing breeders bear the standard in mind when planning matings lest qualities other than speed are lost.

66. *160 yards to go. (Walsh)*

Secondly there is the fact that very few breeders involved in racing have any interest in the show ring. Unlike coursing which has been supported from the beginning by a number of well-known breed prefixes (Laguna, Porthurst, Linknumstar, Ballagan, Dragonhill, Nimrodel, Martinsell, Tweseldown) only a handful of such prefixes spring to mind in connection with racing (Laguna, Russettwood, Martinsell, Chancerick) and the benefit to racing of these bloodlines will be lost in years to come if infusions of quality bloodlines are not reintroduced at regular intervals.

As we have seen when considering the show and coursing history of the breed, the influence of Mrs MacKay's Laguna breeding has also been paramount in racing. The Laguna Kennel has produced dogs which have reached the top in all three fields. There can be no doubt that Laguna bloodlines consistently produce outstanding speed, and, when combined with some of the lines more noted for stamina, exceptional individuals have resulted.

One such dog was Miss Robertson's particolour, WCRA Ch. Madishan Moonlake. A first time whippet for his owner, Moonlake (racing name Luke) not only gained his WCRA title but qualified to run at the BWRA championships running against part-breds. His achievements in the coursing field were perhaps even more spectacular. He won the Nicholl Cup for

67. *Individual traps are used in Club racing so that, by moving traps backwards or forwards, dogs can be handicapped according to weight, or previous performance. (Walsh)*

dogs three years in succession, thus winning it outright, as a result of which it has been renamed the Moonlake Trophy. It is rare indeed that a dog has both the speed to achieve a racing title and the stamina to gain top honours on the coursing field. Moonlake was a perfect example of the combination of the speed and stamina bloodlines. His sire, Ch. Laguna Light Lagoon (Laguna Lightstep — Tantivvey Oriole) bred by Miss Clay, although never raced or coursed himself, proved an outstanding sire of both racing and coursing progeny. Moonlake's dam, Madishan Moonflower was a grand-daughter of Int. Ch. Playmate of Allways, a noted sire and grand-sire of stayers. Moonflower herself was a good performer in the field and also a winner at championship shows and Moonlake's pedigree ably demonstrates how effective the best show bloodlines can be when applied to racing and coursing. Ch. Laguna Light Lagoon also sired two other WCRA Champions in Laguna Lintino and Laguna Linneth, as well as numerous other racing and coursing winners.

68. *On the apex of the bend. (Walsh)*

Group Captain and Mrs Whittingham have bred whippets for many years with coursing and racing chiefly in mind. The foundation of their success in recent years has been the acquisition of three bitches from Mrs MacKay, WCRA Ch. Laguna Lauraine, WCRA Ch. Laguna Lintino, and Laguna Luisa. When Mrs Wittingham used the black WCRA Ch. Chancerick Koh-i-Nor a whole generation of winners resulted, including the outstanding coursing bitch, Culverstreet Concubine and her two sisters, Chianti and Columbine. This combination of bloodlines was again an instance of the speed/stamina combination, Koh-i-Nor carrying the strong Ladiesfield — Dragonhill — Nimrodel working strain.

Miss Rooney's Russettwood Pageant, litter brother to her beautiful Ch. Russettwood Portia (Ch. Laguna Ligonier — Russettwood Rhythm) was another outstanding sire of racing stock. One of his sons, WCRA Ch. Mystic Pepe was a WCRA and BWRA Champion, possibly the only dog to have gained this distinction. Pageant also sired WCRA Chs Patch of Bemerton, Woolmer Wayfarer, Chilworth Pride, Bally Will Will, and Lucky Venture. Mated to the greyhound bitch Sarah he sired two BWRA

69. *38 miles per hour. (Walsh)*

Chs, Melvina B and Mary Mint. Ch. Russettwood Portia herself, when mated to Ch. Laguna Linkway produced WCRA Ch. Russettwood Moonshine.

The Martinsell prefix of Joanna Russell and Caroline Brown is behind some of the fastest racing dogs and bitches running with the WCRA. Shalfleet Saga (Porthurst Cherry Brandy — Wingedfoot Bartette), a quality fawn dog purchased from Barbara Wilton Clark, was the foundation of their racing line. He sired WCRA Chs Kimberley and Vangirl, and was the grand-sire of WCRA Chs Valentine's Link, Fulmen Firefly, and Picketty Witch. The last named was, in the opinion of many, one of the greatest racing bitches in the history of the WCRA. A black and white, bred by Mrs Joyce Keable, Secretary of the Andover WRC, Picketty Witch whose registered name was Karyon Sootican Princess (Abbots Anny Pride — WCRA Ch. Vangirl) won all ten of the WCRA Championships for which she was entered, thus making her a WCRA Champion five times over.

Mrs Meek and Mrs Griffiths whose prefix is Chancerick have also had a considerable effect on the racing scene. Their foundation bitch, Chancerick Nimrodel Rosefinch (Ch. Poltesco Peewit — Nimrodel Wintersweet, a litter

70. *It may be only a lure but it has to be dealt with. (Walsh)*

sister to Ch. Nimrodel Ruff, entirely show and coursing-bred) when mated to that impressive coursing dog, Ebzan Noudini Bey-Noir (Ladiesfield — Fleeting breeding) produced the famous litter in which there were three WCRA Champions, Chancerick Koh-i-Nor, Kondor and Kala, as well as the CC and RCC winner, Chancerick Kaspar. From this mating descend eleven WCRA Champions, Star, Topaz, Carly, Marlin, Nippy Girl, Chancilly Lace, Picketty Witchdoctor, Picketty Spook, J for Jackie, J for Jacko, and Velvetine. Chancerick Koh-i-Nor also, as we have seen, had a great effect on coursing, as well as racing, stock. As a sire of blacks and blues he threw more bone than is generally the case and he will be found in the pedigrees of many of the best of these colour being shown today. Koh-i-Nor himself won his Kennel Club Stud Book number in the ring and might very well have been that rare example of triple excellence had he not been over the height limit for coursing.

In breeding for racing, as in other fields, a balanced view is essential. From the examples which we have examined, it can be seen what an important part classic bloodlines have played in producing successful all round stock, and just as show breeders must not breed for exaggerated breed points without attention to overall balance and soundness, nor must

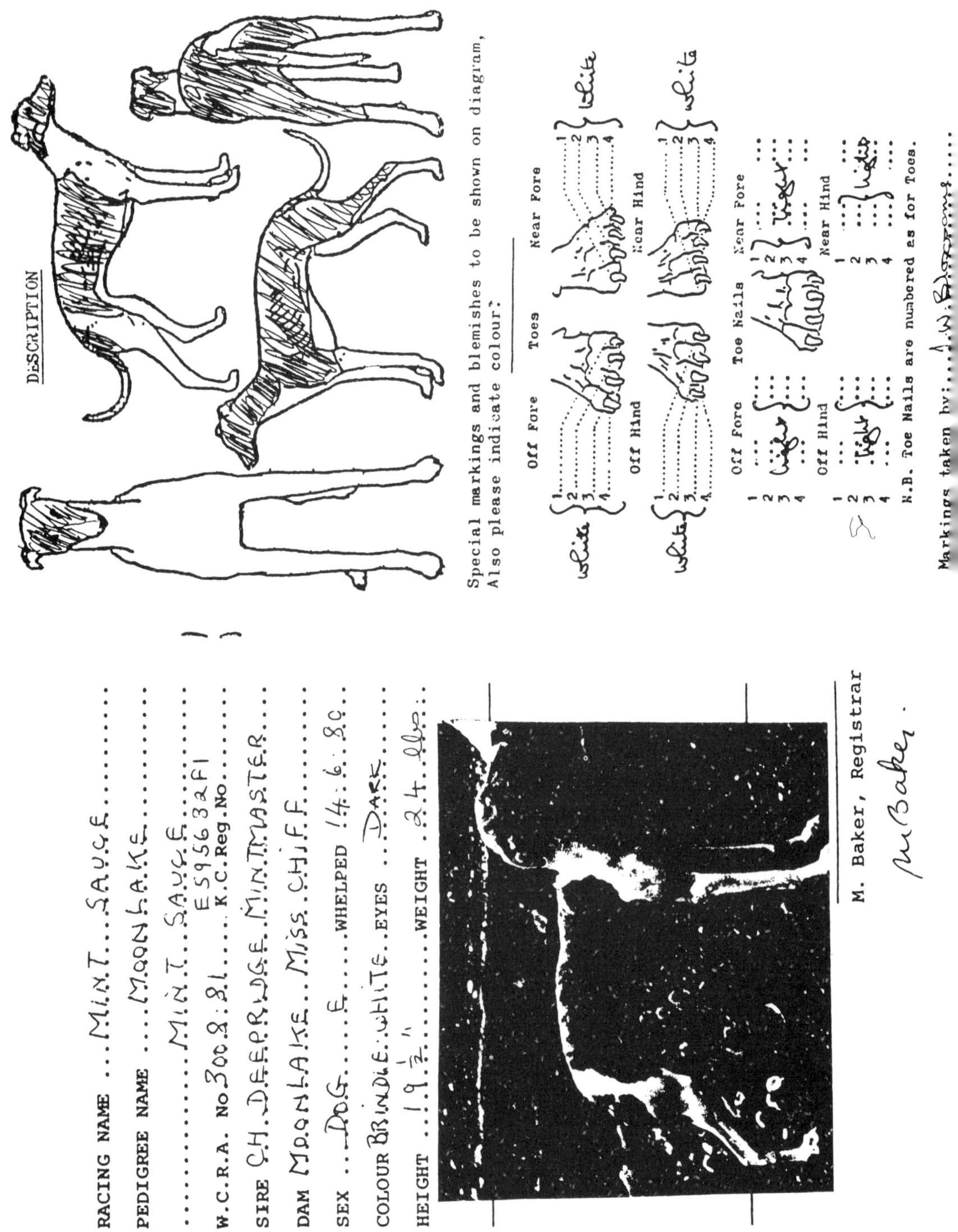

71. *A W.C.R.A. passport. Note the detailed description of the dog, even down to the colour of toenails.*

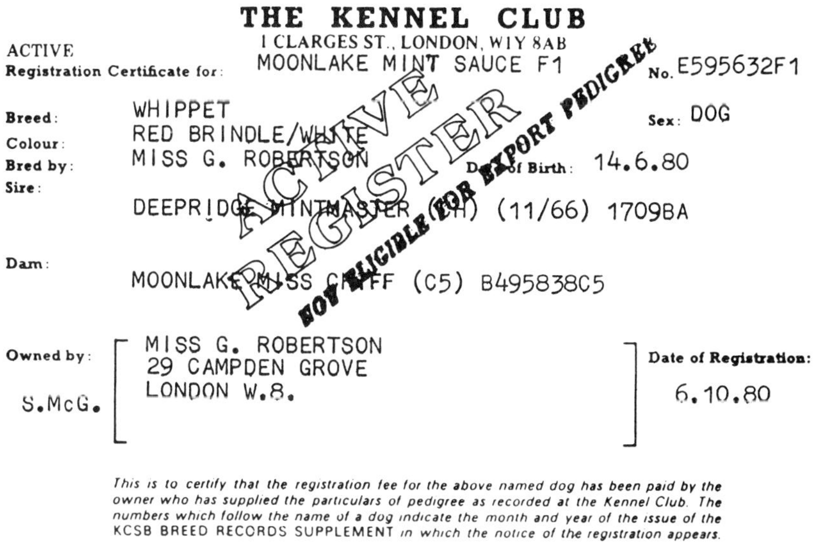

THE KENNEL CLUB

1 CLARGES ST., LONDON, W1Y 8AB

ACTIVE
Registration Certificate for: MOONLAKE MINT SAUCE F1 No. E595632F1

Breed: WHIPPET Sex: DOG

Colour: RED BRINDLE/WHITE

Bred by: MISS G. ROBERTSON Date of Birth: 14.6.80

Sire: DEEPRIDGE MINTMASTER (CH) (11/66) 1709BA

Dam: MOONLAKE MISS C[illegible]FF (C5) B495838C5

ACTIVE REGISTER

NOT ELIGIBLE FOR EXPORT PEDIGREE

Owned by: MISS G. ROBERTSON
29 CAMPDEN GROVE
LONDON W.8.

S.McG.

Date of Registration: 6.10.80

This is to certify that the registration fee for the above named dog has been paid by the owner who has supplied the particulars of pedigree as recorded at the Kennel Club. The numbers which follow the name of a dog indicate the month and year of the issue of the KCSB BREED RECORDS SUPPLEMENT *in which the notice of the registration appears.*

72. *The same dog's Kennel Club registration card. The description could apply to a great many dogs.*

racing breeders consider speed alone to the detriment of the breed standard as a whole. It is an interesting fact that, while racing type today has diverged rather more widely that is desirable from the standard, nor is the breeding as classic as when the WCRA was founded, the times clocked by winning dogs in the championships are no faster now than they were in the early 1970s. If a better constructed, better bred, dog can run faster than one which is entirely racing-bred for several generations, racing breeders should be taking a look at their pedigrees and consider reintroducing some show, or coursing, lines to re-establish some of the breed qualities they have lost.

Training for racing is very much a matter of individual opinion but generally speaking the routine is much the same as for coursing. It is important not to start trialling or training a puppy too young as this can have long-term ill effects. Road walking is the basis of most training and dogs can be walked for anything between two and five miles daily. Diet, again, is often a question of personal preference and the guiding principle must be what proves successful with the individual dog. Race results, and times clocked, will soon tell whether a dog is giving of its best. The same general principles which apply to getting a dog into peak fitness for any activity should be the first consideration. Dogs which are reduced excessively to achieve a certain racing weight may suffer serious long term effects. A good healthy diet and plenty of the right sort of exercise are the best recipe for success.

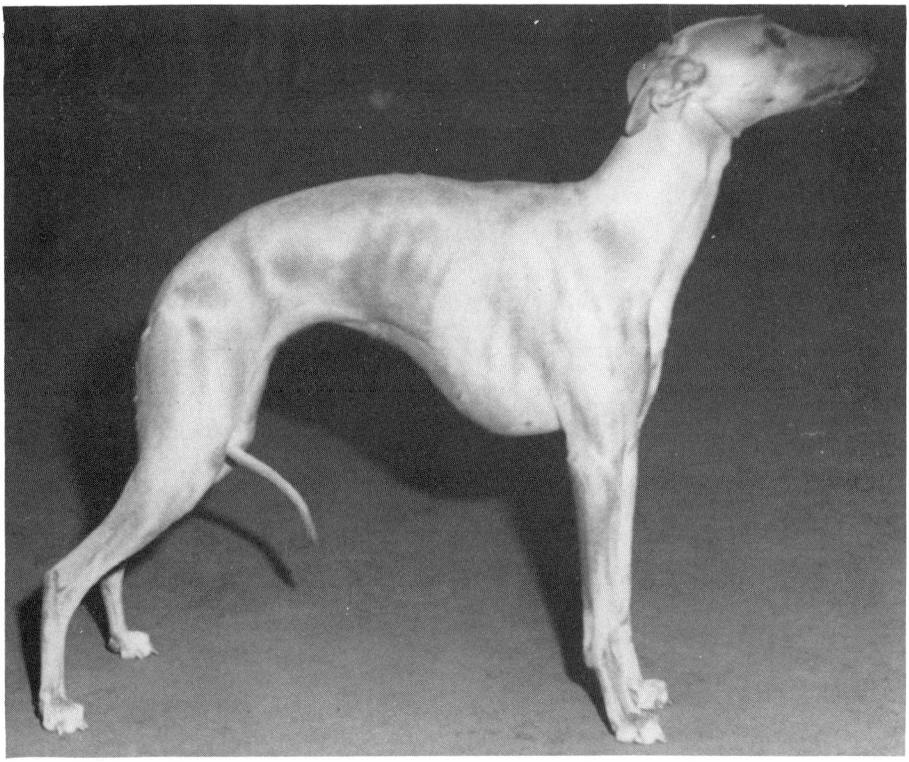

73. *'There are a number of individual dogs who have made their mark in two, if not three fields of activity.' Ch. Nimrodel Willow Daughter, winner of the Hound Group and Res. BIS at Birmingham National; she also won two Open Bitch coursing stakes and was 'Dog of the Day' at the Oxford Whippet Racing Club. She was awarded the Dutch Medal for Dual-Purpose Excellence by Mr Hugenholtz, of the Netherlands Whippet Club. (Cooke)*

Buying a puppy specifically for racing is similar to buying a puppy for any other purpose. Attend a number of meetings, meet and talk to competitors and breeders, and finally place yourself in the hands of a breeder who has made a name for producing winning stock. If racing is your serious objective it will, in all probability, not prove successful to buy a puppy from show or coursing bloodlines. Such a puppy would be likely to have more bone and substance than one which was racing bred so it would start with a weight handicap which it might not be able to overcome. At club racing level, this would not prove a barrier since most club racing is organised to give members and dogs the widest chance of success but at Open or Championship level a puppy from a proven racing strain would be a better prospect. The secretary of your local W.C.R.A. club should be in a position to help with advice about litters and bloodlines; until the novice is familiar with the racing scene he would do well to seek such advice.

74. *W.C.R.A. Racing Ch. Chancerick Koh-i-Nor ('Koko'). (Dierdre Poole)*

75. *W.C.R.A. Racing Ch. Madishan Moonlake ('Luke'). (Jim Meads)*

76. *The ideal brood bitch, Ch. Oakbark Michaela. (Whimpanny)*

CHAPTER 7

Breeding Whippets

'Breeding is the name of the game.' There are many aspects of the world of the pedigree dog, and many people get a great deal of pleasure in contributing in a number of different ways. Without exhibitors there would be no shows, without shows there would be no judges, without judges there would be no winners, without winners there would be no spectators; but without breeders there would be nothing. Breeders can make or mar their chosen breed. A breed which is rich in intelligent, scrupulous, clever and dedicated breeders cannot go far wrong. On the other hand, a breed which is dominated by the wrong sort of breeder, those who are more interested in the financial returns or show ring success alone, can deteriorate in very few generations.

Skilful breeding appears to be a gift and a vocation. It is perfectly possible to be a topflight exhibitor of high quality dogs but not to be capable of breeding them oneself. It is also possible to be a skilled judge of great integrity and yet not be a breeder of dogs at the level of those one judges. The converse of this is true; it is also possible to be a highly successful breeder without having the ability to campaign the resulting stock to the top. Thus it can be seen that there is room for us all in the world of dogs, and each of us should try to have the intelligence to realise just which is the contribution we are best equipped to make.

Breeding dogs, be it for show purposes, coursing or racing (and each field should contribute to the others) requires specific abilities. A breeder must have an eye for stock, great integrity concerning genetic faults, and furthermore, in top breeders there is a sort of sixth sense which lifts the competant breeders beyond the run-of-the-mill into a class of their own. A careful breeder may produce one or two good litters, an inspired breeder will produce generations of stock which bear witness only too obviously to the inspiration which has fired them. We have been very lucky in whippets, in that we seem to have been blessed throughout the history of the breed, with just the right sort of breeder. Perhaps because whippets

77. *Michaela's daughter, Ch. Newbold Kerry Gold. (Whimpanny)*

78. *Michaela's son, Ch. Newbold Muffinman*

are not, in any strict sense, a financially rewarding breed, we have had very few commercial kennels. A large kennel can contribute just as vitally to the progress of the breed as inspired smaller breeders, but a commercial breeder contributes little. In a breed with small financial returns the relative importance of the large kennel versus the smaller breeder allows for the fostering of talent to a greater extent than in a breed where financial rewards further the foundation of large commercial kennels, which, while they may have a head-start in terms of facilities and opportunity, may not breed as selectively as is desirable. In a large kennel where twenty to fifty dogs are kept, a breeder will be campaigning eight or nine puppies a year which will be the pick of anything up to fifty whelps. The smaller breeder, on the other hand, will bring out one or two puppies a year which are a selection from one or two litters only. This sort of breeder, however, rarely makes mistakes; only top class stock is bred from and great care goes into planning matings. If you are privileged enough to secure a puppy from a litter such as this, you will be fortunate indeed.

There are a number of whippet breeders who have come into this category. The Miss Hudsons (Cockrow) bred very selectively and kept only one or two to campaign themselves, yet their stock in the hands of others has had an enormous influence on the breed. The same is true of Mr and Mrs H. Wood (Flarepath) and Mr and Mrs D. Howarth (Newbold). A Newbold or Flarepath bitch has set many a current breeder on the road to success. The late Mrs Cleeve (Dragonhill), Mrs Wigg (Ladiesfield) and Mrs Gollan (Peppard) were breeders of such consistent flair and perception that it is doubtful if present day breeders could rival their capacity for producing stock of the highest quality in every successive generation, stock furthermore, which always bore the Dragonhill, Ladiesfield or Peppard hallmark. Two of the larger kennels which produced consistent type, and whose bloodlines have been the foundation, since 1962, of almost all other breeders were the Allways kennels of Mrs Bobbie Cooke and the Laguna kennels of Mrs Dorrit MacKay. Since that date, and based on those foundations, the most influential prefixes have probably been Mrs Wilton Clarke's Shalfleets, Mr and Mrs Meakin's Oakbarks, Mr Nicholson's Glenbervies, and of course, Mrs Anne Knight's Dondelayos.

Choosing a Foundation Bitch

When choosing foundation stock on which to build your own line as a breeder, there are many advantages in going to a large kennel. The benefit of having a number of choices available from a well-proved strain when it comes to planning future generations, must be obvious. Equally, however, a puppy from one of the breeders in the category I have mentioned might well prove more potent as a representative of a powerful bitch line provided

79. *Ch. Laguna Ravensdowne Astri. (Cooke)*

80. *Astri's son, Ch. Flarepath Astrinaught of Lowglen. (Diane Pearce)*

that future matings follow the carefully thought out progression of the original breeder. Were I buying a foundation bitch today I would take a good look at the classic bitch lines which have dominated the breed over the last few years and consider myself very lucky if I was able to purchase a puppy from a litter carrying the Newbold, Flarepath, Oakbark, or Glenbervie prefixes. Certain kennels are notable for producing either better dogs or better bitches and on the whole, if it is breeding in which you are primarily interested in, you must choose a kennel with a strong bitch line. Always look at the bitch line of any puppy you are contemplating buying, and of any dog you propose to use at stud. I do not mean that such a line should contain a row of Champions but you must ask yourself whether each successive generation were related to winners or other quality stock and that will be the best indication of what your bitch will be able to produce herself. There are certain sires (not necessarily the ones which have produced the highest number of winners) whose daughters are noted winner-producers and if you can obtain a bitch by such a dog you will have laid your foundations correctly.

Ch. Fieldspring Bartsia of Allways is a perfect example of a sire with a classic bitch line. He sired five Champions, but his greatest influence on the breed lay rather in what his daughters produced. Chs Ladiesfield Topaz, Shalfleet Swordsman, Playmate of Allways, Nimrodel Willow Daughter, Laguna Ligonier (currently the top sire ever in the breed) were all out of bitches by Bartsia, as was Black Brocade of Allways who, while not a Champion, has a considerable effect on blacks and blues. Ch. Lowglen Newbold Cavalier is another famous for his beautiful daughters and their influence on the breed has yet to be fully accounted. Ch. Ravensdowne Bright Star, sire of Ch. Laguna Ravonsdowne Astri, Towercrest Ravensdowne Vega and Laguna Ravensdowne Faerie Queen all of whom in turn produced Champions, was another such sire.

The choice of a foundation bitch to show, course or race, may not be necessarily based on the same premises as the choice of one to breed from. Most of us do not acquire our first bitch with anything specific in mind, and it is only later on, as we become more involved and knowledgeable, that we start to apply the criteria I have described, to our original choice. It is very important, if you are considering breeding from your first bitch, to apply to her all the critical assessment which you would do if you had bought her specifically as a foundation brood. If she does not match up with your requirements it is more sensible to forget about breeding from her and to buy another bitch for what you have in mind. The basic requirements of a brood bitch are as follows. She should be of the right age (two to four years old and no older for a first litter), she should be of average size with no outstanding breed faults against the Standard for the breed, she should be in good health, and have a steady reliable

81. *Astri's grandson, Ch. Lowglen Newbold Cavalier. (Diane Pearce)*

82. *Cavalier's daughter, Int. Ch. Savilepark Sweet Harmony.*

temperament. She should also, ideally, have a solid pedigree, that is, one which is the result of several generations of planned breeding. A bitch which is the result of a haphazard mating, carrying diverse bloodlines of different breed types, will be most unlikely to produce typical stock of the standard you require.

In buying a bitch for such a purpose, decide which type of whippet you prefer and put yourself in the hands of an experienced breeder who consistently produces the type you have in mind. You may have to wait a year or so to get the sort of puppy you want but your patience will be rewarded in the long run because if you rush out and buy a puppy from the first litter which is available it may take you several generations to correct the mistake you made initially. I cannot stress sufficiently the inadvisability of breeding from second-rate stock. An indifferent brood bitch will reproduce her failings from one generation to the next. The most important things to look for are good type, coat, ears, movement, especially good temperament, sufficient bone, body and length. She could well be a shade large, or a shade small, perhaps not especially glamorous, or badly marked; these things might prevent her being a winner herself but they will not prevent her producing a good litter to a suitable dog.

Choosing a Stud Dog

When selecting a sire there are some questions you must ask yourself concerning him over and above his suitability as to pedigree. Always choose a dog with a friendly, outgoing temperament. Faults of temperament are almost always hereditary and although you naturally hope you are going to breed a litter of Champions it is more realistic to remember that in every litter there will be a proportion of pet puppies whom you will wish to settle in good homes. No one wants a pet which is nervous or vicious and your pet-market for the non-show quality stock is important to you in order to continue in business as a breeder. The fact that so many dogs have to be resettled by the rescue societies means that there are too many people breeding too many dogs without sufficient care as to whether they will find suitable homes. It is important that, with every litter you breed, you produce typical quality stock which will be in demand as pets, even if they are of no interest to you as show, coursing or racing prospects. In selecting a stud dog, try to see as many of his progeny as possible. This should give you an idea as to whether he is capable of reproducing himself and what lies behind him. Some stud dogs stamp their type on their progeny almost regardless of the bitches they are mated to, whilst others tend to reproduce the qualities of the dam. Either propensity can be useful to the discerning breeder, but it is important to understand which he is likely to do since this factor must influence your final choice.

83. *Ch. Towercrest Flarepath Taurus, a nephew of Astri.*

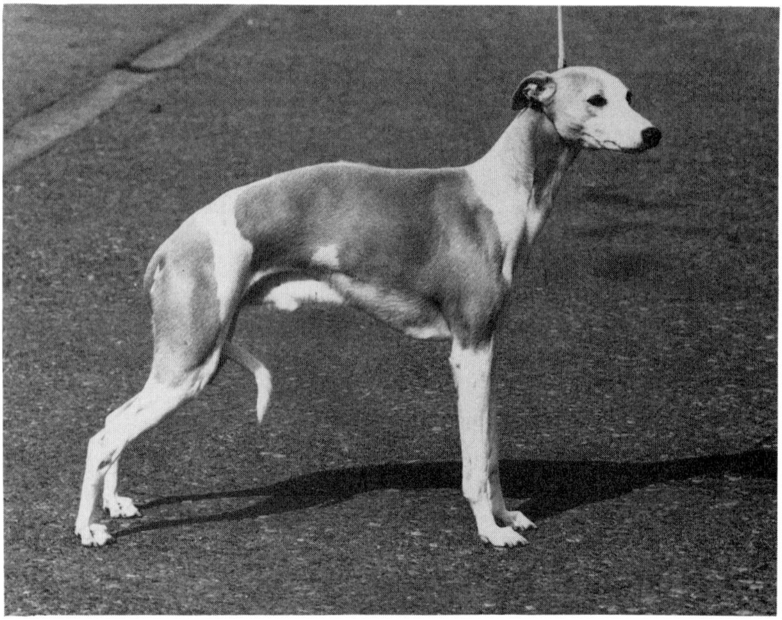

84. *Taurus' son, Ch. Oakbark Melord. (Whimpanny)*

85. *Taurus' daughter, Ch. Oakbark Movie Queen. (Whimpanny)*

Type-breeding and Line-breeding

The Shorter Oxford English Dictionary defines 'type' as 'A species or genus which most perfectly exhibits the essential characters of its family or group, and from which the family or group is named; an individual embodying all the distinctive characters of a species.' An understanding of breed type is the basis on which clever breeding is founded. In reality this must depend on the eye of the breeder. An eye for stock is a talent which some are born with but which it is perfectly possible for others to acquire. A trained eye in any field is a tremendous asset and it can be acquired in the world of dogs as in any other field. With this in mind we have attempted to arrange the pictures in Chapter 9 according to type and bloodlines so that it should be easy to see at a glance the differences in type between well-known dogs of different breeding. There are those who contend that there should be no differences in type within a breed and that the only correct type is laid down in the breed Standard. However, while the Standard lists the correct construction of a whippet and the faults to be avoided there is room within that framework for a certain amount of variation in breed type. Each breeder will have in the mind's eye a picture of a whippet as near their ideal of the Standard as possible, and it is this selective interpretation of breeders, combined with generations of planned matings, which produces consistent breed type. With the most successful breeders it is always possible to look at their stock and to know at once that it is, for instance, an Allways or a Laguna whippet. A careful look at photographs, past and present, will

86. *Choosing a stud dog; Ch. Pilot Officer Prune, sire of ten champions.*

show that there are differences in type between many of the top winners although each individual will have conformed to the standard of excellence. It is only by studying photographs and attending a large number of shows, and by paying attention to the dogs on view, that an eye for type will be developed.

One of the cardinal rules in breeding is 'stick to type'. The reason for this is that if two dogs of different type are mated to each other the result is apt to be a litter of uneven puppies which resemble neither of the parents and are unlikely to inherit the best qualities of either. Type should be working for you rather than the reverse. There are two ways in which type can be maintained in ensuing progeny. The mating of two unrelated but similar dogs (type-breeding) can be perfectly effective, but an even more successful method is the mating of two related dogs (line-breeding) provided that neither has serious breed faults. Just as line-breeding doubles the virtues, so too will it double the faults should they be present in the parents. There is a certain amount of confusion about the difference between line-breeding and in-breeding. Whilst line-breeding is one of the most effective ways of stamping type on a line and producing outstanding stock, too close in-breeding can produce genetic faults, lack of substance, and poor temperament. Briefly, line-breeding is mating dogs with a common ancestor or ancestors, to each other. Thus the mating of half-brother to half-sister,

87. *Three generations of Mrs Chapman's champions: Chs Pilot Officer Prune, Flying Officer Kite and En for Nonsense.*

grand-daughter back to grand-father, etc, are line-breeding. Mating father to daughter, mother to son, or full brother and sister, are in-breeding. In such matings no new blood at all is added to the genetic pool whereas in line-breeding selected genes are doubled on. An 'out-cross' is where unrelated blood is introduced, not to be confused with 'cross-breeding' where a different species altogether is used.

Whether you decide to 'type-breed' or 'line-breed' or a combination of the two, always look for mates which are of the same type and quality. In that way you can hope to produce puppies which resemble their parents and their bloodlines and in very few generations you will find that you are achieving litter after litter of level puppies of good quality. Although the occasional big winner does crop up in a litter where the other puppies are mediocre to poor, the dogs and bitches who have had the greatest influence for good in the breed have generally been those which came from a good litter. This importance is borne out in the next generation since a dog or bitch which is one of a good family is much more likely to reproduce themselves.

Colour Breeding

Colour breeding in whippets is generally taken to mean breeding for blacks and blues, although logically the term must also apply to breeding for any specific coat colour to the exclusion of others. Enterprising breeders have always been attracted by the challenge represented by colour breeding and

88. *Ch. Fieldspring Bartsia of Allways. (Goater)*

while the Whippet Standard, in common with most standards for working dogs, lists colour as 'immaterial' there can be no doubt that a working knowledge of colour genetics can greatly help a breeder both to understand the importance of type, which is discernedly colour-linked, and also to produce an animal which not only conforms to the breed standard in respect of working qualities but has the added glamour of attractive coat colour as well. It is a great mistake to allow considerations of colour to outweigh breed type and excellence and no novice should attempt colour breeding without the advantage of a great deal of advice or expertise gained through long experience. A whippet cannot be a bad colour although some colours may be more favoured in the show ring than others, and some are even preferred for sporting purposes. There is an old greyhound prejudice against white dogs since it was thought that the hare could see a white dog more readily and would turn away, thus favouring a darker coloured rival.

89. *A typical Bartsia litter: five Ballagan puppies out of Fr. Ch. Heathermead Ada.*

Coursing enthusiasts have consequently tended to favour the fawns, blacks and brindles, while poachers are thought to have favoured them for reasons of their own!

Since type is linked to colour more often than not, there are strengths and weaknesses more generally associated with some colours than with others. Brindles tend to have finer or rounder bone than fawns or parti-colours, and in some cases, markedly coarser coats. Blacks and blues have a tendancy to either weediness or coarseness, whilst whites almost invariably have longer textured coats than fawns and many of the parti-colour lines. When exhibiting blacks, blues and brindles there is the added disadvantage of the optical illusion. Just as a woman who is wearing black stockings appears to have thinner legs than one who is wearing white stockings so do blacks and blues tend to look finer in substance than they are. An experienced judge who handles the dogs will, of course, be able to assess the bone correctly, but looking at these colours across the ring can be misleading. Such colours do not stand out against the background of an indoor show, and can therefore be at a disadvantage in this respect. The difficulties involved in breeding top class black and blue exhibits are underlined by the breed records — there have only been five black Champions since the last war (three since 1962) and no blue dog or bitch champion.

Genetically, the subject of colour breeding is a very complicated one. Although a great deal more is known about the different modes of inheritance of coat colour in dogs than was the case in the past, there can be no doubt that, as Burns and Fraser* say (in their excellent and

90. *Ch. Samarkand's Greenbrae Tarragon and his daughter, Ch. Dondelayo Duette. Close in-breeding produced two supreme winners of identical breed type. (Diane Pearce)*

comprehensive book on the subject of the 'Genetics of the Dog') many uncertainties remain. Perhaps one of the reasons why many whippet breeders have known cases which do not seem to follow the rules is that genetically speaking, it is very hard to find a whippet which is pure-bred for colour. The range of colours acceptable in the whippet Standard is very wide and since breeders through the years have, rightly, concentrated on breed excellence rather than colour, dogs and bitches of every permissible shade have contributed to the bank of genes from which we are drawing. A second, less acceptable, reason is the undoubted fact that not all whippet pedigrees are everything they should be. Whippets alone are subject to infiltration, even today, of unregistered racing stock with incorrect pedigrees which can make research very much less than rewarding and produce some of the anomalies which confront the breed expert. Further confusion can be caused by quite genuine errors in Kennel Club records of registration. Many people, when registering a dog, may give the colour at birth which

* Burns, M. and Fraser, M.N., 'Genetics of the Dog' (Oliver & Boyd, 1967; first published 1952)

is not found to be correct as the animal matures, but by then it is too much effort, or too late to have changes made in the registration. Equally, the registration forms may simply be returned with the colour incorrectly recorded, and again the owner may either not notice the fact, or may not think it of importance, or may be in a hurry to pass on the documentation to the new owner, and therefore does not bother to return the forms to the Kennel Club for correction. When drawing up a six or seven generation colour pedigree one such error can cause completely erroneous conclusions from a research point of view. I have personally checked recorded colours at the Kennel Club and subsequently been told by the owners of the bitch in question that it was in fact a parti-colour and not a brindle.

Whilst the Kennel Club Standard for the breed lists colour as 'immaterial' it is perhaps as well to give the colours which a whippet may be. According to C. C. Little* (*The Inheritance of Coat Color in Dogs*) whippets carry the genes to produce all of the following colours:

> 'Black, red, fawn, blue, brindle, cream or white or any combination of the above with white. They may also occur with white spotting, varying through Irish to piebald to extreme white piebald and white itself.'

It is not our intention, nor are we qualified to supply a complete explanation of colour genetics here. To the average breeder colour will be, as the Standard intimates 'immaterial' and for the colour enthusiast there are a number of highly professional and explicit works available on the subject which we list in our Bibliography. In order to understand colour breeding a good working knowledge of genetics is essential, and even then, for reasons which we have gone into, some anomalies remain. While certain coat colours can be said to be 'dominant' (or imperfectly dominant) to others (described as recessive since the presence of the genes for the recessive colour is masked by the visible or dominant colour) the interaction of certain genes on others (such as the gene for brindle and the gene for solid dark pigment) can produce what appear to be surprising results, consequently a simple rule of thumb is impossible to produce.

There are two things of importance to the whippet breeder as far as colour is concerned. Firstly, it must always be remembered, when planning 'colour matings', that all the same criteria as apply to any other mating, must be considered. Type, soundness and pedigree must all apply to 'colour matings' as to any others. The second fact with which the breeder should be concerned is the presence of the recessive genes for dilution, what is called the 'dilute factor'. Since the standard allows the dilute colours (blue and cream, blue resulting from the (d) gene for blue dilution, and cream from the paling

---

* Little, C.C., 'The Inheritance of Coat Color in Dogs' (Howell Book House, New York, 1979; first published 1957)

91. *Ch. Poaching Black Jack.*

92. *Ch. Martinsell Grand Slam. (Lionel Young)*

factor (c-Ch)) pale eyes and light pigment must be expected with these colours and is indeed expressly permitted by the standard. However, since a number of judges would seem to be under a misapprehension that light eyes and liver noses are breed faults (which is not the case) breeders should perhaps take the dilute factor into consideration when line-breeding. Inbreeding and line-breeding to any great extent will give rise to a higher proportion of recessive colours (blue, cream, parti-colour) and from time to time it will be necessary to reintroduce the darker pigment and eye colour

93. *Ch. Fleeting Spean La Calindra, the only tri-colour to gain a title.*

which goes with the dominant colours (black, brindle, fawn). The American standard differs from the English Kennel Club standard in respect of eye colour and pigment which is perhaps why there are those who tend to penalise exhibits in this country with light eyes and/or lack of pigment. It is a pity that this has come about since there is absolutely no doubt that the wide range of whippet colours available is one of the breed's greatest attractions, and the fact that the breed has remained so free of hereditary faults must be due to a certain extent to the fact that, since colour is immaterial, breeders have available the widest possible genetic pool, including all the virtues which dogs of dilute coat colours might have to offer. In some breeds where coat colour or markings are very rigidly adhered to, consequently confining the genetic pool of animals suitable for breeding, hereditary defects are becoming a disquieting factor.

Starting to Breed

Before deciding to breed a litter at all you should ask yourself some very serious questions. Breeding requires certain basic facilities which are not readily available to everyone. In the world of dogs there is plenty of room for people who make ideal dog owners or exhibitors, without necessarily being breeders. Equally there are those who are extremely gifted breeders but whose interests do not necessarily include exhibiting. If you do not have the time, money or facilities to breed a litter, it is far more sensible and satisfactory in the long run to buy a puppy from someone whose speciality this is. No mistake should be made, breeding requires a lot of time, a lot of money, and a degree of dedication which is not always consistent with everybody's life-style.

Firstly, there is no money to be made in breeding whippets. Those who make a financial success of dog breeding depend almost inevitably on boarding or other activities to supplement their income. Most litters of

94. *Four hours before whelping; the outline of a puppy can be seen on the bitch's flank. (Walsh)*

puppies consume every penny of their purchase price long before they go to their new homes. Long-established breeders whose kennels are world famous for producing top-class stock may well have a steady clientele to whom they can be sure of selling any puppies they may breed, but the beginner in the game, unless perhaps helped by the breeder of their bitch, or the owner of the sire, may well find it hard to find good homes for their puppies, certainly in the short term. If you cannot depend on selling your five or six puppies promptly at eight weeks, you must have the space and facilities to 'run them on' until you can find good homes for them. It is all very well to have a bitch and six puppies curled up in a cardboard box in the back kitchen when the puppies are three weeks old, but quite another thing to have six four month old puppies destroying your living room and digging holes in your small garden. Divorces have been known to result from the circumstances I describe. In short, you must make sure that you can be at home all day from the time the puppies are born until they are sold, you must have large enough premises to be able to construct an outside run where they can play and develop when they have reached that stage, and you must be prepared to spend a great deal of money on feeding them the best possible food for anything up to six months; and four or five whippet puppies can eat a lot of food. This does not take into account any veterinary bills or the extra heating you may have to provide. Whippets are not an

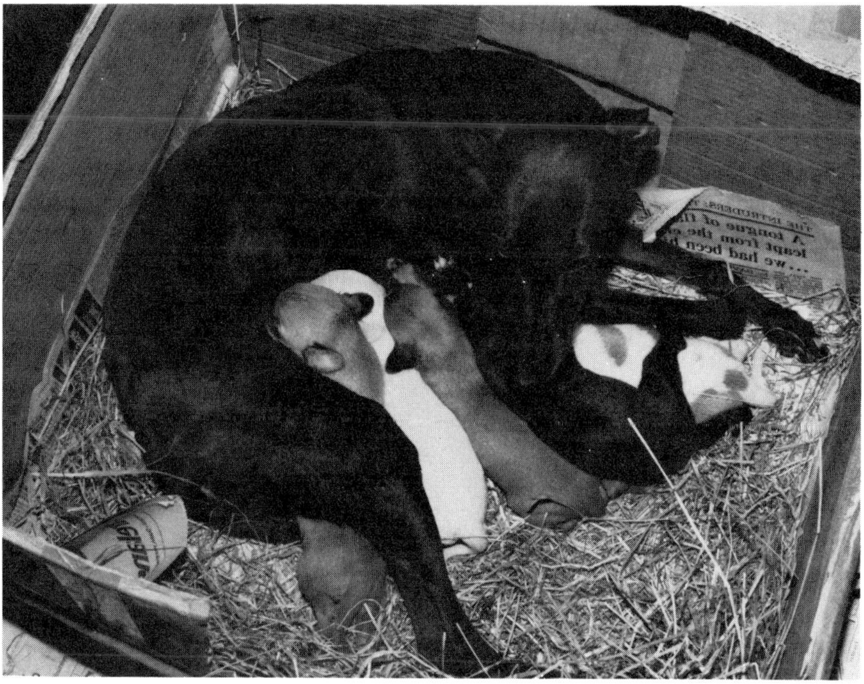

95. *A strong cardboard box makes a very adequate rearing bed. (Walsh)*

expensive breed and the current price for a well-bred, well-reared whippet puppy is anything between £70-£150 so it can be readily appreciated that a litter of four or five, which is average, is hardly likely to show a profit.

Unless you are very sure that you have the support of your family, that your premises are ideal, that you yourself have plenty of time, and that your Bank Manager is a friend rather than an enemy, don't embark on this hazardous undertaking. Buy a puppy instead!

Mating

Having considered well all the pros and cons and decided to mate your bitch at her next season, make sure that all her inoculations, including Parvovirus, are up to date BEFORE she is mated. It is most unwise to have the in-whelp bitch injected during the period she is carrying the whelps, as this can cause deformed puppies or absorption of the entire litter. It is best to make sure that her inoculations are in order about two/three months prior to mating. It is important that a bitch carrying puppies should not be exposed to any infection, injected with drugs, or otherwise interfered with when she is in whelp. The side-effects of drugs on the unborn foetus is not a subject which we are qualified to deal with in depth but prevention is better than cure in this case and therefore great care should be taken

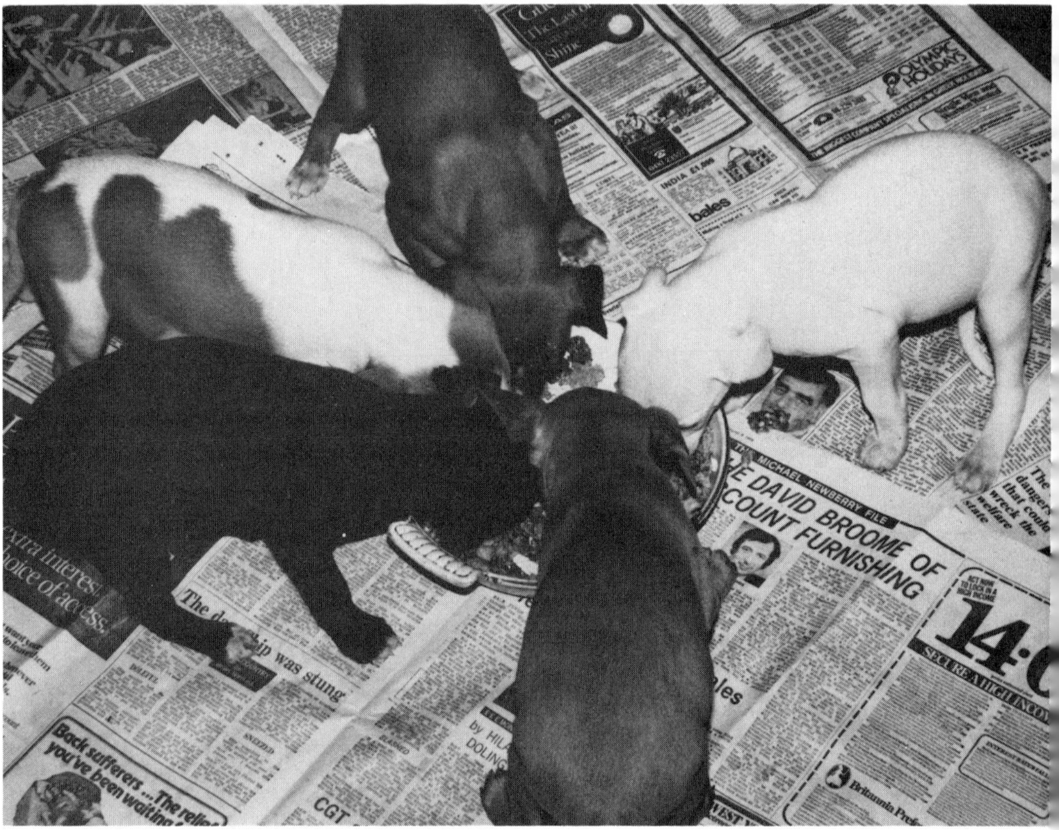

96. *Good appetites at four weeks; the litter is still indoors. (Walsh)*

to safeguard the in-whelp bitch. It is most unwise to exhibit a bitch when she is either in season or in whelp as she will be wide open to infection at that time. If you are unlucky enough to get an infection in your kennel when you have a bitch in whelp, you must naturally take all precautions to protect her well-being but it may have an effect on her litter, so take the precautions first and keep her as free from trouble as possible. The most dangerous period is from three to six weeks but if your bitch is worth breeding from and you expect a good litter it will be worth safeguarding her throughout her pregnancy.

The normal period of 'heat' in a whippet is 21 days but shorter or longer periods can be known and need not be a sign of abnormality. In general, bitches tend to follow the same pattern as their dams, so if you can find out the normal cycle of the dam of your bitch it will give you a guide to her probable pattern. The normal pattern for most whippet bitches is to come in season for the first time between twelve and sixteen months. A bitch should not be bred from on her first season as a general rule, for two reasons. Firstly, a whippet bitch is not fully mature until eighteen

97. *Appetites improve remarkably when the puppies have been wormed and are out of doors. (Walsh)*

months old at the earliest and it is a mistake to breed from an immature bitch; she will have to give the puppies what should be completing her own growth. Secondly, it is as well to establish her 'cycle' (i.e., the length of time between her 'heats') before upsetting her metabolism by putting her in whelp. The normal cycle is anything from six to eight months between 'heats' but in comparison with other breeds whippet bitches seem to be late with their first season (toy breeds often have their first 'heat' as early as eight months and are early maturing as a result) and quite a number of whippets come in season only every ten months or once a year as opposed to the more average twice yearly. This syndrome can be quite an advantage since once a year is quite often enough to mate a bitch and the longer gaps between seasons enables a bitch to be on peak form for showing, coursing or racing for longer periods. A bitch who comes into season regularly every six months is apt to spend half the year in season or recovering from it; some bitches go right off form for the nine weeks following a season, whether they have been mated or not. Coursing and racing enthusiasts know that a bitch will not run normally for the nine week period after her season and it is no good expecting her to do so; her whole metabolism behaves as though she was expecting puppies and even without suffering from a false pregnancy a bitch will often show signs of enlarged teats, slackened

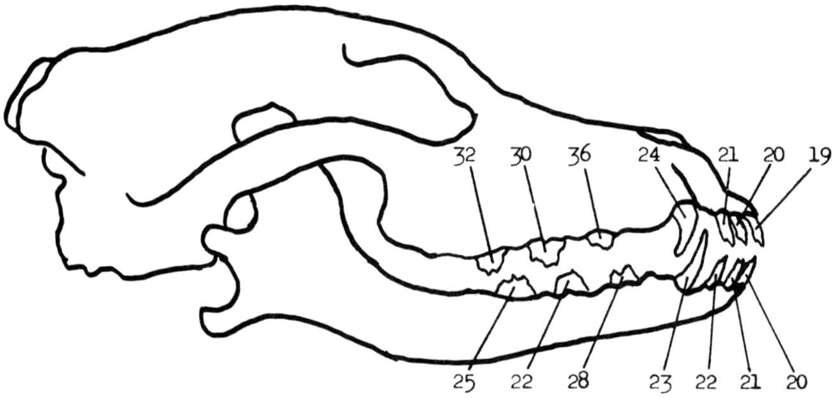

The number of days after birth on which a puppy's teeth usually appear.

The dental formula for a puppy is:

Incisors $\frac{3}{3}$ Canine $\frac{1}{1}$ Premolars $\frac{3}{3}$ Total 28

The dental formula for an adult dog is:

Incisors $\frac{3}{3}$ Canine $\frac{1}{1}$ Premolars $\frac{4}{4}$ Molars $\frac{2}{3}$. Total 42

98. *The number of days after birth on which puppy teeth usually appear. (Walsh)*

muscle and increased weight, all of which will affect her performance in the field and her appearance in the ring.

Breeders vary as to when and how often they mate their bitches. My own practice has been to have a first litter between eighteen and twenty four months, which serves to mature and fulfil the bitch; it also ensures that you will be less likely to have trouble later on. It can be difficult to get a bitch in whelp for a first litter after three or four years old. The showing and coursing can then be enjoyed while the bitch is in her prime (from two to five years old) and have a second and possibly third litter at five and six years old. So, the general rule is, never breed on the first season, never breed on successive seasons (time must be allowed for a bitch to build up her reserves between litters) and do not leave it later than four years old for a first litter. Two to three litters are ideal for a bitch, and risk is greatly increased after seven years of age; but at all times the chief guide must be the general health of the bitch concerned and her propensities as a dam.

The first sign of a bitch coming in season is generally a small, bright red discharge. With later seasons a bitch may be swollen for some days or even a week before there is any discharge but it is usual to count the first day from the first 'show of colour'. Normally the 11th to 13th day from first seeing colour will be right to mate a bitch. But once you have a certain amount of experience it is a better guide to watch the behaviour pattern of the bitch. Generally speaking, a bitch will be ready to mate when the swelling has gone down slightly and the discharge is clear; usually this coincides with the 11th/13th day period but it can be earlier or later. If you have a dog to 'try' her with it is easier to be sure that she will accept the dog you have elected to mate her to, but many people keep only bitches or do not choose to upset their own dogs in the house from whom the bitch will of course have been shut away ever since she came into season. At about ten days the bitch will start to stand to a dog (or to another bitch), that is, she will stretch herself, curl her tail up and sideways, and swing her rump towards another dog, thus indicating clearly what it is she is wanting. This is a sign that she is almost ready to be mated and the time of maximum fertility is usually two or three days after the first indication of being willing to 'stand'. It is important to get the right day since, although the bitch could possibly be covered by a determined dog from the earliest point, mating either too early or too late may result in decreased fertility producing only one or two puppies or perhaps none at all; this is a waste of time and energy, especially if you have to travel some distance to the dog of your choice. As all owners of stud dogs will tell you, it is surprising how many bitches are 'absolutely ready' on Sundays! If you have decided to have a litter and go through all the trouble and expense that this involves it will be worth trying to achieve the best possible mating. With a maiden bitch — that is one that has not been mated before — it is best to use what is called a proven dog, one that has sired litters before, so that you can be sure of his ability at stud and his fertility. Having decided which dog to use you should give the owner of that dog as much notice as possible. Book the bitch to the dog of your choice *before* she comes in season and ring up the owner immediately she *does* come in season. If the dog is young, or untried, have a second choice in mind in case the original choice does not work out for some reason. It will be disappointing if your bitch is ready to be mated and you telephone the owner of the dog only to be told that she is going on holiday. Never take a bitch to be mated in anything but perfect health. For one thing it is not fair to the owner of the dog; it is also not fair to the bitch as she will need all her reserves of strength during the next two months and is unlikely to produce or rear healthy puppies if she herself is unwell.

99. *Play which looks rough, but it is all part of the training which she will give her puppies. (Walsh)*

The In-Whelp Bitch

Once your bitch has been satisfactorily mated she becomes valuable property and must be cared for as such. If the mating takes place on the correct day she will go off heat quickly. Since the bitch in the natural state in the wild has to feed herself for the 63 days of pregnancy Nature has wisely arranged that the embryo puppies will grow slowly to start with and will not begin to show until the fifth or sixth week; even then they will be carried high up in the bitch's abdomen and will not 'drop' until the final week (see Plate 94). So it is not easy to tell if a bitch is in whelp until well on into her pregnancy and even experienced breeders can tell stories of bitches that hunted or coursed within days of producing unexpected puppies.

One guide as to whether the bitch is in whelp is if she goes off her food on the 21st day after mating; it is not infallible but it often happens and she may pick at her food for the next ten days. If she has not been wormed this must be done no later than three weeks after mating or the medicine may affect the puppies. She should not be treated any differently from normal and can be exercised with other dogs until about the sixth week; thereafter she should get all the exercise she needs but it is better that she does not charge out through doors or gates with a lot of other dogs or be allowed to jump down from banks or walls. Do not take her to shows or other gatherings where there may be a risk of infection.

Between the fifth and sixth weeks she will begin to change shape and will show a slight, colourless faintly sticky discharge, a sign that she is definitely in whelp. Now is the time to increase her food gradually, especially the protein content, and she can go onto two meals a day with a higher meat content and less biscuit. From the day of mating she should get a calcium supplement such as Stress, Canovel or Vetzyme, but do follow the makers' instructions; as much damage can be done by over-supplementation as by deprivation.

The length of pregnancy is given as 63 days but many whippets go 60 or 61 days rather that the full nine weeks. For the week before she is due the bitch should have a milk drink at night in addition to her other food; Complan is excellent for this and it is also a very useful food for the three or four weeks after whelping when the bitch is feeding the puppies entirely by herself.

Whelping

Whelping usually takes place at night, for reasons that go back to the wild dog's instinct for concealment. The first signs that the bitch is preparing to whelp are refusing or picking at food, and she will start looking for a nest in some safe, dark place where she will feel secure and private. Many books on dogs tell the reader that when whelping starts the bitch should be left alone to get on with it; that she will do better without a human presence. It is even suggested that a nervous bitch may damage puppies at birth if someone is present in the room; this is possible, but if the bitch is as nervous as this you should not be breeding from her. We offer some reasons why the owner *should* be present during whelping.

Firstly, one needs to know when the 'waters' break and if all the afterbirths have come away; if one afterbirth is retained there will almost certainly be trouble ahead.

Secondly, if any complication should arise one needs to know what stage the bitch has got to. If a particular puppy has not appeared after an hour and a half's straining, professional help will very likely be needed. If the bitch has been on her own until trouble is spotted you will not be able to tell the vet how long the bitch has been straining.

Thirdly, there is the question of vitality at birth which will, or certainly should influence your choice of which puppy to keep or which to put down should it be necessary to do so. Remember that in the wild, canine mortality from predators, disease and accidents can be as high as 70% in the first twelve months so large litters are necessary to allow for wastage. Domestic dogs have no predators, drugs and inoculations take care of disease and

100. *A ten week old puppy can be stood up for a minute, but not more. (Walsh)*

survival of the fittest is no longer the rule. One has only to read the figures issued by the Whippet Rescue Service — let alone figures published by the RSPCA, etc, — to realise that there are too many dogs in the country. Weaklings should *never* be reared, no matter how pathetic and appealing they may look.

Fourthly, — and it affects those who breed whippets for coursing and work, rather than for the show ring — a reason that is not to be found in books but can be important in choosing a working dog. It does not always happen, and one may not see it at all in a litter, but length, symmetry and 'speed' can sometimes be seen for a moment as a puppy is born, while it is still wet. The first two or three may have had nothing particular about them; then one arrives and as it struggles free from its caul you say to yourself, 'That one is going to gallop'. Within minutes the bitch has licked the puppy dry and there is nothing to distinguish from the others except, perhaps, its colour. But that one will almost certainly win courses in the end.

Since most bitches whelp at night and since you will want to keep an eye on her, the most satisfactory place for the bitch to whelp is probably in your bedroom. If this is not possible then it must be a room, or shed, where she can be kept warm, which is free from such interruptions as people

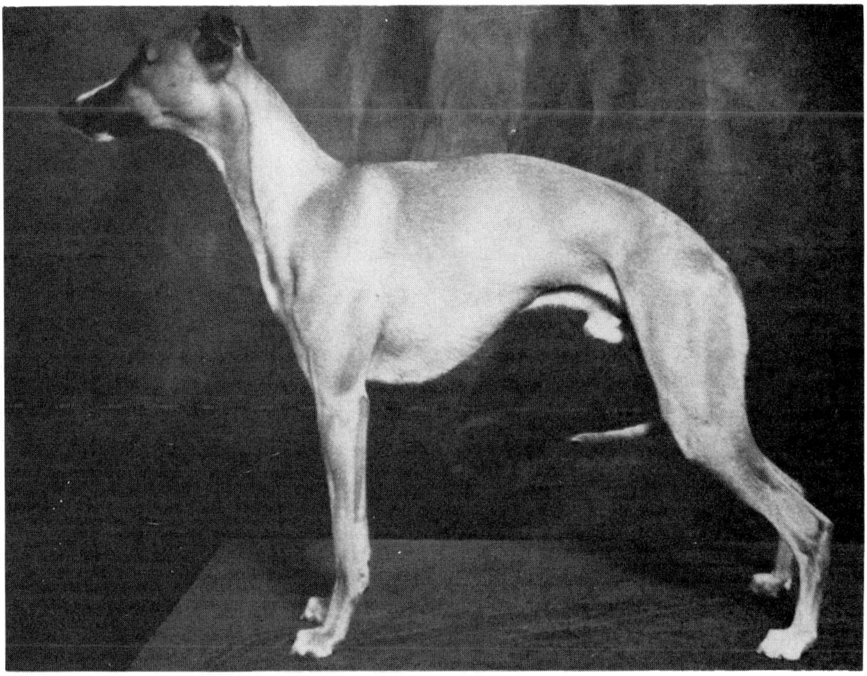

101. *The same dog at twelve months.*

coming and going, and where you can sit and keep her company. It must be secure, and handy enough for you to keep a close watch on her for the first two or three days, the period when something is most likely to go wrong. You must have a whelping box ready; a good sized, strong cardboard box lined with newspaper is perfectly adequate. About two foot six inches square is just large enough for a whippet and such a box will hold the puppies for their first three weeks; but watch the bitch whilst whelping, that she does not tread too hard on puppies already born.

Personally I find it easiest to take the bitch to sleep in my bedroom for the last week of her pregnancy; this means that when anything starts — and it can happen any time during the last seven days — I am at hand to see what is going on and reassure the bitch if necessary. From the point where the bitch starts to 'nest', turning round in the bed and scraping and chewing up the bedding and panting, you should watch carefully for the breaking of the waters. This is important because four hours is the absolute maximum that a bitch should be left without veterinary attention, once this has happened and no puppy has appeared. Once the waters have broken the bitch is in labour; if it should happen and not be noticed, if the bitch is in kennel or not being watched, it is possible that there may be no further signs of whelping and 24 or 36 hours later you realise that you have a bitch very sick with septacaemia, dead puppies inside her and her own life at risk. So watch her carefully.

Whippets are normally easy whelpers due to their narrow heads; nevertheless you should monitor every stage of the whelping so that if anything should go wrong you know when and how to act. Unless you have a memory like a computer we suggest you have a pencil and paper handy; make a note of the time at which anything happens, first signs of straining, appearance of first, and subsequent, puppies, clearance of after-births (some bitches eat these very quickly and you may have to watch closely) and, last but not least, each puppy's will to live, the energy it shows at birth and the efforts — or lack of effort — that it makes to start feeding straight away. The puppy that is looking for food while the bitch is still rolling it around and licking it dry will come to no harm; the puppy that makes no effort to find a teat within minutes of being born should be put down. The next three weeks are going to be a constant struggle for food and warmth, where strength and vitality are all-important, and this puppy will probably fade and die anyway. Do not try and rear it artificially.

Once the puppies have all arrived and the bitch is tucked up, well and happy with her new litter, she will still need regular and frequent attention. At this stage she should have no solid food for 24 hours but should be given four-hourly milk feeds, or egg and milk, or Complan. On the second day she should have a little cooked chicken or fish and only on the third day can she have some brown bread mixed in her food. She should be having five or six small meals a day at this point, alternatively liquid and solid. The reason for this is that during parturition the bitch will eat the after-births which are rich in minerals and protein. In the wild that is all she would eat until she had recovered enough strength to hunt for food again and when the whelps were strong enough to be left for a few hours. At this point her stomach must not be overloaded with other forms of high protein or she will start to scour and this will affect her milk and, through the milk, her puppies. There may, in any case, be a darkish discharge for a day or two after whelping but if the bitch is gradually eased back onto a full diet scouring should not occur.

For the first few days the bitch will be reluctant to leave the puppies and she may have to be lifted out of her box and taken outside to empty herself; this should be done two or three times a day. During this period I give the bitch an extra calcium supplement; ordinary calcium and vitamin D tablets from the chemist are excellent and a whippet can be given 2 to 4 a day. Whelping and feeding a litter are a tremendous strain on the bitch's calcium resources, and, like a human mother, she must get extra calcium and plenty of liquid. When she is back onto a normal diet — in 48 to 72 hours — her two main meals should consist of 4oz to 6oz of high quality meat with a non-abrasive biscuit, or brown bread baked in the oven. All the good that you put into your bitch for the next six weeks will be going into the puppies as milk and there are no short cuts in breeding. Time and money spent now will repay a hundredfold in the months to come; the puppy that has been well-reared from the very start will have an advantage all through its life over the puppy that has been skimped.

After a night or two in your bedroom — if that is where she whelped — you can move the bitch to where she is going to stay for the next few weeks. She must be kept warm and quiet during this period. It is not a good idea for her to be in a living room where there are people coming and going; this will make the steadiest bitch nervous and distracted and will take her mind off her job which is to rear puppies. For the same reason visitors must be kept to a minimum, particularly children. 'Oh, do let them see the puppies' is a common cry but the bitch must be left alone and there will be plenty of time to see puppies when they are weaned. The breeder must also remember that outside visitors can bring infection into a kennel.

During these first three weeks attention can be at a minimum provided that the bitch is really well fed and is let out to empty herself at regular intervals. In winter, if she is not in a heated room she should have a heat lamp — one of the large, red bulbs that are used in piggeries and poultry houses — over the box to make sure that any puppy rolling away from her is not chilled, but it is a mistake to overheat the puppies at any stage. In the natural state the bitch would whelp in a den or tunnel, making a saucer-shaped bed for the puppies. This shape ensures that when they start moving around they sooner or later roll back to the centre of the nest with their brothers and sisters and against the bitch. The same shape should be aimed for in the rearing box, pushing some of the bedding against the walls. Once the bitch has stopped discharging she will keep the bed clean herself, licking the puppies to make them urinate and defecate; again, a natural instinct to keep the den clean so that predators cannot find it by the smell.

Care and Feeding of Puppies

For the first three weeks of their life puppies are the responsibility of their mother. She will feed them, clean them up, keep them warm and pull them back into the nest if they crawl too far — though you should try and make certain that they cannot do so. If the litter is very small, say, two or three, the bitch may feed them for a month; if the litter is very large she may not be able to produce enough milk for them for 21 days. No hard and fast rule can be laid down and you must watch both bitch and puppies carefully.

Dew claws are removed from whippets on the fourth day and a later removal will cause undue loss of blood. Who does the operation depends on experience; a pair of curved surgical scissors are used, pressed up against the leg so that all three joints of the dewclaw are taken off. As soon as each puppy has been done, a dab of mild antiseptic is put on each wound and the puppy is put back in the bed. If you do not feel up to doing it yourself get an experienced friend, or your vet, to do it for you but do not delay beyond the fifth day. If dewclaws are half removed or left on and later taken off it will mean a proper surgical operation under anaesthetic, and the dog will be out of action for a considerable time.

At about twelve or fifteen days after birth the puppies' eyes will begin to open. At first it will merely be a slit that shows a lighter colour — pale blue — and sight will come gradually. At about the nineteenth day the first teeth will start to appear; thereafter teeth will continue to appear, usually in the order shown in Plate 98. The puppies' claws will also grow and should be looked at and trimmed when necessary from about the tenth day. If this is not done they will begin to scratch the bitch when pushing and pummelling against her teats to stimulate the milk flow; this can become too much for the bitch and she may cut feeding sessions short to her own and the puppies' detriment.

Some bitches' milk tends to be acid; this can upset puppies and it is worth while keeping some litmus paper handy, particularly if any puppy shows signs of bare patches on its skin. If a drop of milk turns the litmus paper red the bitch should be given some milk of magnesia or bicarbonate of soda to neutralise the acid.

Eclampsia (Milk Fever)

One of the minerals required for growth is calcium; it is needed particularly for teeth and bones and it is passed to the puppies-in-embryo through the bitch's blood stream and then, after they are born, through her milk. There is, therefore, a steady drain on the bitch's own supply of calcium from about the fifth week of pregnancy until she has finished feeding the puppies herself. Eclampsia, or milk fever, is caused by a sudden acute shortage of calcium in the bitch; it can occur during pregnancy but it is more likely to occur in the second or third week after birth when the puppies are making the greatest demands on the bitch for milk.

Symptoms are restlessness and nervousness, stumbling, a stiffening of the legs; the bitch goes down on her side and kicks violently, often with general body spasms. A fit can wear off but it will come on again and if treatment is not given very quickly the bitch will probably die of heart failure or exhaustion.

Treatment must be given by a vet; it consists of an injection of calcium into the blood stream and in almost all cases the bitch recovers very quickly. It is better that, if possible, she does not feed the puppies herself for 24 hours to give her time to recover fully. If she has been fed properly during pregnancy and whilst feeding puppies she ought not to get eclampsia, but if she does we must emphasize the importance of speed to the surgery.

Weaning

At about three weeks of age the puppies can see fairly clearly and their sense of smell is becoming more acute; although they are still unsteady on their legs they are taking more exercise and taking an interest in what goes on around them. By now, not only is the bitch's milk not enough for them but the supply may be starting to slacken and it is time to give the puppies some extra nourishment.

As they have only been getting mother's milk so far, the first food you will give them will be milk. Not cow's milk alone; a bitch's milk contains 11% to 12% fat, a goat's milk about 6% fat and a cow's milk 3% to 4% so, if goat's milk is not available, either enriched cow's milk or a milk food such as Lactol must be given. A dash of honey can make it more palatable.

The first feed will be a messy one; the puppies have not only got to learn to lap but they are still unsteady on their feet and have not got full control of their heads and necks. However, by dipping your finger in the milk food and smearing a puppy's lips, or even dipping a puppy's muzzle lightly into the liquid they will learn very quickly and we have seldom known a litter not make a good effort at lapping after 24 hours. They will be unsteady for a while yet so the dish must be a fairly heavy one that cannot be tipped over if they stand on the rim.

Milk feeds should be given when the bitch has been away from the puppies for a while — little and often must be the rule all through their early feeding — and then she can be put in to them again. Her milk contains more nourishment than any made-up food and they will continue to feed from her for several weeks yet.

By the end of the fourth week the puppies should be getting four milk feeds a day, two of them being thickened with cereal such as Farex or Readibrek, plus honey. Now is the time for them to start on meat but again, very little to begin with and it must be scraped and not minced. The easiest way to scrape meat is to use an old spoon with one side of the bowl sharpened slightly. Put some shin or beef skirt on a board, hold it with one hand and scrape with the spoon until a small amount — the size of a marble — has been taken off; this is one puppy's ration. Scrape off as many 'rations' as there are puppies, put them on a plate, take a puppy on your knee and put a piece of meat against its lips. The first efforts will be enthusiastic if inefficient, but no matter; there is plenty of time. Do the same next morning and in a day or two the puppies will be fighting for meat. It can now be added to their food which can consist of:

Early morning	Milk feed
Mid-morning	Milk feed with meat and cereal
2 pm	Milk feed

5 or 6 pm	As for mid-morning
Last thing at night	Milk feed

After a couple of days of solid food the puppies will have their first worming and, depending on the time of year, they should then be spending several hours outdoors each day.

Regurgitation

Although the bitch will have finished feeding the puppies regularly they will still take milk from her when she appears in their run until she dries up; they will do this with the bitch standing, the puppies sitting on their bottoms and pushing at her sides with their front feet. Many bitches will also feed their puppies by regurgitation — sicking up their own food — and may be very cunning about it; if you are not watching for it particularly you may not notice anything until the puppies begin to be a bit easy about their evening meal.

Any time from 15 minutes to an hour after her own meal the bitch will jump into the run (and there should be access for her, just as, earlier, she was able to get out of the puppies' reach if she wanted to) and will probably disappear into the house with the puppies. They will push at her mouth with their noses, she will put down her head in a corner and up comes her supper, to be bolted by the puppies. Do not stop her doing this; it is a perfectly natural thing for her to do. But if you do find a bitch feeding puppies in this way make certain that her food is cut up small enough so that the puppies will not choke on it, although it is partly digested; and do give her an extra meal to replace what she is passing on.

Sunlight and Fresh Air

There is no substitute for sunlight for growing puppies. They are growing very fast and their needs from what you, the breeder, can give them will not vary whether they are born in June or December; but the puppies that are born in the spring can be outdoors by May or June and no amount of supplements can do as much for them as the summer sun. Breeders of coursing greyhounds pour large libations to Diana and whatever other gods look after the country sportsman in the hope that their bitches will come in season in February or March; there is a firm belief that spring puppies have the edge on those born earlier or later.

As well as sunshine, the best of food and a dry bed out of draughts which all young dogs need there is one more requirement that is special to the running dog, the Hound Group, in show terms; that is enough room for them to gallop and learn to use themselves. The basics of rearing apply equally to terriers, labradors and running dogs; but a whippet or greyhound reared on the best of food in a small run will never compete in later life with the one that may have been skimped of food but has had unlimited room for exercise. For the first few weeks outdoors the puppies will stumble around, getting stronger and stronger and gaining more control over themselves; then they must be given room to learn to move. Puppies need exercise but it must be exercise that they give themselves; they will play and play in their run until they have had enough, when they curl up in the straw, or in the sun, and sleep.

What sort of run the puppies go into depends very much on circumstances but it should be as large as there is room for. My own run is 30 foot by 70 foot, with a similar area of grass alongside that can be enclosed if required. The corner posts are sawn-off telephone poles and there are straining wires at ground level, at 3 foot and at 6 foot from the ground; angle-iron posts hold the wire at about 6 foot intervals. The bottom 3 foot of the fence is 2 inch mesh Weldmesh and the upper 3 foot is 4 inch mesh wire netting. A path of concrete slabs is laid all round against the wire to stop any digging under the wire and to give the puppies a firm surface to stand and walk on; these slabs came from a well-known firm of concrete garage manufacturers as rejected panels. This run is as escape-proof as one can get for whippets and can be divided off as necessary.

In the run I build a house of straw bales. The walls are made of three layers of bales and 21 bales make three walls of a "kennel" approximately 5 foot by 4 foot internal measurement. The fourth side is made of wood, half being a door; the two side walls project beyond the wooden wall to make wind breaks. An inner ceiling of plywood rests on joists and on top of this are placed polythene sacks filled with straw as insulation; overall is a corrugated iron roof. A house built in this way costs almost nothing; it is rain, wind and draught-proof; with a thick bed of straw I have had a mis-timed litter of whippets outdoors in December frosts and have seldom seen healthier puppies. After two seasons the house is dismantled, the straw is burnt, or composted for the garden, and a new house is built on a different site in the run. But before puppies go outside they should have their first worming.

Worming

There are various worms that dogs can, and almost always do carry, but the two most common are tapeworms in adult dogs and round worms in puppies.

Ascarids, or Roundworms, are the worms that most commonly infest puppies and are seen in their droppings. The worms are white, round in section and sharply pointed at each end; their size can vary from a fine thread to a fat, curling, five or six inches. Adult roundworms live in the intestine and, like tapeworms, nourish themselves by absorption, sharing the food of their hosts. A light infestation may show no symptoms; in a heavy infestation the puppy will have a staring coat, a bloated stomach and roundworms will be seen in the faeces. Part of the life-cycle of the roundworm is spent in the bitch's lungs, brain, liver or eyes and the worm larvae are passed to the embryo puppies through the placenta; so puppies are infested with roundworms before they are born. These larvae take from four to five weeks to develop into adults so if a serious infestation is going to arise it will happen four or five weeks after birth; this is the time when the worming dose should be given.

You will, of course, have dosed the bitch for roundworms and tapeworms before she was mated or, at the very latest, during the first three weeks of pregnancy. Since it is unlikely that any medicine will get rid of every worm you should assume that all puppies have some roundworms and so you dose every litter. No matter how small the infestation, roundworm eggs are passed out in the faeces and will be reingested by the bitch. Later these eggs can be picked up by intermediate hosts or, possibly, by adults and children from handling puppies; another reason for keeping children away from puppies until they — the puppies — have been weaned and wormed. And thus the necessity of worming whether there are external, visible symptoms or not.

Time was when more puppies died from too strong worm medicines than were killed by the worms themselves but nowadays medicines have little or no side effects. If you are not certain what to use get the medicine from your veterinary surgery. We have found that Shaw's 'Earliworm', or Antipar, are both effective without any adverse effects. Since not all the worm larvae grow at the same rate a second dose of medicine must be given two weeks after the first and, on veterinary advice, a third dose may be necessary a fortnight later.

When the puppies have had their first worming dose they are ready to go outside full-time, unless they have been weaned in the winter; in which case they will probably have to stay indoors at night, possibly with some form of heating, but they should spend as much of each day as possible outdoors.

Whatever housing is provided, there must be ample bedding for them to burrow into. At first the space round their house can be restricted with wire netting which may be moved outwards each week to give them more room. If this is done there will always be fresh ground to explore and more space in which to play and the puppies will be less likely to try and escape from the run through boredom. At about the eighth week, when their legs are becoming stronger, I put a low barrier across the run, railway sleepers or straw bales, firmly fixed, so that in their chasing and play they start to scramble and jump without thinking about it.

As they grow and are given more space to play in the puppies will get hungrier and the food must be increased with their appetite; experience will show how much food to give at each meal but so long as they are polishing their dish there can't be much wrong. If they start leaving food, cut down the amount a bit, then increase as they eat up.

A Diet Sheet for Puppies

What puppies are fed on depends on circumstances and availability, but whatever is used must be of the very best quality; nourishment that is missed or skimped now cannot be replaced later on.

6 to 12 weeks

7 am	Milk and egg
11 am	Meat; scraped at first, then minced but it must be butcher's best. Mix with cereal (Farex or Readibrek) or baked brown bread.
2 pm	Milk and egg or milk food (Lactol)
6 pm	As for morning feed; by the 8th or 9th week some well minced raw tripe can be substituted for minced beef. The cereal can be replaced by a good puppy meal, soaked in gravy or Marmite water.
10 pm +	Milk and cereal

12 to 20 weeks

7 am	As before but increase quantity
11 am	As before but replace cereal with puppy meal
6 pm	As for 11 am
10 pm +	Milk and cereal

+ This late feed should be dropped when a puppy comes into the house, otherwise it will be difficult for it to be clean overnight.

From 20 weeks

8 am	Morning meal as before
2 pm	Milk
6 pm	Evening meal as before

Development

The first two weeks of a puppy's life are spent in eating and sleeping. It cannot see or hear, but it is sensitive to warmth and cold and touch and it has a sense of smell for the bitch's milk. When awake it moves with a "swimming" motion, waving its head from side to side in search of its mother's warmth and skin and the milk smell. When not feeding it will sleep in a pile with its brothers and sisters at the bottom of the nest. If possible, a non-slip surface should be provided in the bed — a porous nylon 'sheepskin' which can be washed easily is recommended — to give the puppies' feet a purchase when moving and feeding. The bitch will keep them clean by regularly licking their tummies; this encourages evacuation and the bitch will, in turn, lick up the urine and faeces. It is a natural act to keep the den or nest clean.

In the third week the senses start to develop. The sense of smell broadens, the eyes start to open and the puppy will begin to react to noise. The first teeth will be seen about the nineteenth day and a sense of curiosity begins to show in short exploratory journeys round the bed.

From the 4th to the 7th week the puppy begins to learn what it is: a little dog. In the wild, puppies will start to climb out of the den or nest for brief periods about this age and, if the domestic puppy box has low sides, or a gap on one side, the more adventurous puppies will start to explore out of the box. If low wire netting or mesh surrounds the box the puppies will have to be watched carefully as it is astonishing how a four-week old whippet can climb. During this period the puppies must see and hear as much as possible of other dogs and of humans. It is the 'imprint' phase and experiments have shown that if a puppy is isolated from canine and human contact for these three weeks it will probably remain shy and anti-social. The more puppies see of other dogs and the more they are handled and talked to by the breeder and family the more secure they will become and the easier they will fit in as they grow, or adapt to another home on being sold.

The following notes on the progress of a litter of puppies are offered as a guide to novices on what to expect as time goes on:

11th day	Hind legs starting to take some weight
12th day	Eye slits showing a faint reflection
15th day	Eyes open; staggering around the bed, 'growling' and barging against each other
18th day	Aware of noises; some sight
19th day	First teeth showing in lower jaw
22nd day	Lactol offered and lapped immediately
28th day	2 hours in an outdoor run; scraped meat offered and taken avidly
29th day	5 meals per day, three of milk and two of scraped meat and Farex
30th day	First worming
33rd day	In outdoor run by day and night; coming readily to call
35th day	Scraped meat replaced by mince
42nd day	Ragging and inciting each other to chase; very keen scent

	for the bitch's presence and that of the breeder but uncertain about picking up humans by sight 35 yards away
44th day	2nd worming.

From the 8th to the 13th week is the time when the puppy starts to learn its place in the community; fighting for its pecking order starts now. It makes no difference whether the community is the home where it was born, a new home where there are other dogs or a new home that is dogless. This is the period of adjustment and, in the dog family, when discipline is implanted. The bitch starts to play more roughly with the puppies, she will suddenly pounce on a puppy and sieze it by the neck, jump away and pounce back from the other side (see Plate 99). At first the puppy will try and play as before but very soon it will be rolling on its back, waving its feet in the air and waiting for the storm to blow over. The storm does blow over for that puppy but the bitch has pounced on another and has got that one by the neck. It looks murderous and it sounds murderous but the puppies get to their feet none the worse and are ragging with each other straight away. What the bitch is doing is teaching the puppies to play with adults; to take a buffeting and bounce back but also to know their place in the family pack.

This play period with the bitch is extremely important for the puppies' development and it is therefore a great mistake to wean the puppies completely from their dam. Though she will eventually finish feeding them, even by regurgitation, she still has a lot to teach them up to about 10 weeks of age when they will start to go to their new homes — you hope. So, just as she should have had somewhere to escape to when they were small, she must have access to them several times a day in their outdoor run, or in the garden or orchard or meadow, or wherever they are let out to play. Eventually the puppy, or puppies, that you keep will follow her further afield and she will teach them their business as hunters.

When a puppy is sold to a home where there are other dogs this natural process will be repeated by the resident dogs and the puppy will soon learn its place in the pack. It will play — or try to play — until things get rough and then, accustomed to being rolled over by its mother it will roll onto its back as a sign of submission at a snarl or rumble from an older dog and by so doing it will avoid retribution. Play, the natural instinct of the growing puppy, is the guide to new owners. A puppy acquired between 8 and 12 weeks of age should be played with several times a day whether there are other dogs in the house or not. Puppies deprived of play at this period find it difficult to play with other dogs or with humans thereafter and so do not grow up "whole dogs".

Discipline and Training

Like greyhounds, whippets are not as biddable as, for instance, sheep dogs or gundogs, nor have they the same inherited ability to learn. But whippets are not fools — anymore than are greyhounds when properly reared, despite their reputation — and many of them can be trained to a high standard; we well remember Mrs Caroline Brown's Martinsell Slippery Sam beating all manner of highly trained dogs in the Obedience Test at one of the early Lambourn Lurcher Shows, much to the disgust of their owners. It is no use expecting to be able to stop or recall a whippet that is in full flight after a rabbit or a hare unless the dog has already reached a much higher state of training than most owners ever dream of; but basic training is not difficult and it is important for two reasons. Firstly, an obedient dog is a much better companion than the mindless tearaway that is out of control the moment it is let off a lead; secondly, unless you are the lucky owner of broad acres, or you never take your whippet out of town you will, inevitably, be exercising your whippet on other people's land (with, we hope, their permission). England is a very overcrowded island and thousands of acres of farmland disappear every year under, or blighted by, tarmac and concrete; demands for access and pressures on the countryside increase yearly. Trouble from dogs, bullocks frightened through a fence or the slightest suspicion of sheep-chasing let alone sheep-worrying can and does strain the goodwill so freely given by so many landowners and farmers. Equally, a loose dog in a built-up area is a menace to itself and to other road users.

So, whether a whippet lives in town or country it should, at the least, know its name, go to its bed when told to, walk on or off a lead, come when called under normal circumstances, follow across country without having to be helped and be absolutely safe and reliable with all farm stock, chickens, sheep, cattle and horses.

Naming

You will, of course, call your whippet any name you choose, but in choosing remember that dogs hear sibilants and vowels and do not notice other consonants; that a two or three-syllable name is picked up easier than one syllable; that the syllables should sound different from each other and that the name should not be confused with any other name in the house or kennel or with any command. As a very simple example, if a dog's name is Rover it is of little use using the command "over" when you want him to cross the road or jump over a fence!

'Bed'

When a puppy is first brought into the house it will be excited by new sights and smells; it will inevitably get under people's feet and in their way and it must learn where its own corner is. When it has had its run-around and is beginning to look sleepy, pick the puppy up and put it into its bed using any command you like; 'bed' or 'get into bed' is usual , but since the puppy doesn't speak English, 'Happy Easter' would do just as well provided that it is the command that will always be used. So long as you are firm and tactful and, once in bed no one calls or entices the puppy to get out again, it ought not take more than a couple of days for the message to sink in; but your family, especially children, must not interfere in this, or in any other dog training. If they do you will end up with a muddled and confused dog that obeys no one.

Coming when Called

Coming when called starts almost at weaning. If you have bred the puppies you will have called them every time you put down a bowl of food. Sitting in the run talking and playing with them, the puppies soon get used to names, they come when called since a human is someone else to play with and it is all fun. If you buy in a puppy it has got to get used to new voices, the sights and smells are new and fascinating and the human voice is ignored in favour of something else that is more interesting. Be tactful and try to avoid too many confrontations; if the puppy can see you but doesn't take any notice, sit down, kneel, squat or even roll on the ground and cry; do something to attract the puppy's attention and make a fuss of it when it comes to see what is going on. Above all, *never* punish a puppy for not coming when called; it will merely not come the next time.

House Training

We have left this until last of the essentials as we have never known any trouble with whippet puppies. Perhaps we have been lucky but any puddles on the floor have been the result of not letting out a young puppy often enough and they have otherwise been clean from the first day in the house. If you are in doubt, put some newspaper on the floor near the door when you got to bed and the puppy will almost certainly use it if required.

This completes the absolute necessities; a whippet can perfectly well be taught to sit, stay, retrieve and all manner of other things if you are interested. If you do not know how to set about training there is certain to be a dog training group, class or club somewhere not too far away. Join them. But for your own purposes, remember that tact and forethought will avoid many confrontations; a puppy can run and dodge much faster than you can so try and put yourself into a position where it will come towards you, not away. Train it in a passage or a small yard where there is no escape and no distractions. If you have to punish, and you almost certainly will have to at some time or another, don't beat a whippet with a stick; if you must beat, use a belt or the end of a lead but make absolutely certain that the whippet knows what the beating is for. Dogs cannot reason nor do they connect one action with another unless they are almost simultaneous. A far better way of punishing is to pick up the dog by the scruff of the neck with both hands, tell it in no uncertain terms what you think of it and give it a good shaking; this is what the pack-leader would do and it is what a dog understands. Remember that to one whippet or a dozen whippets you are — or you very well should be — the pack-leader and, as such, you do the punishing just as you lead them out hunting or whatever you do with them and you provide the food. Your dogs must wait on you and look up to you and if they don't then you are in for trouble sooner or later.

Cross-country

There is one other form of training — it is almost self-training — that is required for any whippet which is going to be used for anything active in the country; that is mobility, or getting across country. The whippet that can't or won't get over or through or round an obstacle is a bore to say the least. How do you deal with this has to vary with circumstances so I will merely describe my own methods. I am lucky in having a three acre garden, mostly rough, with hedges, shrubs and trees; this is a big enough to keep a lot of dogs interested. I also have access to farm land over the garden fence and at about four or five months I start taking puppies out into the first field; they come along happily with other dogs for a hundred yards or so and then, as likely as not, a fit of agoraphobia starts and the puppy bolts for home and safety. This phase does not last long and in a day or two they are investigating everything in the field, sheep or cattle droppings included. From here on they arc taken very gradually further and further, never being over-faced with any obstacle but never being helped over or through anything. They are never asked to jump anything until they are at least six months old, merely to creep and crawl and slide; at places where there is no way through the other dogs go round and the puppies soon follow on. By the time they are nine months old they have learnt their way about at least two farms and know the way home in daylight or dark. When the time comes for chasing hares or rabbits they follow through hedges and fences with no thought of stopping; wire netting is learnt about the hard way, by bumping into it and rebounding. Barbed wire is an occupational hazard. Some whippets are hardly ever cut or torn, others are constantly being stitched. I believe that it has a lot to do with the dog's character, the bash-on ones going blindly through whilst others take just that extra second of care and there is little the owner can do about it.

Finding homes and choosing what to keep

Finding homes for the puppies you have carefully bred and lovingly reared can be the most fraught part of the whole exercise. It is a good idea to have one or two homes lined up before you decide to have a litter at all, or be sure that at the time you decide to mate your bitch that there will be a demand for her puppies. If you are a novice breeder the best way to go about this is to consult either the breeder of your bitch or the owner of the sire, and try to establish from them what the state of the puppy market is likely to be. It must be remembered that whippet puppies do not find a ready market and that you will certainly have to run on one or two of a large litter beyond the ideal 10/12 week stage before you can settle them satisfactorily. If you plan to keep one of the litter yourself you may well find it practical to keep another one with it until four or five months, since a puppy on its own misses a lot of playing and learning and can actually meet with damage by trying to play with older dogs.

Choosing your own puppy

In some litters it is obvious very early on, almost from the moment when the puppies are wet, which one or ones are outstanding. Very often it is the one which first discovers everything, that puppy which, whenever you look at it, seems to draw your eye like a magnet. In some litters however, the puppies may be so even in quality that it is hard to pick out which is which unless you count their white toes or other distinguishing markings. If you have a litter where they are hard to tell apart you can be sure that it is a good litter! It is a good idea to persuade the owner of the sire to have a look at the puppies when they are about nine weeks old since it is probable that past experience may be a helpful guide when sorting out the progeny of an individual dog. As a basic guide, choose the longest of the medium sized ones — generally the largest is a mistake, and the smallest is a mistake, so look for the one of middle size that seems to have the most scope and quality about it and allow yourself to be influenced by temperament as well. Never choose the shyest or weakest since they are less likely to be satisfactory in other ways when mature.

Finding homes for the others

From ten weeks on you will be wanting to part with those puppies which you are not going to keep. The best homes, of course, come from personal recommendation, and any applicant for a puppy, if unknown to you, should be very thoroughly grilled to make sure that they really can offer your puppy a long and happy life. Advertising is a somewhat two-edged weapon as it can produce the wrong sort of home and it is sometimes difficult to be really sure about people who answer advertisements, about whom you may not have much time to make up your mind. Perhaps the most practical way to set about advertising your litter is firstly to tell the owner of the sire as soon as the puppies arrive (you should do this in any case since the owner of any stud dog will want to keep records of resulting progeny) and to keep him or her posted throughout development. Then, should they have suitable enquiries for their stock, they may be able to pass them on to you. Secondly, an advertisement in the dog papers when the puppies are only a week or two old will let other people in the whippet world know that your litter has arrived and whippet people are notoriously generous in trying to find suitable puppies for new owners and suitable buyers for new breeders. The wording of any advertisement needs to be quite carefully thought out if it is to produce the right sort of response. Always give the breeding of the litter and do not make extravagant claims which may not be fulfilled. One often sees litters advertised as being of championship show quality; one has only to look at the breeding or the name of the breeder to know that the puppies are unlikely to come into that category. Something like this would be appropriate:-

> Promising litter of brindle whippet puppies born 18/8/82. By Ch. Sleek Simon ex Solihull Susannah. Only genuine loving homes will be considered. Name, address and Tel. no.

Never advertise puppies as adorable pets or suggest that they might be reasonably priced or you will certainly get the wrong sort of applicant. Never, never, NEVER under any circumstances sell puppies to a dealer or a pet shop, since you cannot be sure where they will end up. If you cannot find personal homes for your puppies you have no business to be breeding them at all. Always ask a reasonable price for a puppy; if you know the prospective owners well you may decide to let them have a puppy cheaply or indeed as a present, but in general it is a safeguard to charge a fair and reasonable price — if people are not willing to pay such a price for a puppy then they should not be buying one. Try and find out as much as you can about the new owners. If they are the right sort of people they will not object to your enquiries since it will demonstrate how much you care about the future of the puppy you have bred. Find out who will be feeding and looking after your puppy and make sure it will not be left alone all day whilst its owners are out at work. If the husband is buying it, make certain that the wife wants it too — she will probably be the one who has to look after it! A small puppy which is left alone all day soon becomes bored and destructive and after its new owners have had their furniture and carpets destroyed they will be ringing you up to say that the puppy is impossible and asking you to take it back. Of course you will have to take it back since the thought of it being discarded on the motorway or turned loose in the streets is not to be borne; but the puppy you get back will not be the one you sold. You will find that you have a thoroughly unsettled, neurotic dog on your hands which will be much harder to settle second time round, and this could have been avoided if you had taken greater care in the first place. You must never forget that each and every puppy you breed is YOUR responsibility and it is not fair to expect the overburdened rescue services to have to cope with resettling stock which breeders have sold to unsuitable homes and refused to take back themselves.

Make sure that the new owners understand all the peculiar whippet characteristics and if they have small children do not fail to impress on them that a young puppy needs peace and quiet while it is growing and therefore must have long periods of the day when it is not exposed to children. Whippets are very good with children but no puppy benefits from being constantly mauled and played with and its growth, both mental and physical, will be affected by such treatment. Always make sure that you give the new owners a detailed diet sheet of exactly what the puppy has been eating and what it will need to eat in the months to come up until the time when it will be fully mature. A bag of food for the first day or so is helpful since the puppy will not then have to suffer the trauma of a change of diet as well as a change of environment. Always impress on the new owners that if they get into any difficulties of any kind whatever you are available to them for help and advice at any time. The more you care about your puppies the more likely the new owners are to adopt the same attitude.

You will find, as the years go by, that through breeding healthy, happy puppies and settling them into new homes, you have made a large number of good friends. There is nothing more rewarding for a breeder than to get a telephone call asking for a second or third puppy to join the original one which has been 'such a success'. What is more, whippet puppies are very loyal, they never forget their breeder, however long they have been with new owners. It is very endearing to meet, years later, a whippet which you sold as a puppy, which takes one look at you and hurls itself into your arms!

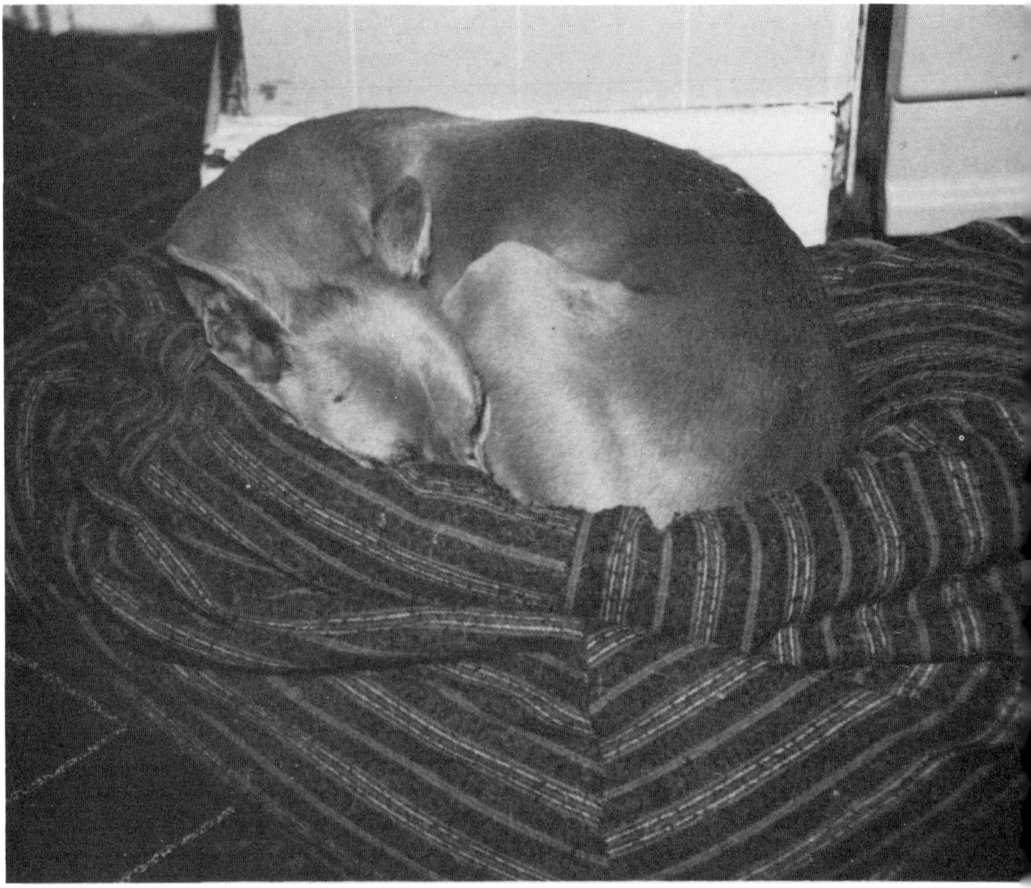

102. *Many whippets will scratch up a bed until it is comfortable, so beds containing polystyrene 'bobbles' must have thick covers. (Walsh)*

Chapter 8

Looking After Whippets

This is not a veterinary handbook nor is either of us qualified to write one. In keeping *working* dogs as well as show dogs we have, in the natural course of events, learnt a certain amount about everyday damage and how to recognise it and deal with it so long as it is not too serious; to know, for instance, when a wound that may look terrible at first sight may be left unstitched, and when the smaller wound must be dealt with by a professional.

There are many veterinary text books for dog owners on the market and some of them are excellent. The important thing for the layman is to be able to recognise certain symptoms and we hope that we have outlined some of the commoner troubles that the whippet owner may come across. Up to thirty or forty years ago there were virus diseases which killed thousands of dogs annually and for which there were no known cures; good nursing for those dogs which survived an attack was all that anyone could do. Dogs can now be inoculated for all these diseases and there is no excuse for the dog owner who does not get his dogs protected; but it must be remembered that there are still dog owners who do not bother and there are always some dogs about that may be carriers of disease.

If you do not take your dog to your veterinary surgeon when something is wrong which you cannot deal with immediately you may be saving yourself some money; but the dog may pay in pain or with his life. It is better to be safe than sorry later on.

Daily Care

Have a good look at your whippets first thing in the morning. Note how they come out of bed or kennels; they should be 'bright eyed and bushy tailed' and if they are not, look for a reason. Watch to see what their droppings are like when you take them out to empty themselves. Faeces will vary according to how the dogs are fed. A meat diet produces small,

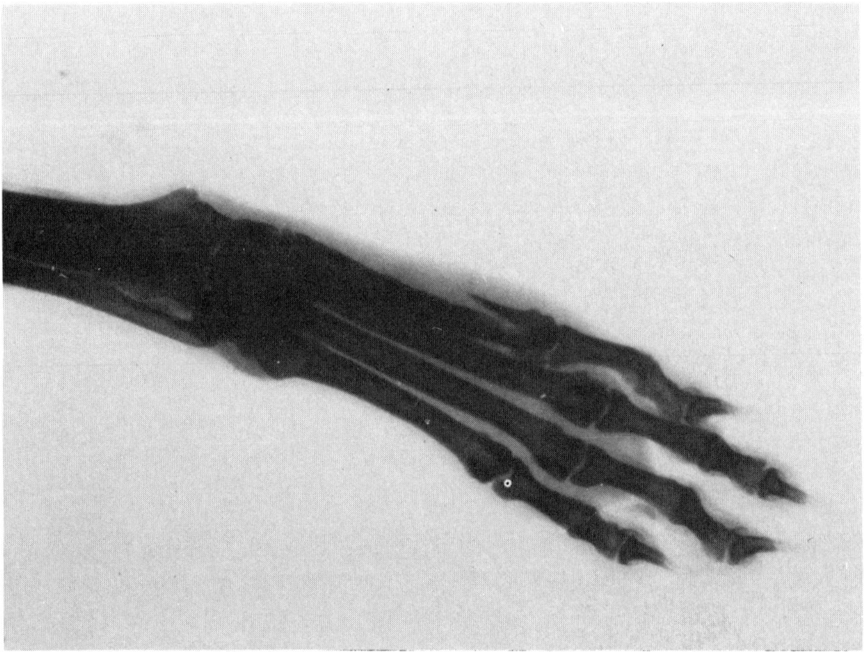

103. *A fracture of the inner metacarpal bone. The foot was strapped up until the break healed, and the whippet, Nimrodel Ent Wife, continued her very successful coursing and hunting career with no further sign of lameness. (Stuart Hastie)*

firm droppings; they will be larger and break up easier if the food is mainly carbohydrates. A dog that has been eating bones produces hard, crumbly white faeces. If your dogs show any sign of looseness or diarrhoea they must be watched during the day; if the looseness persists put the dog onto water alone for 24 hours; add some honey to the water if you like. The other sign of trouble to check for daily is any weeping or discharge from eyes or nose.

A whippet ought to be brushed daily though this is not easy to fit in if you have a lot of dogs. But daily brushing, even for a minute or two, does help to keep coat and skin in condition and gives you a chance to remove any mud that the dog has not licked off for itself; you may also find small thorns or prickles that are hidden in the coat. Most whippets take a lot of trouble to keep themselves clean and will spend a lot of time in licking sessions when they come in from the wet. Some bitches are compulsive lickers — sometimes to excess — and this can be put to good account with sores and wounds. We think it may run in families but we have always had at least one bitch that would take care of cuts and wounds on other members of the pack. Just occasionally a bitch of this habit will show you a sore place that you have not spotted on another dog by licking at it.

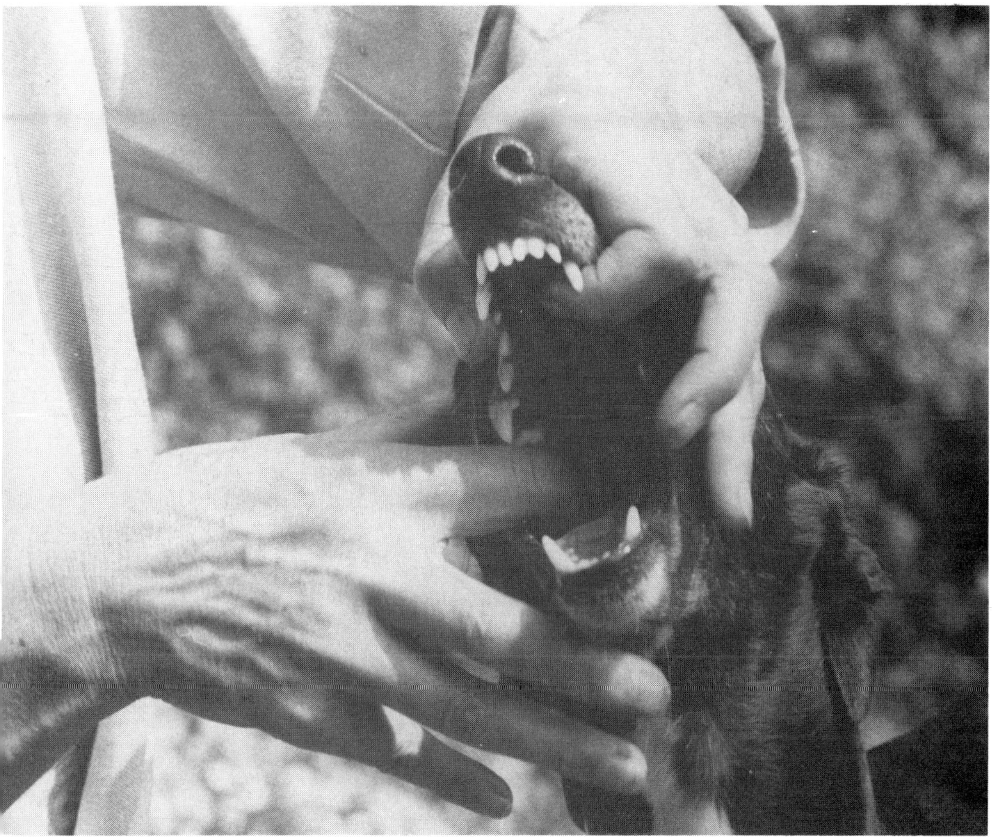

104. *Giving a pill; open the dog's mouth, drop the pill on the back of the tongue and give it a push. (Walsh)*

Keep an eye on toenails. Different dogs wear them down at different rates and even the four nails of one foot will wear differently. Road work will not always keep them as short as they should be and you will have to trim them from time to time. Use the sliding type of nail-clippers (see Plate 106) and cut to within about 1/8th of an inch of the 'quick', which shows pink in an uncoloured nail; with black nails the quick is impossible to see and nail clipping should err on the side of too little rather than too much. A whippet will let you know quickly and loudly if you cut too close and you may lame the dog.

Wherever your whippets are kept, in house or in kennel, make sure that they have access to a bowl of clean water at all times; use non-spill bowls and change the water — and wipe out the bowls — daily.

Kennel or House?

Where your whippets sleep depends on you and your house. Whippets will

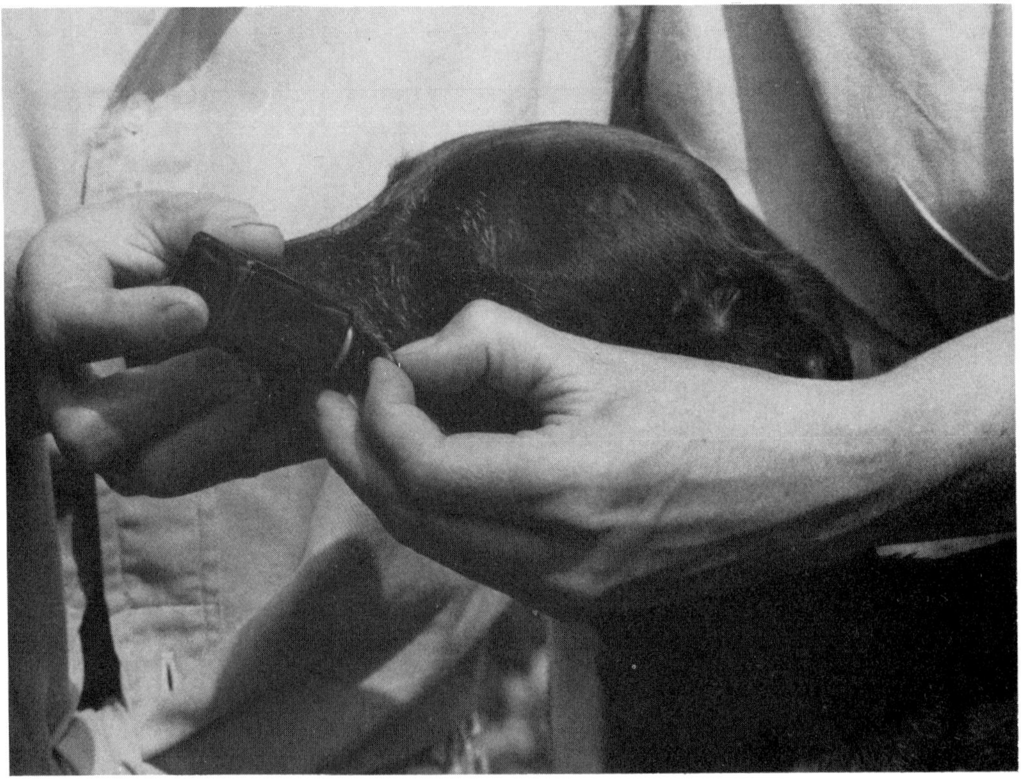

105. *Giving liquid medicine; put the liquid in a small bottle, pull out a pocket of skin at the corner of the dog's mouth and pour in the liquid slowly. (Walsh)*

stand a surprising amount of cold but with their fine coats they cannot be kept in open kennels in winter like sheep dogs or farm dogs; so, if they do not sleep in the house, the kennels or sheds where they live must be light, weatherproof, insulated and free from draughts. The ideal are stables or barns which can be converted. The floor must be impervious to wet both from above and from underneath which rules out wooden floors; the best of all are blue stable bricks but if not already in position they would now be prohibitively expensive so the floor must be of properly laid concrete. In winter a degree of heating will be needed; the amount will depend on the building but it must not be overdone and, provided that there is sufficient bedding for the dogs to burrow into, the only heating necessary will be enough to keep the frost out. The most satisfactory form of heating from most points of view is the red, 250 or 300 watt heat lamp as used in pig farms and poultry farms. It is perfectly safe, cannot be knocked over, dogs cannot burn themselves against it and it can be raised or lowered from the ceiling depending on the amount of heat required.

Beds should be of wood and must be raised off the floor; a raised edge will be needed to keep the bedding in place. Beds must be movable so that the complete kennel can be washed down or disinfected as and when required. Straw is the traditional form of bedding but it does break up, it becomes dusty and can harbour vermin. Shredded paper is good from almost every point of view but it must be the properly shredded type, not just long strips which can easily be pulled off the bed onto the floor. Probably the best bedding is wood-wool, which is dust-free, does not break up, and which does not harbour pests but it must not be used for small puppies. Whatever bedding is used must be changed regularly.

Beds in the House

Whatever is used for whippets which sleep in the house, the important thing is that they should know where their beds are. Beds should be in a permanent place, a place that the whippet knows is his and to which he goes when told to 'Get into bed'. If it can be under a table, so much the better. There are many commercial dog beds on the market but perfectly good beds can be improvised. I have seen a whippet who slept in an old leather top hat box; he allowed no other dog near it and to get into bed he used to jump, curl up in the air and land in the hat box lying down. One used to be able to buy ex-Army canvas baths which would hold three or four whippets but they seem to have disappeared off the market; large, strong cardboard boxes make perfectly adequate beds. Whatever is used, fairly high sides will prevent draughts.

Bedding, like dog beds, is available in many forms. 'Bean bags' filled with polystyrene bobbles, as are sold by 'Dognests' of Market Harborough, are bed and bedding in one but we recommend that denim covers are bought. Whippets are great bed-makers and will scratch and pull a bed about to make a nest before settling down; a small hole scratched in a cotton-covered bean bag will allow the bobbles to escape but this will not happen with the thicker covers. Blankets can sometimes be bought at local auctions quite cheaply; nylon 'sheepskins' make good beds and can be washed easily but they are a bit expensive. The choice is wide, but ease of cleaning and washing should be considered when buying bedding.

In, but not Out

There is one important point that must be remembered when thinking about housing whippets: they are very affectionate and sensitive dogs and they do better when in close company with humans. A whippet that has been kept outside in a kennel will thrive if it is brought inside as a house dog but the whippet that has lived as a house dog cannot be put outside into

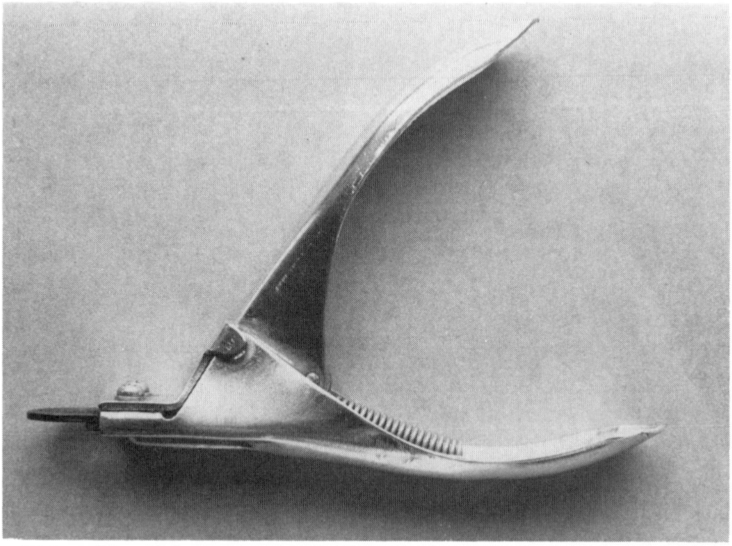

106. *The sliding type of nail clipper which cuts cleanly and does not crush the nail. (Walsh)*

a kennel (except, of course, into a boarding kennel for a limited period) without trouble, both mental and physical. So, if you keep your whippets outside think carefully before taking on an adult whippet that has lived indoors.

Feeding the Adult Whippet

The whippet is a carnivore — a meat eater — and in the wild the dog eats meat as and when it can get it, supplemented by anything it can pick up that is edible. Foxes were traditionally thought to live on rabbits but when myxomatosis killed off 99% of the rabbits in England in the early 1950's it made no difference whatsoever to the fox population. To continue the example, foxes eat a very wide selection of food, from earthworms to dead sheep. They are fond of fruit and will eat a lot of windfall plums and pears when they can find them and, as every farmer and gamekeeper knows, they will take any bird when the opportunity offers.

The dog's dental and digestive system is designed for a meat diet: to tear pieces off a carcase, swallow them whole or with the minimum of chewing, and sleep off the meal; and by a 'meat diet' we do not mean just the red meat of muscles. A dog fed on red meat, or heart or liver alone, soon shows signs of dietary deficiency. Watch three or four whippets that have caught a rabbit. Each grabs as big a mouthful as it can and they pull and strain against each other until the rabbit is pulled apart. Then each dog lies down and eats what it has managed to get, fur, skin, meat, bones and intestines and their contents. It is not long before the rabbit has

107. *Clipping toe nails; stand over the dog, pick up a foot and clip the nails towards the front of the foot. (Walsh)*

disappeared and the dogs are sniffing round in the grass to see if any bits and pieces remain. The whole rabbit — or whole chicken or pheasant — provides all the dog's requirements which nutritionists break down into proteins, carbohydrates, fats and salts; and, moreover, it was an old country belief that a rabbit skin, fur and all, would clear worms out of a dog.

Watching dogs eat such a meal should give a clue as to how a whippet should be fed; one meal a day consisting of meat, offal and bones and, since the hunting dog does not kill every day, a fast day once a week. So long as the dog, fed this way, has access to a garden or the countryside, it will eat as much grass or herbs as it needs to balance the meat diet. The trouble is that as life becomes more 'civilized', sources of meat become fewer and what is available becomes more expensive. At one time most village butchers did their own slaughtering and one did not have to go far for a source of cheap dog food. As with many other things in life the country has unfortunately been tidied up; sheep and cattle are now taken many miles by lorry to one of the relatively few abattoirs where most of the bits and pieces that could once be bought cheaply are collected in bulk and turned into expensive 'pet' food.

In feeding adult dogs — or puppies for that matter — it must be remembered that the wild dog will eat what is available, to the extent of gorging until he can eat no more; the next meal is something beyond his imagination. The domesticated dog has inherited this instinct and he does not *know* that his owner will provide another meal tomorrow and the day after that; he will, therefore, usually eat whatever is put in front of him even if it is far in excess of his actual requirements. Hence the number of grossly over-weight dogs to be seen at any time in any town. The dog owner *must* restrict meals to what will keep the dog fit, not fat, and adjust quantities according to the work being done.

Remembering that the dog's digestive system, with its short, straight and simple gut, is not adapted to chewing food or breaking down fibres and grains by bacterial action like the herbivores, what are the dog's requirements for growth and maintenance? They are:-

Proteins: These are necessary for growth of muscle and replacing wear and tear on the system. Proteins are not abundant in Nature and are therefore relatively expensive to produce. Cereals may contain up to 10% protein; pulses up to 20%, fresh meat or fish up to 25%, and hard cheese, 30%. Dried meat or dried fish can contain 75% protein; they are, therefore valuable sources but should be fed with discretion. Too much protein is as damaging as too little.

Carbohydrates: are fuel, producing heat and energy. The dog's digestive system cannot break down cereal grains — look at the droppings of a dog which has been stealing the chickens' corn — and in the wild the dog obtains most of its carbohydrates from the contents of its preys' intestines. For the domestic dog, cereal grains have to be cooked and fed as biscuits or meal. The amount of carbohydrates to be fed depends on the work being done. Foxhounds and sheepdogs, whose working day is long — 50 miles in the day's hunting is, or was before the days of hound vans, quite usual for a hound — are usually fed greater amounts of carbohydrates than the dog whose work consists of short, violent bursts of energy followed by periods of rest.

Fats: these, like carbohydrates, are a source of heat and energy and are more easily assimilated by the dog. Moreover, certain fat-soluble vitamins — vitamins which dissolve more easily in fat that in water — are vital in small amounts to the dog's welfare.

Minerals: calcium and phosphorous are both essential for growth, particularly growth of bone.

Having seen what the nutritional requirements are, what do we feed our whippet on? The best food is raw meat but it must be a mixture of red meat, tripe, offal and bones; the bones need not be given daily. What meat you use depends on availability. Butchers' meat is now far too expensive except for the 'best mince' which puppies are brought up on, so one has to look around for a reliable source of 'pet food'. Blocks of frozen meat, meat and tripe, etc, are available from most pet stores and the larger quantity you can take at a time the cheaper it should be; if you have several whippets it will probably be worthwhile getting a small freezer for dog food. Game of all sorts makes good dog food and they will do well on it but do feed it whole, skin and all. A hare will chop into pieces for seven or eight whippets and one of mine always takes the head and neck, if she can get it, in preference to the better looking bits. Rabbits are good dog food and can be boiled whole, in the skin, to kill tapeworms. Other meats that can be used from time to time include oxcheek, which is tough, and sheep heads which, cooked slowly with a handful of pearl barley, and onion and carrot added towards the end of the cooking time, make a wonderful winter meal for whippets and are very useful for a dog that is thin and out of condition. The barley is too heating for summer use. Do not use pork for dogs unless it is very well cooked.

The most important of the offals is tripe; not the butcher's white honeycomb blanket that transforms miraculously into tripe and onions, but green, unwashed bullocks' stomachs, weighing from 20lbs to 40lbs each and smelling to high Heaven. Most dogs, faced with a pound of best steak and a lump of green tripe will wolf down the tripe and then take the steak if there's any room for it. Unwashed tripe still has some half-digested green stuff between the 'leaves' and a lot or a little fat adhering to the outside, depending on the slaughterhouse. I used to buy three or four paunches a week from my local butcher and cut them up as required. Then the butcher was forced to close his slaughterhouse and I now buy coarse-minced tripe, ready-frozen in 5lb bags, from a major abattoir some 20 miles away. A 200lb load just fills the dogs' freezer and I must admit that it simplifies handling, especially in hot weather. The dogs are fed on this, raw, with a small amount of soaked biscuit or rusk and they keep very fit and well on it. Lambs tripes are sometimes available in numbers in the late summer or autumn but should be cooked and not fed raw.

Other forms of offal *can* be fed to dogs, heart, liver, lights, melt. Many dogs will not eat the latter and heart and liver should not be given as the sole food as they lack many of the ingredients of meat and tripe. Whilst not strictly offal, breast of lamb is cheap and is useful for fattening up a dog that has lost condition.

For carbohydrates, biscuits and meal are offered in many forms by the trade and in varying qualities at varying prices. What you use for your whippets is probably a question of convenience buying but make certain that what you get is a known, named brand; a lot of rubbish is sold in unnamed bags. For many years I have bought wheatmeal biscuits from

Roberts of Dunchurch; they compare well in price with other makes, especially when delivery is taken into account. Other parts of the country will have other reputable suppliers.

When biscuits are fed with meat they should be soaked in just enough water to be taken up, an hour before feeding time. If fed alone they can be fed dry.

Of dairy products, cheese, if available, is a very good source of protein and very few dogs will refuse it. Some dogs cannot or will not drink milk but for the majority a small amount daily does no harm. Eggs are pounced on with delight. We have whippets that are expert at finding where the bantams and Muscovy ducks are laying in our 3-acre wilderness and they almost always find these outlying nests before we do. The clues are cleaned-out egg shells and a whippet with a suspiciously bright shine to its coat.

Many dogs will eat raw vegetables and there is little point in cooking vegetables for them unless they have no access to grass and herbs; and even then, raw vegetables are better than cooked. Potatoes baked in their skins can be used as an occasional change from biscuits; they can be roughly chopped and mixed in with the meat.

All dogs will eat grass from time to time; sometimes it is to make them vomit up something that is lying uncomfortably, sometimes as a self-administered medicine. Some dogs do so at every opportunity, especially in late winter and spring. The grass usually eaten is couch grass (Agropyrum repens), otherwise known as twitch or squitch. The exact medicinal use for dogs is not certain, though it is said to be diuretic. What is certain is that dogs will eat young couch for pleasure and not just as an emetic; it is the older, coarser leaves that are used for that purpose. The other plant that almost all dogs will eat greedily is cleavers (Galium aparine), otherwise called goosegrass or Sticky Willie. To humans it has no smell but does have a bitterish, somewhat astringent taste. The chemical constituents are starch, chlorophyll, tannic acid and rubichloric acid and it is said to be a diuretic and a tonic, especially a skin tonic. It had a very old reputation in the treatment of skin cancer.

With the amount of grass eaten by dogs it is very important that you use weedkillers extremely carefully in your garden. The most dangerous spray is paraquat but none of the other weedkillers, or fungicides, are beneficial to dogs so if you are spraying, keep dogs away from the sprayed area until the weeds and grass have gone brown — or pink, depending on the chemical used.

So we come to tinned and processed foods. There are a great many brands of dog foods, some well-known for their advertising, some not so well known; the advertising is aimed at the dog's owner, not the dog, but that is another matter. Tinned dog foods vary very much in quality and an interesting test is to tip the contents of a tin into a saucepan, heat it and see how much firm meat is floating in the watery liquid. Dry, all-in foods are also widely advertised. Laboratory tests 'prove' that dogs thrive on them and that generations of dogs have been fed and bred on all-in diets without any ill effects. Many boarding kennels use them as it is quicker and easier to pour out pellets or fill hoppers than make up a lot of separate feeds every day. Some gundog kennels use them and some greyhound trainers too. We do not question the laboratory correctness of such diets and the claims that they contain everything a dog needs for nutrition; we also understand that laboratory tests have shown that a blown-up balloon in a dog's otherwise empty gut will give the impression of satiety. But, next to hunting, meal time is the high spot of a dog's day and we cannot imagine that there is much excitement in being faced with a bowl of pellets; also, some of these foods lack roughage and fats, resulting in poor coats. Some of them are only partly digested.

Dried meat and fish are high in protein and should not be over-fed. When using dried meat, hot water, just off the boil, should be poured over the meat some hours before feeding.

Despite our advice to feed meat and tripe, fresh or frozen, some tinned meat should be kept for emergencies; meat may not always be available and freezers have been known to break down. Some dried meat is also a useful standby; it will keep for a long time in a bin with a tight fitting lid. Whilst puppies are being reared they should be given an occasional meal of tinned food so that it is not something strange and suspicious when they are offered it later on.

Supplementation

Supplementation is largely a matter of commonsense. A dog in the wild needs no supplementation. For the domestic dog, a regular supply of flesh combined with good quality wholemeal biscuit should provide most ingredients for a healthy diet. However, many dogs are fed on various processed foods and natural supplements can be destroyed by either cooking or freezing so some form of supplementation may be needed.

Firstly, it is important to find out exactly what a dog's diet consists of in order to decide whether supplements are necessary and, if so, what. Most dog biscuits are enriched in one way or another containing trace elements, phosphorous, linseed oil, flaked maize or other additives. Secondly it is very important not to overdo supplementation since this can, curiously enough, lead to the same symptoms and malformations as deprivation. It is a common fallacy to think that if two pills daily will do good, four pills daily will do better. This is not the case; far from doing good you may actively do harm.

Experience of breeding, rearing and living with whippets to old age leads us to the following conclusions.

The average adult whippet, if fed as recommended, should not require any additives to its daily food with the possible exception of seaweed powder which supplies minerals which are not usually available in normal diets. Seaweed makes for good coats, clean digestive tracts and absence of skin problems.

The bitch in whelp will need a calcium and vitamin D supplement while in whelp and extra calcium after whelping and while nursing a litter. Growing puppies should have some calcium supplement and possibly cod-liver oil if reared in the winter months when they cannot benefit from sunshine. Further supplementation should only be herbal — all Denes' herbal remedies are excellent and both Buster Lloyd Jones and Juliette de Bairacli Levy have written informative and useful books on natural rearing methods.

The guiding principle in all animal husbandry must be to keep diet and living conditions as wholesome and natural as possible. The dog which is well fed, groomed, and exercised should live a happy and natural life. The quality of the food and exercise are of prime importance and giving regular supplements is no substitute.

How Often and When?

How often you feed your whippets depends on the whippets; when you feed them depends on you.

Puppies' meals gradually decrease from five meals a day down to two and by the age of 18 months a puppy can usually go onto one meal a day. Most adult whippets do well on one meal a day but there are tricky feeders and some nervy dogs who do better on two feeds. If you have one of these by all means feed twice a day but do not overfeed; let the total be what the whippet would have got in one feed. Old dogs sometimes need feeding twice a day as they can find it difficult to take in enough in one meal. But remember that with age and less exercise the older dog needs less food than when he was young and active.

When you feed your whippets depends on your own comings and goings; if you do not get back from work until 6pm you cannot feed your dogs at 5. Whippets should be fed after their daily exercise, and not too late in the evening or they will not have an opportunity to empty themselves before shutting up time. But at whatever time you do feed your dogs, let it be the same time every day. Dogs are creatures of habit and random feeding times can lead to troubles.

General Care

Whippets are normally very healthy dogs. They do not suffer from the many inherited diseases and unsoundnesses that affect many other breeds of 'pedigree' dogs. Because of their active nature they will, from time to time, strain a foot of a leg, or tear themselves on wire or stakes; but because of their lightness, agility and strength they do not suffer so much of the damage that their heavier cousins, greyhounds and lurchers, can do to themselves.

You are unlikely to be able to do everything for your dogs throughout the whole of their lives on your own; as early as the third month a puppy will have to go to the veterinary surgeon for injections against virus diseases and, depending on what sort of a life your whippet lives, future visits will be more, or less, regular. It is not so many generations ago that the dog owner had to rely on guesswork, the local cow-doctor, what Grannie said, and various books on animal management which varied from wishful thinking to downright lethal. Now we have a veterinary service that is second to none and since the discovery of protection against virus diseases there is no excuse for dogs dying of the many infections that decimated kennels up to the early 1950's.

Unless you are a hypochondriac, exceptionally lucky or just callous, you will, as a dog owner, know your veterinary surgeon better than your doctor; the relationship will be just as personal and probably more emotional. Your choice of a veterinary surgeon is partly limited in that you do not want to drive enormous distances for every visit, however minor; but there are few places out of reasonable reach of a surgery and the only advice we would give is that, all being equal, you should go to a vet with a small animal practice. A great many vets are usually busy with large animals, you only see them by special appointment and their surgeries are sometimes staffed by young assistants who will be fully qualified but may be short on the experience that means so much in diagnosing trouble, and in some practices they tend to come and go.

If you are lucky enough to have a small animal specialist within reasonable reach, cling to him or her through thick and thin and do not change to anyone else without a very good reason. Lucky above all is the whippet owner who has access to an experienced greyhound vet. It is surprising how few vets, other than such specialists, have ever seen a running dog at work; have seen the strain imposed on legs and feet at speed over rough ground; have seen a dog go down with cramp while running — a frightening sight to a novice since, at a distance, it looks like a broken front leg — and not many vets can talk authoritatively about it; and not many vets have seen a dog return utterly, if temporarily, exhausted having picked up a second, or even a third hare after a course.

But, having found your good veterinary surgeon you must remember fees and the costs of medicines. Like doctors, vets have to go through a long course of training, they lack many of the back-up services that human medicine provides and no advice or surgery treatment can be cheap; they have the right to charge for their skills. So you do not want to make unnecessary visits to the surgery if you can avoid them and if the matter is one that you can deal with yourself. Though a little knowledge can be dangerous, a basic knowledge of the dog's anatomy, what its daily needs are, recognition of impending trouble and some knowledge of animal nursing can keep the bills down and can make diagnosis quicker when you do have to consult your vet; but remember that it is your whippet who will suffer if you get it wrong.

The Healthy Dog

The owner whose whippets are with him all the time, who knows them in and out and who has some basic stockmanship, can often see trouble, almost before it starts, by changes in a dog's behaviour. There are certain signs to look for.

The Eyes:	are clear and bright. Watch for any weeping or discharge.
The Nose:	should be cold and slightly moist. A hot, dry nose often means trouble.
The Mouth:	should be damp with uniformly pink gums. A dry or cold mouth can mean trouble and pale gums may be a sign of anaemia.
The Teeth:	should be white and clean.
The Skin and Coat:	are probably the most important and obvious sign of health. The skin should be loose and pliable and a raised pinch of skin should return instantly. A tight, dry skin with a harsh coat and hair standing up can be a sign of trouble.
The Faeces:	have already been mentioned on pages 187 and 188.
Temperature:	a healthy dog's temperature, taken at rest, should be between 100.9 and 101.7. A temperature of over 102 means a sick dog. The temperature is taken at the rectum using a rectal thermometer. The thermometer should be shaken sharply to bring the mercury into the bulb and slightly lubricated with soap or vaseline. Get an assistant to hold the dog, hold the dog's tail and elevate it slightly, insert the thermometer at a slightly upwards angle. Leave it for three minutes but do not let go of it; after three minutes, remove the thermometer, wipe it on a piece of

tissue, rotate it at eye level until the mercury is visible and read the number at the head of the column.

Pulse: this is not such an accurate indicator as the temperature since the latter is shown by a figure of mercury whereas the former is felt with the fingers and may mean different things to different people; and, the pulse may range from 80 to 120 beats a minute. In addition, dogs, particularly whippets, have an irregular double beat which makes the pulse difficult to count. What is more important is the force of the heart-beat; a fast, hard pulse can be a sign of shock but a thin weak pulse is more serious still. There are five places where the dog's pulse can be felt, but the best to use is inside the hind leg where the large femoral artery crosses over the *femur,* the thigh bone. It should be felt for where the leg joins the body or just below this point.

Respiration: again, like the pulse, this is not a very accurate indication of trouble since the breathing rate can depend on the ambient temperature and it can increase if the dog is in anyway nervous. It must be counted when the dog is at rest and a normal rate can be from 10 to 30 a minute. But remember that the dog cannot perspire through the skin except between the toes and it cools itself by panting, passing cooler air over the throat, mouth and tongue. So unless breathing is markedly slow, very fast and shallow, harsh or rasping it is only a secondary sign of trouble.

The Medicine Cupboard

Even with only one whippet you will, sooner or later, need some simple implements and medicines; you may not use them for weeks on end but when you do want them it may be urgent and you will not have time to go shopping. Also, remember that veterinary help is usually expensive and you want to avoid unnecessary visits to the surgery so the medicine cupboard becomes essential. The following list has served well over many years with never less than half a dozen dogs in the house, all hard working and who inevitably damage themselves from time to time:

Implements

Clinical thermometer
Two pairs blunt ended scissors, one straight, one curved.
Broad-ended tweezers (or a pair of locking artery forceps).
Nail clippers
Coarse nail file.

Bandages, etc

2 × 4″ bandages
2 × 2″ bandages
Large roll of cotton wool
Elastoplast
Packet of lint
Tin of sterile gauze
Safety pins

Medicaments

Antibiotic ointment
Antiseptic
Embrocation
Friars Balsam mixed 70/30 with Tincture of Myrrh (for feet)
Eye Ointment and Optrex
Green Oil (a pint tin)
Iodine
Kaolin poultice
Kaolin suspension
Worming liquid
Sulpha powder

Damage to Tissue

From their very nature as active dogs, whippets are prone to tears, cuts, wounds, strains and, occasionally fractures. So unless you never let your whippet off a lead — in which case you should leave whippets alone and take up knitting or some other innocuous pastime — you will sooner or later have to deal with damage of some sort.

Bleeding

Bleeding can be *external* where it can be seen, and may be arterial, venous, capillary or a mixture of these three; it may also occur from the nose, mouth, ears or rectum. Or it may be *internal* either into the tissues or into a cavity as a result of injury, disease or poisoning (Warfarin). External bleeding is usually obvious but internal bleeding may not be apparent for some time; the signs are listlessness, pale or white gums, rapid and feeble pulse and a rapid drop in temperature.
Arterial bleeding: since the arteries carry the blood outwards from the heart, blood from an artery is bright red and issues in spurts timed with the heart-beats; the force depending on the size of artery that is damaged.
Venous bleeding: blood on its way back to the heart is dark red and issues

as a steady flow, again depending on the size of vein damaged.

Capillary bleeding: since the capillaries lie in and under the skin there will be capillary bleeding from scratches and minor wounds; the blood is red and oozes from the wound with little force.

If *untreated,* bleeding will eventually slow down or stop due to:

1. retraction of the cut ends of the blood vessel, reducing the size of the opening, lessening the flow of blood and allowing a blood clot to form,
2. reduced circulation due to lowered blood pressure with less blood reaching the wound,
3. clotting both in the wound and in the blood vessel, preventing a further flow of blood.

Treatment of Bleeding: depends on where and what type of bleeding it is:

1. Direct pressure on a wound using fingers and thumb is quick and usually effective but it can introduce germs — from dirty hands — or press a foreign body deeper into the wound.
2. Pad and pressure bandage where a gauze and cotton wool pad is placed on the wound and bandaged firmly in place; if bleeding continues a second pad can be placed over the first which should not be moved. Ideally this is all done with sterile dressing but we have successfully stopped blood pumping out from a cut in a whippet's neck by using three large handkerchiefs and a head scarf!
3. Pressure points of which there are three useable ones:
   a. the brachial artery where it passes over the inner side of the *humerus* about an inch above the elbow, to stop bleeding from the foreleg or foot,
   b. the femoral artery where it passes over the *femur* on the inside of the thigh, to stop bleeding below the stifle,
   c. the coccygeal artery on the underneath side of the tail to stop bleeding from the tail.
4. Tourniquet, constricting a limb by tightening a loop round it, thus stopping the blood supply. This should only be used for major wounds where the bleeding cannot be stopped by other means. A tourniquet can be made with a handkerchief, a tie or a belt, tightened up with a bit of wood or even a biro; but is must *never* be left in place for more than ten minutes at the most without being loosened. Once a tourniquet has been put on, a pressure pad should be bandaged over the wound and the constriction loosened a bit to see if the bleeding has stopped.

Wounds

With their fine coats and thin skin, whippets tend to tear easily. The wounds you may be faced with will vary from a small, triangular nick from touching barbed wire, to the deep, jagged wound from a large spike or a fight with a bigger dog.

In general, where the cut is straight and the underlying tissues are not damaged the wound can be left to heal on its own, particularly if it is where the dog can get at it with his tongue; this is better than any antiseptic. Probably the only action you will need to take will be to clip the hair round the edge of the cut and wash out any grit or dirt. Barbed wire tears are usually triangular, with a piece of skin folded back exposing an area of muscle. Depending on the size of the tear it may or may not need stitching. The exception is a cut or tear under the chest, inside the elbows, on the abdomen or inside the thighs where movement will allow air to get in under the skin. These wounds must be stitched by a professional

When not only the skin but also the underlying tissue — muscles — have been damaged you must get the dog to your veterinary surgeon as quickly as possible as a local — or possibly general — anaesthetic will be needed before stitching begins. Try and telephone before you leave home, or from a box on the way, to give the surgery some notice. *Puncture wounds* may occur from the dog running into a stake in a hedge — the most usual — or from a fight, be it with rats, a fox or another dog. The danger of puncture wounds is that the top of the wound heals, or closes and gives the impression of healing, whilst germs are hard at work underneath. If left unattended the result is an abcess which can be very large and will take a long time to clear up. If the wound is deep it will be a job for your vet. If it is not deep, clip the hair round the hole, flush out the wound with dilute antiseptic (peroxide of hydrogen is as good as anything for this) using a hypodermic syringe without the needle, and squeeze in an antibiotic. Then see that the wound is kept open to drain.

Bruises, Sprains, Dislocations and Fractures

If you work your whippet at all it will sooner or later suffer from bruises and sprains as well as tears and cuts. These things usually happen when you are furthest from professional help and the difference between them is that a wound is usually obvious straight away but damage to muscles, ligaments and tendons — and even small fractures — are often not noticed until some time later. The dog that bruises a muscle or sprains a toe joint may go on working for an hour, showing no signs of lameness; it is warm and intent on what it is doing. But when you get home and the whippet has rested for a while it comes out of its bed on three legs.

Lameness

An otherwise lame dog may go sound on grass and there will be a temptation to take him out for a walk or something more energetic. For this reason an area of gravel, be it a yard, or drive or even a path, is almost essential to any kennel. There is nothing like pea-gravel for showing up sore toes and damaged toenails.

The point of lameness may be obvious from a swelling but sometimes this is not so and there are ways of finding out where it is. As a general rule, the shorter the stride, the higher the seat of lameness. The lame dog takes a shorter stride with the sore leg; if the leg is hardly brought forward at all you may have to look at the shoulder or above the stifle. Examine the whole leg carefully from the toenails upwards; if you find nothing obvious and there is no noticeable swelling or heat, flex each joint up tight in turn and watch the dog for any wincing. If you can get someone else to watch the dog's expression so much the better as it is easy to miss a change when you are handling the various joints.

Bruises

These may occur anywhere but with working whippets a fairly common bruise is on the foreleg between knee and elbow, usually caused when going through a hedge or fence after something. The leg swells up surprisingly quickly and the dog may or may not go lame. Put on his collar and take him home. Treatment consists of either standing the leg in water as cold as you can get it, several times a day, or applying green oil three or four times a day; personally I prefer the green oil. Not only will it deal with any break in the skin, no matter how small, but most dogs will lick at green oil on their skin and the dog's tongue is the best natural massage.

Sprain

A sprain is the stretching or tearing of the ligaments and tissue surrounding a joint. The joint is forced too far out of line and the synovial membrane — the dense membrane which surrounds many joints and holds the synovial fluid — may be damaged. The commonest sprain in the whippet is what is called a 'knocked-up toe'; typical symptoms are heat, swelling, inflammation and pain. An X-ray photo *may* show a broken bone but the usual cause is a very temporary dislocation of one of the toe joints, where the joint has been wrenched apart sideways or upwards and has slipped back into position, leaving damaged ligaments and tissue round it. Fluid will collect and if it is not dealt with can turn into fibrous tissue leaving a thickened and perhaps permanently stiff toe. The treatment is straight-forward:

Rest
Reduce inflammation
Massage

but the most important of these is *rest.* The dog must not be let off a lead until it is quite sound again, otherwise the damage will increase.

To reduce inflammation in a bad case, use a kaolin poultice. Heat a tin of kaolin in a saucepan of water until you can just bear your own elbow in it. Put a bit of cotton wool between the toes of the foot (this must always be done when a foot is bandaged) and spread the hot kaolin on a piece of lint large enough to cover the foot. Wrap the foot in the lint and bandage over, fastening with Elastoplast below the knee. Such a poultice must be changed every twelve hours.

In milder cases the inflammation may be reduced either by painting with iodine four times a day or, if the skin is broken, rubbing with green oil. As soon as the inflammation has subsided the joint should be massaged with the thumbs, using an embrocation, and also manipulated — bent and stretched — to prevent stiffness. Occasionally a dog that is lame may not show signs of trouble in the toes but there will be heat and swelling below and behind the knee or hock. The treatment is the same as for toes.

Dislocations

These *can* occur almost anywhere but with whippets are usually only found in the toe joints and occasionally the point of the shoulder, the elbow or the hip. If noticed soon enough a toe joint can be clicked back into position using a firm grip on both sides of the joint and the treatment is as for a knocked-up toe. Major dislocations are a job for your vet as a general anaesthetic will be needed; get the dog to the surgery as quickly as you can because the longer the joint is out of place the more difficult it is to put back again. Once the dislocation has been reduced the dog must be rested for a long time to ensure that the ligaments round the joint can recover. A shoulder once dislocated may well go again if the dog is exercised too soon.

Fractures

A 25lb whippet does not suffer the damage, the snapped foreleg or the shattered hock, that can happen all too easily to a 70lb greyhound; you are unlikely to have to cope with a major fracture except from a kick from a horse or if the dog is hit by a car. If it does happen it will be a job for your vet and the most you can do is to keep the leg immobilised until the dog is on the surgery table. The problem is that fractures will happen when you are a long way from a first aid box. Still, if the worst comes to the worst, a small branch from the hedge and two handkerchiefs can make enough of a splint to hold a leg steady enough for the dog to be carried.

Lesser fractures you will probably come across are broken toes, or broken metacarpal or metatarsal bones, the bones beneath the knee or hock. Plate 103 shows a break of this sort, the inner metacarpal bone of the off fore leg. The leg and foot were strapped until the bone had knitted and the whippet — Nimrodel Ent Wife — continued her very successful coursing career for another four years without any sign of lameness.

Shock

Shock is a circulatory failure — the heart and blood vessels are not providing the body tissues with oxygen — accompanied by slowing down or loss of vital functions. The brain is starved of oxygen and does not respond to signals from the nerves. The whippet is not in control of its movements and its senses are not working properly.

Shock can happen from various causes; haemorrhage, a traffic accident, a dog fight, burns, scalds, an electric shock or poisoning. Signs of shock can include a weak, irregular or rapid pulse, a blue tinge to mouth and tongue, cold and shivering, sub-normal temperature, shallow breathing and lack of response to sights and sounds.

Treatment must be undertaken by a veterinary surgeon as, almost certainly, a saline drip or blood transfusion will be needed, but first aid given immediately may well save a dog's life that would otherwise die before reaching the surgery.

Obviously, bleeding must be stopped unless it is very minor in which case don't waste time on it. Make certain that there are no broken bones — if there are you must be very careful how you lift the dog — then get it warm, but not hot, and keep it warm by whatever means are immediately to hand; however good and expensive your coat is it can always be cleaned. Above all, keep calm yourself and talk to the dog; quick reassurance may do more to combat shock than later, expert, attention. Once you have got the dog into a vehicle go straight to the surgery, if possible getting someone to telephone that you are on your way.

Eyes

The working whippet will be lucky if it goes through life without some form of eye trouble; thorns are the worst, grit or grass seeds can be washed out but nettle stings when ratting or rabbiting are common. If you see your whippet rubbing its eyes with a front leg have a look, and think where you have been: in the nettlebed? If you can see nothing on the surface of the eye wash it out with cold tea or a weak saline — one teaspoon of salt to a pint of warm water. Use an eye dropper or a hypodermic without the needle by all means but a piece of cotton wool worked to a point will drop liquid just as well and will not damage the eye if the dog moves its head suddenly. Keep a tube of eye ointment in the dogs' medicine cupboard; Optrex is also useful.

If the whippet keeps its eye closed and continues to rub it take the dog to the surgery for a proper examination; and in particular any trace of clouding on the surface of the eye *must* be examined by a vet to see if there is any damage to the cornea.

Ears

Other than tears or cuts from hedgerows or from fights, whippets seldom suffer from ear troubles. Their ears are thin and fine, there are no long hairs and, apart from anything else, I have found that they will clean each other's ears out by licking if they think it necessary. In the rare case of canker, use benzil benzoate; or one can do worse than use the 'Shooting Times' remedy, so-called from the number of times it has been printed in that Journal over the years:

1 oz boracic powder
1 oz zinc powder
1 drachm iodoform.

keep it in a tightly stoppered bottle; massage one saltspoon daily into the base of the ear until the trouble is cured.

Feet

We have discussed the shape of whippets' feet in Chapter 2 and damage to the bones of the feet elsewhere in this Chapter; but however good the feet are, whippets' pads do get damaged, the amount depending on how hard they are, how much road work the whippet was given as a puppy and how much autumnal hardening up has been done.

Minor cuts and sore feet from galloping on a hard surface such as a road or an old aerodrome runway are treated with Friars Balsam, mixed 70/30 with Tincture of Myrrh. It is sticky stuff to get off one's fingers and the cap of the bottle may get stuck but methylated spirits will dissolve it. Dab the mixture on the dog's feet after work for small cuts and sores. A deep cut is another matter and if it is through the keratinised layer it may need stitching to bring the edges of the cut together.

Thorns can be a constant trouble, especially with the modern farming practice of 'cutting' hedges with tractor flails; these mash up the clippings and spray thorns both into the hedge and for yards on either side. A dog can run a thorn into a pad, or between the toes, and not be seen to be lame straight away; by the time you notice the dog going lame the tip of the thorn has probably broken off inside the foot. Soaking the foot in a saturated solution of Epsom salts, as hot as you can bear your finger in, will sometimes bring a thorn to the surface but it can take time.

In a very wet winter when dogs are being coursed or worked on arable, particularly winter corn that has been sprayed, they can get sores round the base of the toenails if their feet are not washed immediately after work. Again, soaking in Epsom salt can help, followed by a squeeze of antibiotic ointment round the base of the nail.

Euthanasia

Whippets can, and do, lead long and healthy lives, the actual length much depending on what sort of lives they are. Many whippets who do not do very much will live happily to fourteen or fifteen but they are getting into borrowed time; ten to thirteen years is probably the average. Whippets that live hard, that are always hunting, may not get to ten years; some have to be put down because of injury, some die of heart attack. But, as with all living things, the time comes when the body must fail and you must remember that when you take on a whippet you take on the responsibility of seeing that its latter days are comfortable. The older dog will — or ought to — eat less food and it will take as much exercise as it wants. Where there is pain, disease or the inability to perform natural functions the decision is straight forward. It is the slowly deteriorating dog that may present problems; it can happen that the person who is with the dog, day after day, is the last to see the change in condition but it is only the owner who knows the dog in all its moods who can tell when the time has really come.

No dog should be kept alive on drugs just to suit its owner's feelings; modern methods of euthanasia are painless and very quick. If you can, get your vet to come to your house; if this is not possible, the old dog needs your reassurance in the clinical atmosphere of the surgery so take him there yourself and stay there, holding him until the injection is done. After all he has done for you the very least you can do is to see that his last moments are as dignified and unworried as possible.

108. *Ch. Samarkand's Greenbrae Tarragon. (Sally Anne Thompson)*

109. *Ch. Dondelayo Roulette. (Diane Pearce)*

CHAPTER 9

The Show Ring, 1962–1989

There can be no doubt that during the last twenty-seven years, 1962–1989, whippets have steadily increased in popularity in each of the three fields of activity which we have discussed, showing, coursing and racing. Entries in all three spheres achieve new records, year by year. At general championship shows the whippet entry is usually the second highest—to Afghan hounds—in the Hound Group. At representative shows this can mean as many as 180 dogs, and at most other shows a championship entry is seldom less than 100. Curiously enough, this rise in entries does not reflect a similar rise in Kennel Club registrations over the same twenty year period. In 1962, 1,903 whippets were registered. In the early 1970s, registrations were at a peak with over 2,000 dogs registered in 1972, putting whippets into the 'Top Twenty' breeds league for numbers registered, an event which many breeders regarded with some dismay. However, during the late 1970s the numbers fell off dramatically, dropping to 663 in 1977 when the ill-fated, two-tier registration system was in operation, and levelling out at 1,399 in 1978 and 1979. The figure in 1982 was 1,247, considerably lower than the 1962 figure of 1,903, while overall show entries are very much higher than they were in those days.

It is difficult to know what conclusions to draw from these figures. It would be encouraging to think that breeders are breeding fewer litters more selectively and that the net result is higher entries of higher quality. On the other hand, the drop in registration figures may simply reflect the fact that, due to the sharp rise in Kennel Club fees, breeders do not necessarily register all, or even most, of the puppies in each litter. Since the foundation of the W.C.R.A. a fair share of the total registration figures must be due to racing breeding, since the W.C.R.A. requires all whippets eligible for a W.C.R.A. passport to have Kennel Club registration, as do the whippet coursing clubs. Previously, racing whippets were not necessarily Kennel Club registered; many were pure-bred but many were not. Tempting though it may be to think that the lower figures are attributable to more selective breeding, there are two factors which point fairly conclusively in the opposite direction. Firstly, the J.R. Whippet Rescue Service, which was founded by Mrs

110. *Ch. Robmaywin Stargazer of Allways. (Fall)*

Joanna Russell (Martinsell) to fulfil an urgent need, and which is supported by the Whippet Breed Clubs, is responsible for finding homes for a really horrifying number of abandoned whippets every year. This does not argue for selective breeding or for careful disposal of stock. Secondly, show reports by experienced whippet judges, who have received record, or near record, entries at recent shows, have indicated a lack of quality in depth which the discerning whippet owner and breeder should view with alarm. Looking back at photographs of winners from the early 1960s one cannot feel that there is room for much complacency. We may have much larger entries at our shows now but we do not necessarily have the same strong level of competition. The best we can breed are very good indeed, but the highest standards are not being applied overall, and it is necessary to look deeper into the results and breeding patterns to discover a reason for this. We hope that there are some lessons to be learnt from such an examination and that there will be an improvement in the breed over the next twenty years.

The early 1960s

Looking at show catalogues for the early 1960s, the breeding of the majority of exhibits was dominated by two kennels, the Allways kennel of Mr and Mrs

111. *Ch. Harque the Lark. (Newark Advertiser)*

F. Jones, and the Laguna Kennel of Mrs D. U. McKay. The two most important sires of the 1950s (see Appendixes 1 and 2) were Ch. Pilot Officer Prune and Ch. Wingedfoot Marksman of Allways, both of whom sired ten Champions apiece. Prefixes such as Fleeting, Seagift, Hillgarth, Test and Wingedfoot were the foundations on which the 1960s were able to build. Mrs Chapman's famous Ch. Pilot Officer Prune sired Ch. Bellavista Barry, in turn the sire of, amongst others, Mrs McKay's Ch. Laguna Ligonier, who holds the record for top sire in the breed. Since Mrs Chapman has never used a prefix and has also steadfastly refused to judge, her long line of beautiful champions, with their distinctive names which are her hallmark, have often been overlooked in the annals of the breed but have, nevertheless, been of immense importance to whippet history. The Wingedfoot and Test prefixes, closely allied to and based on the Allways line, produced numerous champions in the 1950s. The same breeding is behind the enormously successful Shalfleet kennel of Mrs Wilton Clark, as well as other prefixes such as Walkabout, Worthmere, Velroza, Ballagan, Iniskelltr, Brough and Poaching. Mrs Garrish's Fleeting breeding, which has had such an influence in the U.S.A. and Scandinavia, has also, through Fleeting Fancy Free (dam of Int. Ch. Tantivvey Diver and

112. *Shalfleet Skyliner. (Fall)*

grandam of Ch. Laguna Light Lagoon), descended through the Cockrow, Baydale, Crysbel, Crawshaw and Nevedith breeding to the present time. Mrs Whitwell's Seagift prefix is directly behind all Dragonhill, Poltesco, Tweseldown, Nimrodel and Martinsell lines, all of which have combined successfully with Allways, and retained their consistent type throughout the years. The Laguna lines were the foundation, chiefly through Ch. Samarkand's Greenbrae Tarragon and Ch. Laguna Ligonier, of the Samarkand, Dondelayo, Oakbark, Ravensdowne, Flarepath, Newbold, Lowglen, Towercrest, Deepridge and Hardknott prefixes. Many other prefixes were, of course, a combination of two or more of the prefixes we have mentioned, and indeed, it would be hard to find a top winner who did not, at some point in his pedigree, include common ancestors. Nevertheless, it is, broadly speaking, possible to draw a line down the middle and say that even twenty-nine years later most exhibits fall on one side or the other of this line. This is well demonstrated by the seven record holders in the breed who fairly represent these two bloodlines.

The Record Holders in the Breed

The breed record for number of CCs won has been held over the years by four dogs and three bitches. Ch. Robmaywin Stargazer of Allways won 17 CCs as did Ch. Samarkand's Greenbrae Tarragon, although both won duplicate CCs under

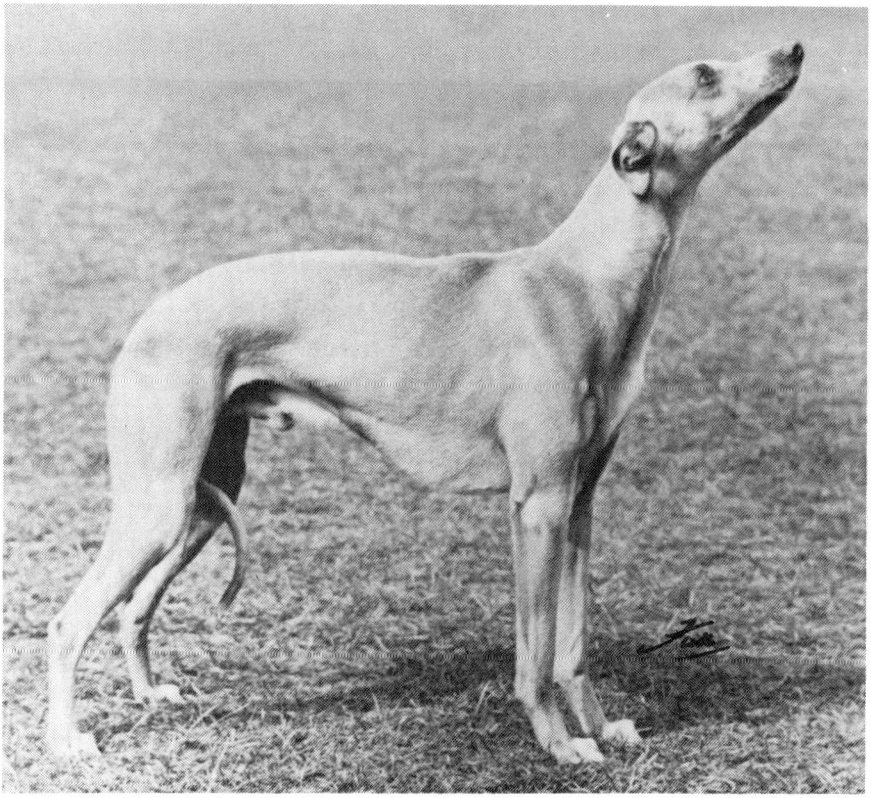

113. *Ch. Shalfleet Sailing Free. (Fall)*

certain judges. This record was then surpassed by two bitches, Ch. Harque the Lark and Ch. Dondelayo Roulette. For some time their record stood level at 19 CCs each until finally, at the mature age of seven, Ch. Dondelayo Roulette won her twentieth CC under Mr Dennis Meakin, thus setting the record for CCs each won under a different judge. This record was overtaken in 1987 by Ch. Selinko Another Lady who won 25 CCs, 24 of them under different judges. Meanwhile the dog record, held jointly by Stargazer and Tarragon, had been defeated in 1986 by Ch. Welstar Royal Mint who won 19 CCs and whose record has only been defeated in 1989 by his grandson, Ch. Nimrodel Wanderer, who gained his twentieth CC during the year.

1989 has also been the year of Ch. Nutshell of Nevedith, whose meteoric rise to fame has included an unbelievable total of 6 Hound Group wins, 6 Reserve in Group wins, 2 All-Breed Championship Show BIS awards and 2 Reserve BIS awards. Nutshell is currently the winner of 19 CCs thus equalling Ch. Harque the Lark and threatening both Ch. Dondelayo Roulette's and Ch. Nimrodel Wanderer's totals and, since Nutshell is very much in her prime, representing a serious threat to the overall breed record held by Selinko Another Lady. There are

114. *Ch. Sequence of Shalfleet. (Fall)*

many breeds where the breed record is 30 CCs or more but in whippets, where competition is fierce, the achievement of the breed record is underlined by the very few dogs or bitches which have gained more than 10 CCs in the last 25 years. In dogs, Ch. Roanbar Star, Ch. Deepridge Mintmaster, Ch. Ambassador of Algarth, Ch. Beseeka Knight Errant of Silkstone, Ch. Nimrodel Ruff, Ch. Novacroft Madrigal and Ch. Nevedith Paperweight are amongst the top winners. In bitches, Ch. Lily of Laguna, Ch. Laguna Ravensdowne Astri, Ch. Sequence of Shalfleet, Ch. Tweseldown Whinchat, Ch. Jubilant Lady of Tygreen and Lowerdon and Ch. Baldrey Limited Edition of Juneric are amongst the select few.

It is interesting to take a look at these seven record holders and the breeding behind them. What makes a dog or bitch a multiple winner in a breed as hotly contested as whippets? It usually takes a good dog or bitch to become a Champion but to do the sort of winning these seven achieved requires something extra. Roulette and the Lark were campaigned simultaneously and Roulette won 13 RCCs to the Lark. What sort of record might either have set up had she been whelped earlier or later? Royal Mint shared several seasons with his grandson and both would have appealed to the same kind of judges. All seven were fawn, which some consider the dominant colour for the breed and, although fawns were probably more general in the breed ring in the days of Stargazer, Tarragon, Lark and

115. *Ch. Shalfleet Sequilla. (Fall)*

Roulette, that has not been the case in the last decade when Another Lady, Mint and Wanderer were oversetting the records.

Nutshell is, in fact, the first really big winner amongst the parti-colours and to the extent that she is also the biggest Group winner to date in a breed which is not generally considered Group material, her exceptionally glamorous markings, combined with her breed excellence, have probably given her an edge in that respect. Personality plays a great part in keeping a dog at the top with such frequency and over such a period of time. The campaigning of a dog at this level requires a great affinity between dog and handler; if the dog has not got the desire to please and the ability to participate in the game, then it will not be a really great winner. Presence, that indefinable 'something', which turns a good whippet into a hound of commanding elegance and dynamic force, is an essential requirement. Some dogs have this quality in abundance and thereby win despite quite serious breed faults; others may be so lacking in presence that good construction and breed type is not enough to carry them home. It must be said here that the temperament and also, perhaps, the circumstances of the owner will also play a large part in such campaigning. The passionate desire to win, the mental toughness to survive setbacks which beset even the best, and the financial ability to travel the length and breadth of the land; all these factors are contributory. Six of the record holders have wins at Group level, several of them a substantial number of such wins, so they must have possessed that elusive quality which enabled them to dominate the ring. They were, if you like, the 'essence of whippet' and it must have been just that which led so many judges, by no means all of them breed specialists, to reward them so richly.

Ch. Robmaywin Stargazer of Allways (Plate 110)

It is important to study the breeding of these seven record holders because all seven, especially the four dogs, have had a lasting influence on the breed. Ch. Robmaywin Stargazer of Allways, bred by Mr Robbins, owned and campaigned by Mr F. Jones, was the result of that most classic of all matings, half-brother to half-sister. His sire, Ch. Evening Star of Allways, was by Ch. Wingedfoot Marksman of Allways out of Ch. Fieldspring Betony, litter sister to Ch. Fieldspring Bartsia of Allways and Int. Ch. Wingedfoot Fieldspring Bryony, thus carrying the dominant bitch line back through Brekin Willow Pattern to Ch. Brekin Spode and Ch. White Statue of Connevan. As we discuss other breed influences we will see how often this line, very often doubled or tripled, appears in important pedigrees. Stargazer's dam, Ch. Mistral's Mrs Miniver, also by Marksman, was out of Fleeting Frieze who was by Ch. Sapperley Kinsman, sire of Marksman. Thus Stargazer had two lines to Marksman plus a third line to his sire, Kinsman. His litter sister was also a Champion, Ch. Robmaywin Quicksilver of Allways.

Stargazer sired only two champions, Ch. Shalfleet Selbrook Daylight and Int. Ch. Playmate of Allways, who figures in a large number of pedigrees despite being exported to Australia quite early in his career. However, Stargazer's influence on the breed began to make itself felt in his grandchildren and subsequent generations. Shalfleet Skyliner, doubly line-bred to him, being by Stargazer out of Ch. Shalfleet Story, a daughter of Ch. Shalfleet Selbrook Daylight, sired three champions, Ch. Shalfleet Sailing Free, Ch. Selbrook Bracelet and Ch. Shalfleet Sultan of Sherrimere. Another son, Trevelmond Starsign, sired Ch. Ravensdowne Bright Star, sire of five champions, a sire whose daughters were spectacular winner producers. Int. Ch. Playmate of Allways sired Mrs Chapman's Ch. Telstar Moon and Ch. Playfair. Playmate also sired Apbrenin Piquet, who is behind many of the leading coursing winners, Black Brocade of Allways, a black who contributed a great deal to many of the best blacks and blues, and Nagrom Feola, the dam of Ch. Oakbark Dondelayo Storming. Stargazer's chief wins included the Hound Group at Crufts (the first whippet to achieve this honour) and BIS at Three Counties Championship Show and BIS at the Northern Counties Championship Show in a then record entry under visiting judge Anton Rost.

Ch. ROBMAYWIN STARGAZER OF ALLWAYS	Ch. Evening Star of Allways	Ch. Wingedfoot Marksman of Allways	Ch. Sapperley Kinsman
			Bolney Starshine of Allways
		Ch. Fieldspring Betony	Fleeting Hillgarth Sovereign
			Brekin Willow Pattern
	Ch. Mistral's Mrs Miniver	Ch. Wingedfoot Marksman of Allways	Ch. Sapperley Kinsman
			Bolney Starshine of Allways
		Fleeting Frieze	Ch. Sapperley Kinsman
			Fleeting Filigree
Ch. HARQUE THE LARK	Harque to Beaumont	Ch. Runway Controller	Ch. Allways Wingedfoot Running Fox
			Evening Mist
		Ch. Wingedfoot Tu Whit Tu Whoo	Ch. Wingedfoot Marksman of Allways
			Eh for Adorable
	Rosaday of Knotkum	Ch. Allways Wingedfoot Running Fox	Ch. Wingedfoot Marksman of Allways
			Perpetual Motion
		Brimhurst Thimble	Cornish Rhapsody
			Fleeting Flicker

116. *Ch. and Aust. Ch. Playmate of Allways. (Fall)*

117. *Ch. Playfair.*

118. *Ch. Telstar Moon. (Cooke)*

119. *Ch. Harque to Pegasus.*

120. *Ch. Harque Yonder. (Cooke)*

Ch. Harque the Lark (Plate 111)

Ch. Harque the Lark shares Stargazer's main bloodlines. The Lark was bred, owned and campaigned by Mrs Anne Argyle who has, over the years, consistently produced a line of high quality, correct sized whippets, including numerous champions. The Lark was by Harque to Beaumont out of Rosaday of Knotkum, a mating which produced two other champions in different litters, Ch. Harque to Gamecock and Ch. Harque to Rosa. Harque to Beaumont was by Ch. Runway Controller (Ch. Allways Wingedfoot Running Fox by Marksman), out of Ch. Wingedfoot Tu Whit Tu Whoo (by Marksman), while Rosaday of Knotkum was also by Ch. Allways Wingedfoot Running Fox so that the Lark, like Stargazer, was strongly line-bred to Ch. Wingedfoot Marksman of Allways. Her record is staggering. She was BIS at Chester, the Hound Show and Birmingham National, and Reserve BIS at the L.K.A. (Ladies Kennel Association) and at Bath Championship Shows. She also found time to produce a Champion daughter in Harque Yonder, by Ch. Dondelayo Buckaroo, litter brother to the record holding Roulette, an interesting combination of bloodlines.

Ch. Samarkand's Greenbrae Tarragon (Plate 108)

Ch. Samarkand's Greenbrae Tarragon was bred by Alicia Yerburgh, owned and campaigned by Mr R. M. James. He was by Ch. Laguna Limelight (Ch. Fieldspring Bartsia of Allways-Ch. Brekin Ballet Shoes) out of Ch. Greenbrae Laguna Lucia (Ch. Runway Controller-Ch. Laguna Leading Lady). Leading Lady was a full sister to Ch. Laguna Ligonier, and her dam, Ch. Lily of Laguna, was litter sister to Ch. Laguna Limelight, so Tarragon was entirely Laguna-bred, with double lines to the Bartsia/Ballet Shoes combination. An added strength was that Bartsia and Ballet Shoes were already closely bred, since Bartsia was out of Willow Pattern out of Ch. Brekin Spode, whilst Ballet Shoes was out of Ch. Spode herself. Ch. White Statue of Connevan, the dam of Ch. Spode, was thought by many to be one of the greatest and most influential brood bitches in the history of the breed, and a comprehensive examination of today's pedigrees will reveal that particular bitch line behind a number of top winners and successful kennels. It is no wonder that the Bartsia daughters, carrying that bitch line, have had such an influence on the breed. Tarragon sired five Champions but his great strength and influence came in the next and subsequent generations, and from the fact that in-breeding and line-breeding to him had such spectacular results. From the mating of his son, Ch. Cockrow Tarquogan of Glenbervie to his daughter, Ch. Dondelayo Rue, came the outstanding litter which included the record holding bitch Ch. Dondelayo Roulette and her brother Ch. Dondelayo Buckaroo, one of the leading sires, plus another champion bitch, Ch. Dondelayo Ruanne of Charmoll, dam of three further champions.

Perhaps because he was not backed by a large kennel, or because he lived off the beaten track, Tarragon was not used at stud as widely as he might have been. He

Ch. SAMARKAND'S GREENBRAE TARRAGON	Ch. Laguna Limelight	Ch. Fieldspring Bartsia of Allways	Fleeting Hillgarth Sovereign
			Brekin Willow Pattern
		Ch. Brekin Ballet Shoes	Ch. Balaise Barry
			Ch. Brekin Spode
	Ch. Greenbrae Laguna Lucia	Ch Runway Controller	Ch. Allways Wingedfoot Running Fox
			Evening Mist
		Ch. Laguna Leading Lady	Ch. Bellavista Barry
			Ch. Lily of Laguna
Ch. DONDELAYO ROULETTE	Ch. Cockrow Tarquogan of Glenbervie	Ch. Samarkand's Greenbrae Tarragon	Ch. Laguna Limelight
			Ch. Greenbrae Laguna Lucia
		Cockrow Lady Kate	Trevelmond Imp of Allways
			Laguna Little Lady
	Ch. Dondelayo Rue	Ch. Samarkand's Greenbrae Tarragon	Ch. Laguna Limelight
			Ch. Greenbrae Laguna Lucia
		Linknumstar Lizard	Ch. Laguna Linkway
			Laguna L'Etoile

had also to contend with competition from his son, Tarquogan, and his near relative, Ligonier, both with large and successful kennels behind them. It was only relatively late in his career when Mrs Knight, with great flair and instinct as a breeder, used Tarragon on whom to base a whole breeding programme with such dramatic results that other breeders began to realise his potential. The combination of Tarragon and Ligonier was subsequently to prove the single most powerful influence on the breed for years to come and other breeders were able to double back and use variations of this combination with outstanding success. Ch. Akeferry Jimmy (the second highest rating sire of the period after Ligonier) was a perfect illustration of a Tarragon-Ligonier pedigree. Tarragon's champion grandchildren and great grandchildren are almost too numerous to count. For the purposes of breed records it would be simpler to list those champions who do not carry either Tarragon or Ligonier (or both) in their pedigrees. Tarragon himself, as Mr James has testified, was one of those dogs who threw himself heart and soul into the show ring. Besides gaining his record 17 CCs he was twice runner-up in the Hound Group at Crufts and BIS at Chester (where his granddaughter, Ch. Dondelayo Roulette, and daughter, Courthill Country Life, were later BIS and Reserve BIS respectively). He was also BIS at the Whippet Club Championship Show. His ability to pass on his qualities of showmanship is underlined by the fact that more of his direct progeny have won Groups and BIS awards than any others.

Ch. Dondelayo Roulette (Plate 109)

We then come to Ch. Dondelayo Roulette, bred, owned and campaigned by Mrs Anne Knight. Roulette, like Stargazer, was the result of a half-brother/half-sister mating, being by Ch. Cockrow Tarquogan of Glenbervie (Ch. Samarkand's Greenbrae Tarragon-Cockrow Lady Kate) out of Ch. Dondelayo Rue (Ch. Samarkand's Greenbrae Tarragon-Linknumstar Lizard, by Ch. Laguna Linkway-Laguna L'Etoile, a sister of Ligonier). Thus Roulette was that combination of Tarragon/Ligonier bloodlines which was to prove itself so potent, both in this country and overseas. The half-brother/half-sister mating is one of the most successful ways in which a breeder can fix type and quality in a line provided that the original stock had no dominant faults to pass on. Mrs Knight's flair as a breeder, in deciding to inbreed to Tarragon, was later to prove more than justified as winner after winner emerged from the Dondelayo kennel, to take not only their titles but awards at Group and BIS level. The mating which produced Roulette also produced her brother, Ch. Dondelayo Buckaroo, one of the leading sires, and another champion bitch, Ch. Dondelayo Ruanne of Charmoll who, in her turn, produced three champions, Ch. Charmoll Clansman, Ch. Charmoll MacTavish and Ch. Charmoll Bonnie Prince. When Roulette was mated back to her double-grandsire, Tarragon, she produced Ch. Dondelayo Duette, Ch. Courthill Dondelayo Tiara and S.A. Ch. Dondelayo Minette of Oldwell. Ch. Duette won the highest award ever won by a whippet at Crufts, that of Reserve BIS. She also won the Hound Group and BIS at Peterborough. Roulette herself, besides winning her 20 CCs, all under different judges, won BIS at Bournemouth and at Chester, Reserve BIS at Chester and the Hound Group at Windsor. Mrs Knight has bred or owned a total 47 Champions of whom 15 have their English titles and 32 have titles abroad; but it is, perhaps, the achievements of Roulette and Duette (Roulette as a record holder and Duette for her Reserve BIS win at Crufts) which must earn the Dondelayos a very special place in whippet history.

Ch. Selinko Another Lady (Plate 167)

This beautiful fawn bitch represents everybody's dream. Bred by her owners, Carol and Barry Kennett, she came from their first litter and was virtually their first show whippet. Her pedigree is one of those happy accidents which can, just occasionally, prove all the experts wrong. Her sire, Ch. Marlins Duskie Miller of Iniskelltr, while carrying some solid, old fashioned lines including both Shalfleet, Allways and Laguna – through Deepridge Mintmaster – was by no means closely bred although his sire, Iniskelltr Escort, represented a long line of Miss Ussher's very typical breeding. Another Lady's dam, Silver Bambi of Selinko, carried both colour lines and racing lines, unrelated to each other although amongst them is another line to Mintmaster. However, it is interesting that in her pedigrees are the four factors shared by her two contemporary male record holders, Royal Mint and Wanderer: all three carry lines to Ch. Shalfleet Starstruck, Ch. Deepridge Mintmaster, Ch. Iniskelltr Lovely Silver and Ch. Nimrodel Ruff or Rosefinch. As we shall see later on, the combination of these lines, particularly Ch. Iniskelltr Lovely Silver and Ch. Nimrodel Ruff, produced numerous champions throughout the eighties.

Anyone who saw Another Lady handled by Barry Kennett in the ring would have to agree that a very high degree of affinity existed between them. Another Lady was a classic bitch built on smooth flowing lines and her effortless movement and statuesque stance made her hard to overlook in any company. She won 25 CCs in all, 24 under different judges, representing almost every championship judge in the breed, plus the Hound Group at Birmingham, Reserve in the Hound Group at Crufts and BOB at Crufts 1985, 1986 and 1987. She was top winner in the breed for 1984, 1985 and 1986.

Ch. Welstar Royal Mint (Plate 163)

Royal Mint was bred by Linda Jones and was owned and campaigned by Gwen Hempstock whose prefix, Brough – later changed to Broughland, had already produced, with very selective breeding, some high class stock. Mint was sired by Ch. Nimrodel Wiveton out of Ch. Welstar Minted Model. Both parents were Hound Group winners and Wiveton was Reserve BIS all breeds at Bournemouth Championship Show. Although the mating between Wiveton and Minted Model

Ch. SELINKO ANOTHER LADY	Ch. Marlins Duskie Miller of Iniskelltr	Iniskelltr Escort	Iniskelltr Crispin
			Iniskelltr Bewitched
		Marlins Turkey Brown	Ch. Shalfleet Sailing Free
			Marlins Tippet and Black
	Silver Bambi of Selinko	Pioneer of Sheerhatch	Chancerick Koh-i-nor
			Wirrawon Fancy Free
		Charnwood Twinkletoes	Ch. Deepridge Mintmaster
			Charnwood Nanny Nippy Toes

Ch. WELSTAR ROYAL MINT	Ch. Nimrodel Wiveton	Bartonia of Brough	Ch. Iniskelltr Lovely Silver
			Mistrey of Test
		Nimrodel Wissendine	Ch. Nimrodel Ruff
			Nimrodel Withywindle
	Ch. Welstar Minted Model	Ch. Shalfleet Silver Knight of Skyboat	Shalfleet Schelle
			Shalfleet Silver Mint
		Rasaday Amber	Ch. Deepridge Mintmaster
			Rasaday Oakbark Mirreille

was a relative out-cross, both carried lines back to the old classic Allways winners of the 1960s and both produced other champions, Wiveton being the sire of Ch. Mithrandir Gambit of Dhahran and Ch. Gainscliffe Chase the Ace whilst Minted Model produced Ch. Welstar Winning Dream from a subsequent mating to Ch. Nimrodel Ruff, Wiveton's sire. Royal Mint was Gwen Hempstock's first champion in the breed but she and her husband, Frank, had bred and owned Wiveton's sire, Bartonia of Brough (Ch. Iniskelltr Lovely Silver-Mistrey of Test), a beautiful dog who was little shown but who put up some very fast times on the track. Sadly, Bartonia died relatively young but in siring Wiveton and Ch. Wipstych Courbette through both of whom numerous champions descend he has turned out to be of great breed importance. Royal Mint was an immensely impressive dog. Although on the large side his classic conformation and outstanding quality combined with great ring-presence and a close affinity with Gwen Hempstock made him a very difficult dog to overlook in any company. Of his 19 CCs no less than 8 were won when he was eight years old, including the CC at Crufts (his second) and 3 BIS awards at Club Championship Shows. He proved to be an important sire, especially of bitches, producing two champions for his owner, Ch. Brough Lady Devine and Ch. Broughland Gina of Baldrey, from whom all the winning stock in that kennel descend, and Ch. Nimrodel Rare Magic out of Ch. Wipstych Grandiflora. His unshown daughters proved equally important, Nimrodel Wanton being the dam of Ch. Nimrodel Wanderer, Welstar Amber Royale the dam of Ch. Woolsocks Summer Blaze and Crufts BOB Woolsocks Morning Glory and Rasaday Royal Charm, the dam of some good winners for Jill Chapman, including the lovely CC winner Rasaday Namesake. Like his grandsire Bartonia, Royal Mint died tragically young and at a point where he undoubtedly still had a great deal to offer the breed, but the legacy he left behind is considerable and his record of 19 CCs has as yet only been beaten by his grandson, Ch. Nimrodel Wanderer.

Ch. Nimrodel Wanderer (Plate 170)

Wanderer, like Dondelayo Roulette, is a grandchild of a previous record holder, Royal Mint. He was bred by the Author and owned and campaigned by Mrs June Minns who also owned his sire, Nimrodel Dragoon, the winner of 3 RCCs. Unlike Another Lady and Royal Mint, Wanderer is tightly line-bred to Ch. Poltesco Peewit and Bartonia of Brough, the combination which is behind numerous champions made up in the 1970s and 1980s. Wanderer's dam, Nimrodel Wanton, was by Ch. Royal Mint out of his aunt, Nimrodel Wissie, litter sister to Ch. Nimrodel Wiveton. His sire, Nimrodel Dragoon, was by Ch. Nimrodel Ruff out of a daughter of Ch. Danegeld Piper's Tune and Ch. Dragonhill Tawny Owl, both being grandchildren of Ch. Ladiesfield Topaz. Piper's Tune was a very beautiful dog who was little used at stud but who carried a very strong bitch line, his dam being by Ch. Robmaywin Stargazer of Allways out of Ch. Porthurst Atlanta by Ch. Mars of Test – also the sire of Bartonia's dam, Mistrey of Test. Wanderer thus represents many generations of line-breeding along lines well proven to be highly successful winner producers.

Like his grandsire, Wanderer has an air of arrogance and superiority which rewards him well in the ring. Amongst his 20 CCs he is the winner of a Hound Group and two Reserves in Group and he is also a CC winner at Crufts. He has already sired a top winning bitch in Ch. Baldrey Limited Edition of Juneric (winner of 13 CCs), a Green Star winner and a CC winner, Nimrodel Eagle Wings, amongst other quality stock. Since, like Nutshell, he is still a young dog it can be hoped that his record both in the ring and at stud may be added to.

Ch. Nutshell of Nevedith (Plate 168)

Whilst Nutshell is, at the time of writing, strictly speaking not a record holder in the sense of the dogs and bitches we have just looked at, she has set up a record of her own and earned the right to a place in whippet history. Ch. Nutshell of Nevedith is by Ch. Nevedith Uptown Guy, a dog who was exported to Mrs Newcombe whose Pennyworth kennel is famous in the USA, shortly after gaining his title in the UK. Her dam, Chilka Dairy Maid was by Ch. Oakbark Middleman and she was bred by Mr and Mrs Barker (Chilka), owned by Mrs Editha Newton Reid and campaigned by Nev Newton. Nutshell has swept the board in the show ring during 1989. She has won to date 19 CCs, and in the course of so doing she has also won more Groups, Reserves in Group and BIS at all-breed championship shows than any other whippet in the history of the breed. She is currently Top Dog (all-breeds) in the Pedigree Chum Top Dogs League, an achievement hitherto unknown in breed history. Whilst we who breed and show whippets consider them to be the epitomy of canine beauty it has always been a generally accepted fact that it is difficult for a whippet to look impressive in a Group against many other larger or more coated breeds. Nutshell, however, with her very glamorous brindle and white markings, her graceful outline and superb free movement, seems to be able to dominate the big ring to an extraordinary degree.

Unlike the previous three record holders we have considered, Nutshell is heavily line-bred to the classic Tarragon/Ligonier combination that, as we have seen, has been so successful in the past. On her sire's side she descends from Ch. Akeferry Jimmy, the foundation sire of the Nevedith Kennel, and on her dam's side from Ch. Baydale Cinnamon, whose dam, Cockrow Merle, was a half-sister of Cockrow Partridge of Chawshaw, sire of Ch. Akeferry Jimmy. It is clear that with the necessary introduction of new blood these lines are still producing the results, which, after all, is what clever line-breeding is all about. For good measure Nutshell also carries, through Ch. Hillsdown Tobique, the great Glenbervie bitch-line; what a brood bitch she in her turn should prove to be. In the course of winning her 19 CCs (18 with BOB) she has also won 6 Reserve in Group, 2 BIS and 2 Reserve BIS at all-breed championship shows, and 2 BIS at Breed Club Championship Shows. This is an incredible achievement, for her, for her breeders Mr and Mrs

Ch. NIMRODEL WANDERER	Nimrodel Dragoon	Ch. Nimrodel Ruff	Ch. Poltesco Peewit
			Nimrodel Wintersweet
		Nimrodel Dipper	Ch. Danegeld Pipers Tune
			Ch. Dragonhill Tawny Owl
	Nimrodel Wanton	Ch. Welstar Royal Mint	Ch. Nimrodel Wiveton
			Ch. Welstar Minted Model
		Nimrodel Wissie	Bartonia of Brough
			Nimrodel Wissendine

Ch. NUTSHELL OF NEVEDITH	Ch. Nevedith Uptown Guy	Ch. Nevedith Paper-weight	Nevedith Merry Monarch
			Whitbarrow Mini Mist
		Sakonnet Alfalfa	Ch. Akeferry Jimmy
			Sakonnet Black Mustard
	Chilka Dairy Maid	Ch. Oakbark Middleman	Ch. Charmoll McTavish
			Oakbark Moving Picture
		Pearl of Aconite at Chilka	Ch. Black Knight of Carmodian
			Ch. Hillsdown Tobique

Barker, and for her handler Nev Newton. By the time this new edition of *The English Whippet* goes to press, Nutshell's record will in all probability be out of date.

We hope that Appendixes 1 and 2 will enable the reader to see at a glance the pattern of awards in terms of numbers of Champions bred and made up and to see from the list of sires and their progeny where the greatest influence has lain. However, there is another factor which should be taken into account when considering breed records. As George Orwell might have said, 'Not all wins are equal and some are more equal than others.' Some exhibitors are able to travel further and more regularly than others and are, perhaps, more skilled in presenting their dogs in the right place and in the right condition than are others. It is equally true that there are judges who, by consistently putting up their own stock or stock sired by their dogs, are able to turn the record to their own advantage. Needless to say, a dog does not become a multiple winner in any other way than through sheer excellence but a dog or bitch can be lucky in gaining the three qualifying CCs which make a champion, thereby adding possibly undeserved prestige to the breeder and to the sire. There are, on the other hand, a number of breeders who have not campaigned in any sense of the word yet whose stock has been enormously influential in the breed. The prefixes of Cockrow, Flarepath, Newbold and Ravensdowne spring readily to mind. Equally there are sires who have never gained their titles, indeed who may never have won a CC yet whose progeny are up to or exceed the quality of other more famous or well known winners. Examples of these would be Shalfleet Skyliner, Oakbark Pyramid, Black Brocade of Allways, Selbrook Brandy of Shalfleet, Cockrow Partridge of Crawshaw and, more recently, Oakbark Mister Blue and Ballagan Whipcord. So, whilst the records can be considered an indication of breed excellence, it must not be forgotten that they present only a part of the picture. When a dog is at public stud it makes an enormous difference where he lives as to the number, and possibly the quality, of the bitches that come to him. A stud dog cannot produce winners all by himself; I suspect that many a good dog with a good pedigree has never had a chance to show what he could do given the right type of bitch. In this respect a dog backed by a large kennel is at a distinct advantage since the owner has opportunities to use him on home stock and the resulting progeny, if impressive, will persuade others to try the same experiment.

Ch. Laguna Ligonier (Plate 122)

The greatest sire in the breed to date has been Ch. Laguna Ligonier, bred, owned and campaigned to his title by Mrs D. U. McKay, with whom he lived throughout his life. Ligonier sired eleven English champions and numerous foreign ones who went on, in their turn, to be record breaking sires in their countries of adoption. By Ch. Bellavista Barry (Ch. Pilot Officer Prune-Brekin Bright Spark), out of the very

121. *Ch. Lily of Laguna. (Cooke)*

122. *Ch. Laguna Ligonier.*

123. *Ch. Russettwood Portia. (Cooke)*

lovely Ch. Lily of Laguna (Ch. Fieldspring Bartsia of Allways-Ch. Brekin Ballet Shoes), Ligonier has proved himself over and over again to have been the most consistent sire of top quality stock in the history of the breed. He was not a particularly spectacular winner himself, and indeed, while absolutely correct in all essentials, was not the most eye-catching dog. Definitely small by today's standard, he was a blue-brindle particolour and, as a glance at a list of his champion progeny will show, he sired champions out of bitches of varied breeding. His sire, Ch. Bellavista Barry, sired eight champions and his grandsire, Ch. Pilot Officer Prune, sired ten, the then joint record shared with Ch. Wingedfoot Marksman of Allways. Ch. Bellavista Barry and Ch. Lily of Laguna were out of sisters, Brekin Bright Spark and Ch. Brekin Ballet Shoes, both out of Ch. Brekin Spode. Lily's sire, Ch. Bartsia, was out of Brekin Willow Pattern, again, a half-sister out of Ch. Spode. Therefore Ligonier carried three lines to Ch. White Statue of Connevan, the line which, as we have already seen when studying Tarragon's pedigree, has been of such paramount importance in the breed. Considering this pedigree it is not really so surprising that not only did Ligonier sire more champions in this country than any whippet before or since, but his sons abroad proved themselves to be a formidable force. In the U.S.A., Ch. Greenbrae Barn Dance held the record for number of champion progeny for a considerable time, as did Ch. Laguna Leader in Scandinavia. In this country Ligonier's most successful sons were Ch. Deepridge Mintmaster and Ch. Towercrest Flarepath Taurus. Ch. Tantivvey Diver was, most unfortunately, exported to the U.S.A. before he had time to fulfil himself; nevertheless he left behind two champions, Ch. Fleeting Flamboyant (who later went to Sweden where he was very successful in the ownership of Bo Bengtson) and Ch. Cockrow Pheasant whose virtually unshown litter brother, Cockrow Partridge of Crawshaw, went on to sire four champions. Out of the litter sisters, Laguna Ravensdowne Faerie Queen and Flarepath Ravensdowne Vega, Ligonier sired three champions, Int. Ch. Laguna Leisure and Ch. Laguna Lunanute out of Faerie Queen and Ch. Towercrest Flarepath Taurus out of Vega. One of Ligonier's early champions was Ch. Peppard Premium Bond (out of Peppard Tit Bits). Premium Bond went on to produce the famous litter by Ch. Ballagan Prince Charlie of Briarcliffe which contained Ch. Peppard Highland Fling and Ch. Peppard Faithful Flora, and a third bitch, Peppard Preston Pans who won 2 CCs and was unlucky not to gain her title. Mated to Ch. Deepridge Mintmaster she, in turn, produced Ch. Peppard Royal Victory.

Ch. Akeferry Jimmy (Plate 140)

Second to Ligonier in the number of champion progeny is Ch. Akeferry Jimmy, who was bred, together with his brother, Miss Clay's Ch. Tantivvey Akeferry Crusader, by Mr Pendleton, owned by Mrs Editha Newton-Reid and campaigned by her father Mr Nev Newton. A rich brindle-particolour, Jimmy was a consistent winner, always showing with freedom and personality in great harmony with his

Ch. LAGUNA LIGONIER	Ch. Bellavista Barry	Ch. Pilot Officer Prune	Happy Landings
			Silver Nymph
		Brekin Bright Spark	Ch. Balaise Barry
			Ch. Brekin Spode
	Ch. Lily of Laguna	Ch. Fieldspring Bartsia of Allways	Fleeting Hillgarth Sovereign
			Brekin Willow Pattern
		Ch. Brekin Ballet Shoes	Ch. Balaise Barry
			Ch. Brekin Spode
Ch. AKEFERRY JIMMY	Cockrow Partridge of Crawshaw	Ch. and USA Ch. Tantivvey Diver	Ch. Laguna Ligonier
			Fleeting Fancy Free
		Cockrow Tarradiddle	Ch. Samarkand's Greenbrae Tarragon
			Cockrow Lady Kate
	Eegee Jane	Ch. Samarkand's Greenbrae Tarragon	Ch. Laguna Limelight
			Ch. Greenbrae Laguna Lucia
		Eegee Anita	Ch. Laguna Ligonier
			Harque to Dreamgirl

124. *Ch. Laguna Leading Lady*

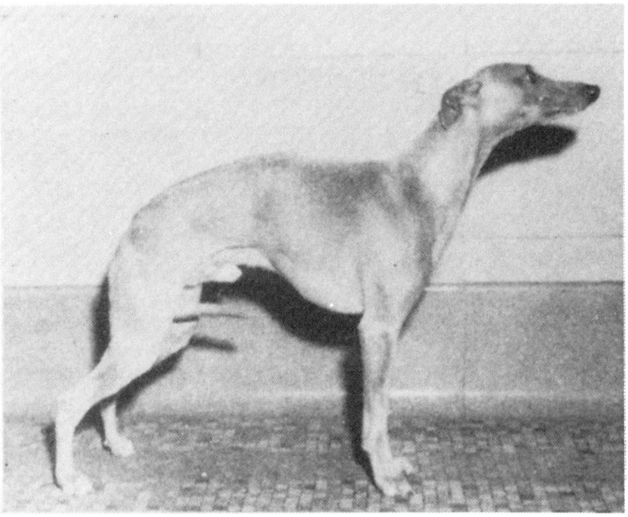

125. *Ch. Laguna Linkway.*

126. *Ch. Laguna Porthurst Moonlight Sonata. (Cooke)*

127. *Ch. Deepridge Mintmaster.*

128. *Ch. Deepridge Minstrel. (Cooke)*

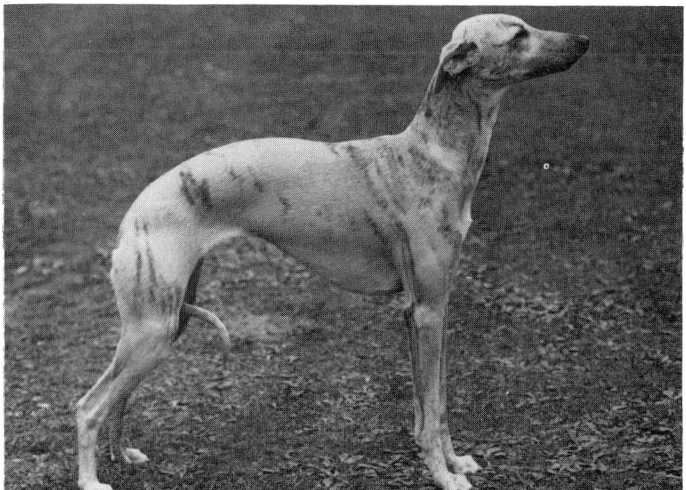

129. *Ch. Deepridge Minniva. (Cooke)*

130. *Ch. Peppard Premium Bond. (Fall)* 131. *Ch. Peppard Winter Queen. (Cooke)*

132. *Peppard Preston Pans.*

133. *Chs Peppard Highland Fling and Peppard Faithful Flora.*

handler but, more than that, he proved to be an outstanding sire and a look at his pedigree will show why this is so. By Cockrow Partridge of Crawshaw, litter brother to Ch. Cockrow Pheasant (Ch. Tantivvey Diver-Cockrow Tarradiddle) out of Eegee Jane (Ch. Samarkand's Greenbrae Tarragon-Eegee Anita by Ligonier), Jimmy's pedigree was strongly line-bred to that combination of Tarragon and Ligonier which had already proved so dominant a force. Jimmy sired ten English champions and his breeding has proved successful abroad, particularly in Scandinavia. Several of his champion sons are currently at stud in this country and could emerge as useful sires in their own right. His daughters have already proved their ability to breed on: Ch. Ruegeto Nina of Nevedith is the dam of Ch. Nevedith Hill Breeze, and Ch. Crysbel Skylight of Nevedith is the dam of Ch. Houghtonhill Night Starry Sky of Chatwig. Jimmy also sired, amongst his other champion progeny, the brother and sister, Chs. Sakonnet Devil's Cub and Sakonnet Sprig Muslin.

Ch. Cockrow Tarquogan of Glenbervie and Ch. Dondelayo Buckaroo

Ch. Cockrow Tarquogan of Glenbervie and his son, Ch. Dondelayo Buckaroo, sired nine and ten champions respectively. Both had the advantage of large home kennels behind them and both showed themselves capable of producing multiple champions in single litters or repeat matings. Ch. Cockrow Tarquogan of Glenbervie was bred by Miss Anne and Miss Elizabeth Hudson who, despite breeding very sparingly and campaigning hardly at all, have had a great influence on the whippet scene. Not only did Tarquogan prove himself a superlative producer for his owner, Mr A. B. Nicholson, but Cockrow Tarradiddle, his litter sister, was the dam of Ch. Cockrow Pheasant and of Miss Wright's Cockrow Partridge of Crawshaw, who sired Ch. Akeferry Jimmy, Ch. Tantivvey Akeferry Crusader, Ch. Pimlico of Crawshaw, and Ch. Belinda of Hardknott. Cockrow Merle, a half-sister by Tantivvey Diver, was bought by Mrs Fenwick and her mother Mrs Blair, and when mated to Ch. Samarkand's Sun Courtier produced Ch. Baydale Cinnamon. Tarquogan's nine champions were out of only three different bitches. Chs. Sky Gypsy of Glenbervie, Gypsy Moth of Glenbervie and Gunsmith of Glenbervie were out of the lovely fawn bitch, Ch. Hillgarth Sunstar of Glenbervie, bred by Mrs Sheffield. Chs. Denorsi Moon Dust of Glenbervie, Denorsi Moonduster of Glenbervie and Another Rose of Glenbervie were out of White Gorse of Glenbervie and the famous litter containing Chs. Buckaroo, Roulette and Ruanne were all out of Ch. Dondelayo Rue. Apart from Mrs Knight, Tarquogan seems to have been little used outside his home kennel, but his stock were of a consistent type and quality and Mr Nicholson was always generous in parting with good stock so that there are a number of breeders who have been fortunate enough to found a successful line on a Glenbervie bitch.

Tarquogan's son, Ch. Dondelayo Buckaroo, sired ten English champions and large numbers overseas. He produced no less than four champions for Mr Nichol-

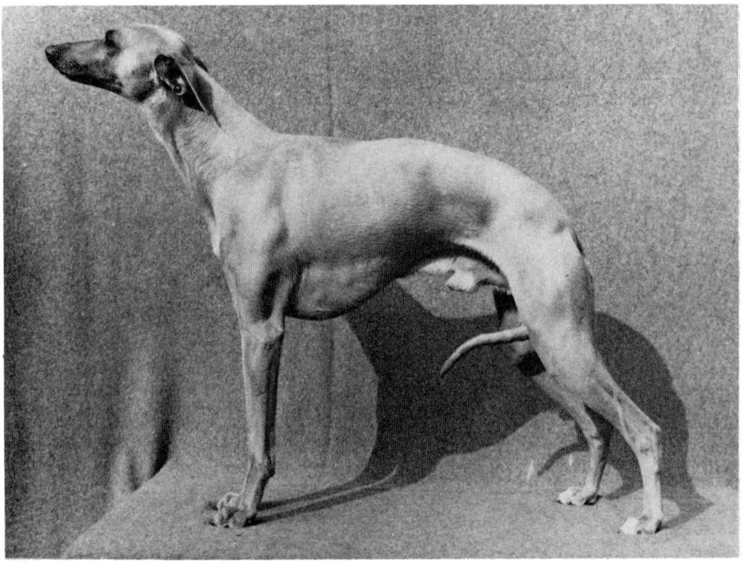

134. *Ch. Ballagan Prince Charlie of Briarcliffe.*

135. *Ch. Ballagan Annie Laurie. (Fall)*

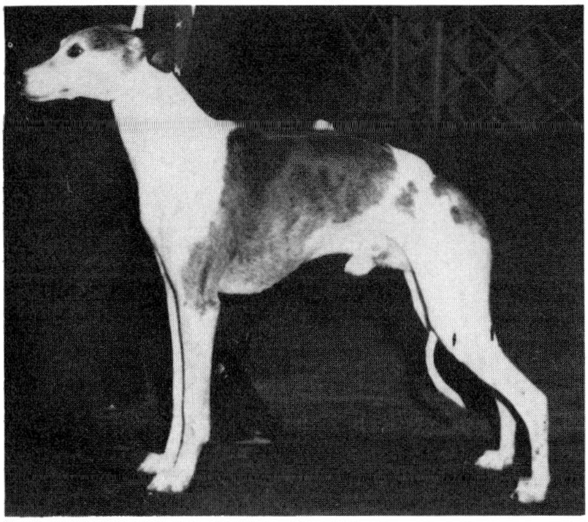

136. *Ch. Tantivvey Diver in old age. (Booth)*

137. *Ch. Fleeting Flamboyant.*

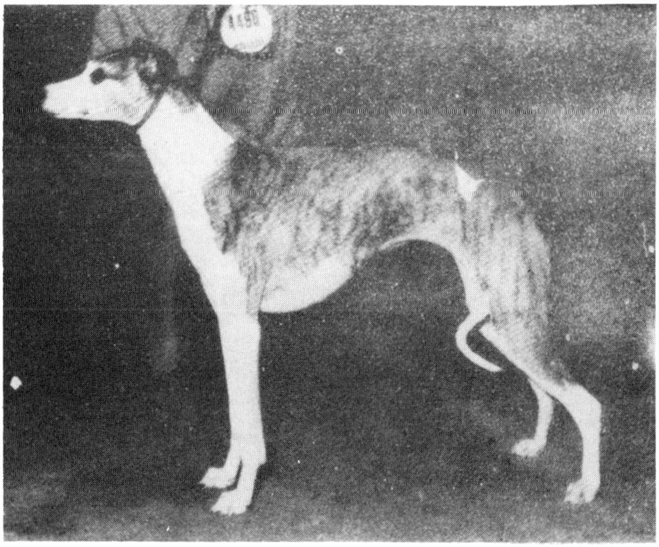

138. *Ch. Cockrow Pheasant.*

son out of Whitebridge of Glenbervie, namely Chs. Gypsy Picture, Pathway, Solid Silver and White Frost, all of Glenbervie. Ch. Denorsi Quickmatch of Glenbervie was also bred by Mr Nicholson out of Tarara of Glenbervie. Mr Morrison bred the beautiful parti-coloured bitch, Ch. Laura Love by Buckaroo out of Dondelayo Lauretta. The only champion which Mrs Knight campaigned herself by Buckaroo was the brindle bitch, Int. Ch. Dondelayo Reinette, out of Ir. Ch. Dondelayo Marianette of Seltaeb. Reinette had a spectacular career in this country winning BIS at Three Counties and at the Welsh Kennel Club Championship Show. She was then exported to Australia where she quickly gained her Australian title and further honours at Group and BIS level.

Ch. Lowglen Newbold Cavalier (Plate 81)

Another potent sire who produced nine champion offspring was Ch. Lowglen Newbold Cavalier. Cavalier, a glamorous parti-colour, bred by those discerning breeders, Des and Margery Howarth, was purchased by Mr Fred Nicholas and handled by his wife Patsy (one of the most accomplished and sympathetic handlers in the breed, who has led a large number of champions to their titles). Cavalier was by Skydiver of Lowglen (Ch. Towercrest Flarepath Taurus-Crystal of Hardknott by Ch. Laguna Light Lagoon) out of Flarepath Caprice (the result of a father/daugher mating between Ch. Ravensdowne Bright Star and his daughter, Ch. Laguna Ravensdowne Astri) thus carrying three lines to Bright Star, added to which Astri's grandam was Little Lucy Locket of Laguna, a sister of Ligonier, giving Cavalier the Ch. Ballet Shoes/Ch. Spode/Ch. White Statue bitch lines on both sides of his pedigree. Not surprisingly, Cavalier sired amongst his champion progeny some outstandingly beautiful bitches who have, in their turn, proved able to breed on. Mrs Barbara Robinson bred the two champion sisters, Chs. Savillepark Sweet Harmony (now also an Italian Champion) and Savillepark Summer Season, who in the joint ownership of Patsy Nicholas and Freda Broadbent won BIS at the L.K.A. Cavalier was also the sire of the almost perfectly matched brother and sister pair, Ch. Allgarth Envoy and Eidelweiss (out of Shalfleet Stylish). Envoy was another dog who was exported before he had a chance to prove himself at stud in this country, but Eidelweiss was the dam of Ch. Lowglen Singing Bede who in her turn was the dam of Ch. Lowglen Blue Mink at Dennydene. Another very lovely Cavalier daughter was Mr Morgan's Ch. Ynsfor Aphrodite (out of Lowglen Donna's Daydream) who was a very consistent winner for her owner-breeder.

Ch. Bellavista Barry

It is hard to overestimate the influence which Ch. Bellavista Barry has had on the breed. By Ch. Pilot Officer Prune out of Brekin Bright Spark, Barry sired Ligonier, Ch. Laguna Leading Lady the dam of Ch. Greenbrae Lucia the dam of Ch.

Samarkand's Greenbrae Tarragon and Ch. Courtenay Fleetfoot, a dog whose influence in America, both as a winner and as a sire, is legendary. He also sired Ch. Blik's Ringmore Bardolph and U.S.A. Ch. Ringmore Finisterre. Ch. Poltesco Peewit was out of Poltesco Clemwade Merry Maid, the result of grandfather/granddaughter mating to Ch. Bellavista Barry. While somewhat overshadowed by the records of his progeny, Ch. Bellavista Barry must hold an important place in the history of whippets.

Ch. Towercrest Flarepath Taurus and Ch. Deepridge Mintmaster (Plates: 83 & 127)

Ch. Towercrest Flarepath Taurus sired six champions and Ch. Deepridge Mintmaster sired five, with several other CC winners. These two parti-colour sons of Ligonier were the most successful of his offspring at stud in this country, and both were considerable winners in their own right.

Ch. Towercrest Flarepath Taurus was bred by Harry and Irene Wood who bred relatively sparingly but produced stock of such exceptionally high quality. In the hands of his owner, Mrs Elsie Watson, Taurus quickly gained his title and his wins included a CC under the world renowned judge, Fru Carin Lindhe, and BOB at Crufts under Mrs Judy de Casembrut. His effectiveness as a sire was quickly apparent. Amongst his champion progeny were the glamorous brother and sister, Ch. Oakbark Melord and Ch. Oakbark Movie Queen.

Ch. Deepridge Mintmaster, bred, owned and campaigned by Miss E. Hawthorn, whose Deepridge prefix has produced such consistent and quality stock over so many years, gained his title at only fifteen months, won a total of 12 CCs and 2 Hound Groups. Like Taurus, he produced a brother and sister champion pair in Ch. Deepridge Minniva and Ch. Deepridge Minstrel. Mintmaster's progeny has proved more than capable of breeding on in succeeding generations. His son, Ch. Oakbark Armfield Joker, sired Ch. Oakbark Mr Magic of Silstone who, in turn, sired Ch. Gainscliffe Renown and Ch. Palmik Starsign. Another son, Selbrook Brandy of Shalfleet (out of Ch. Shalfleet Bracelet), sired Ch. Shalfleet Sequilla, Ch. Shalfleet Story Writer, and, out of his half-sister Ch. Deepridge Minniva, Ch. Deepridge Mosaic. The two litter-sisters by Mintmaster, Rasaday Amber and Rasaday Alisa, produced respectively, Ch. Welstar Minted Model and Ch. Denhill's Delectabelle. Minted Model, in turn, produced Ch. Welstar Royal Mint and Delectabelle was the dam of Int. Ch. Dondelayo Statue who has done so much winning and winner-producing in Australia.

Ch. Ravensdowne Bright Star

Ch. Ravensdowne Bright Star, bred by Miss Fair, owned and campaigned by Mrs Irene Wood, was by Trevelmond Starsign (Ch. Robmaywin Stargazer of Allways) out of Samarkand's Sea Nymph. Mated to Little Loo of Laguna (Ch. Laguna

Liege-Little Lucy Locket of Laguna, a sister of Ligonier) he produced the three outstanding bitches, Ch. Laguna Ravensdowne Astri, Laguna Ravensdowne Faerie Queen and Flarepath Ravensdowne Vega, each of whom, in turn, produced champions. Astri, one of the most beautiful and top-winning bitches of her day, a Hound Group and BIS winner, was the dam of Ch. Flarepath Astrinomical (by her nephew, Ch. Towercrest Flarepath Taurus), Ch. Flarepath Astrinaught of Lowglen (by Aust. Ch. Lowglen Oakbark Mastermind) and his sister Flarepath Aquaria, who produced three champions for Mr and Mrs Meakin, Ch. Oakbark Melord, Ch. Oakbark Movie Queen and Ch. Oakbark Must Love. Another Astri daughter, Flarepath Caprice, was the dam of Ch. Lowglen Newbold Cavalier. Laguna Ravensdowne Faerie Queen, mated to Ligonier, was the dam of two Laguna champions, Int. Ch. Laguna Leisure, sire of Ch. Mancot Petruchio, and Ch. Laguna Lunanute. The third sister, Flarepath Ravensdowne Vega, was the dam of Ch. Towercrest Flarepath Taurus who, as we have seen, sired six champions, also of Flarepath Orion, the sire of Mr and Mrs Gwyn Hughes' Group winning Ch. Summerbourne Stargazer. Bright Star also sired Ch. Flarepath Tambillo Tarquin (bred by Mrs Evelyn Radcliffe out of Ballagan Shining Star, by Ligonier) who sired Aust. Ch. Lowglen Oakbark Masterminde and Ch. Oakbark Michaela, the dam of Ch. Newbold Muffinman, and Ch. Newbold Kerry Gold.

Ch. Baydale Cinnamon and Ch. Charmoll MacTavish (Plate 150)

Ch. Baydale Cinnamon and his son, Ch. Charmoll MacTavish, sired five champions apiece. Cinnamon, bred by Mesdames Blair and Fenwick and owned by Mrs Oddy, was another whose pedigree carried the classic Tarragon/Ligonier lines, being by Ch. Samarkand's Sun Courtier (by Tarragon) out of Cockrow Merle (by Diver by Ligonier). Mated to Ch. Dondelayo Ruanne of Charmoll, Cinnamon produced three champions for Mr and Mrs Dempster, Chs. Charmoll Clansman (who went to America where he became a top winner and sire), Charmoll MacTavish and Charmoll Bonnie Prince. Ch. Charmoll MacTavish, until his early death, was the leading sire in the breed having sired five champions and a number of other CC winners. Two of his sons now at stud promise, in their turn, to be winner-producers. Mrs Patsy Nicholas and Mrs Freda Broadbent's Ch. Novacroft Madrigal is not only one of the current top winners, having won 12 CCs and the Hound Group and Reserve BIS at Driffield, but is the sire of Mrs Sedgeley's Ch. Lowglen Blue Mink at Dennydene as well as a number of other promising winners. Ch. Oakbark Middleman, another MacTavish son, has already sired CC winning stock.

Ch. Poltesco Peewit (Plate 153) *and Ch. Nimrodel Ruff* (Plate 155)

Ch. Poltesco Peewit and his son, Ch. Nimrodel Ruff, were two of the very few leading sires who carried neither Tarragon nor Ligonier in their pedigrees.

139. *Cockrow Partridge of Crawshaw.*

140. *Ch. Akeferry Jimmy.*

141. *Ch. Harque to Equerry. (Diane Pearce)*

However, Peewit's dam, Poltesco Clemwade Merry Maid, was the result of a granddaughter/grandfather mating to Ch. Bellavista Barry, Ligonier's sire. Peewit, bred and owned by Miss Ironside, sired four champions and his full sister, Ch. Greenbrae Poltesco Dusky Maid, also gained her title. Like Tarragon, Peewit has proved a sire to whom it is possible to line-breed closely and his descendants include 32 English champions and a number of foreign ones. The current dog record holder, Ch. Nimrodel Wanderer, carries five lines to Peewit.

Peewit's son, Ch. Nimrodel Ruff, out of a Ch. Dragonhill Woodpecker daughter, Nimrodel Wintersweet (3 RCCs), won 10 CCs and 10 RCCs and was twice top winning dog in the breed and twice top sire, also winning BIS at two Club Championship Shows. Ruff was the sire of six English champions and his daughters also bred on, Ch. Wipstych Grandiflora being the dam of Ch. Nimrodel Rare Magic and Ch. Nimrodel Peerless, and Nimrodel Wissendine being the dam of Ch. Nimrodel Wiveton, a Hound Group and Reserve BIS winner. Ch. Welstar Winning Dream was also a Hound Group winner as was Ch. Tweseldown Whinchat, another Peewit granddaughter and grandmother in her turn of Ch. Tweseldown Summer Chord by Ch. Woolsocks Summer Blaze by Ruff. This line, relatively restricted in descending straight from the older Seagift, Dragonhill and Tweseldown breeding and not sharing the influential Laguna background, has nevertheless produced numerous good winners whilst retaining a very predictable breed type. All Poltesco, Nimrodel and Tweseldown stock are line-bred to Peewit and these lines have combined well with other – chiefly Allways based – prefixes, such as Brough, Welstar and Wipstych.

Oakbark Pyramid

Oakbark Pyramid, bred by Dennis Meakin, who has produced so many good ones, also sired four champions despite being relatively little shown and not carrying his title. By Ch. Samarkand's Sun Courtier out of Laguna Lynda (by Ligonier) he was the sire of Ch. Denhill's Delectabelle, the dam of Int. Ch. Dondelayo Statue, who won the Hound Group and Reserve BIS at W.E.L.K.S. before being exported to Australia where he has been extremely successful both as a sire and competitively. Pyramid was also the sire of the beautiful brother and sister pair, Chs. Newbold Muffinman and Newbold Kerry Gold. A Pyramid daughter, Newbold Startime, is the dam of Ch. Lowerdon Soldier Blue, the sire of Ch. Lowglen Singing Bede, the dam of Ch. Lowglen Blue Mik at Dennydene.

Cockrow Partridge of Crawshaw (Plate 139)

Like Pyramid, Cockrow Partridge of Crawshaw was virtually unshown, but this did not stop him from proving to be a very useful sire. Litter brother to Ch. Cockrow Pheasant, bred by the Miss Hudsons and owned by Miss Wright, Partridge sired four champions, his most famous and influential son being Ch. Akeferry Jimmy

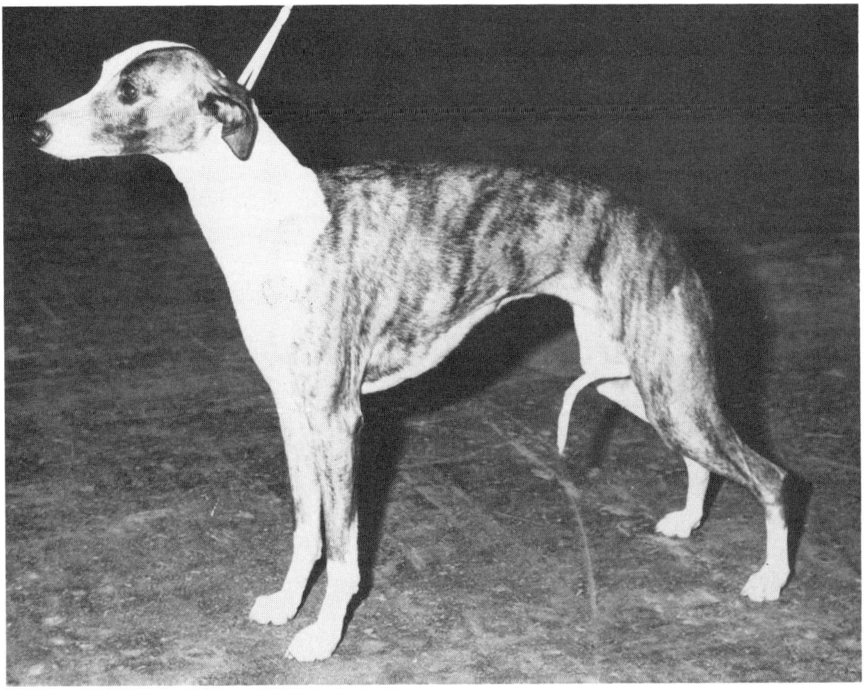

142. *Ch. Crysbel Skylark. (Lionel Young)*

143. *Ch. Crysbel Skylight of Nevedith.*

144. *Ch. Sakonnet Devil's Cub.*

145. *Ch. Sakonnet Sprig Muslin.*

146. *Ch. Gypsy Moth of Glenbervie. (Diane Pearce)*

whose record we have already examined. Partridge's latest champion offspring is the beautifully marked orange brindle and white bitch, Ch. Belinda of Hardknott. Belinda has already produced a winning litter by Ch. Novacroft Madrigal including a young dog, Hardknott Maestro of Bohem, imported into America by Bo Bengtson, where he is already a champion and where his valuable bloodlines have proved extremely useful.

Ch. Samoems Silent Knight of Shalfleet (Plate 165)

Silent Knight was bred by Mr Tim Teillirs, of the Netherlands – whose Samoems prefix is world famous for both whippets and salukis – and imported into England by Mrs Barbara Wilton Clark whose Shalfleet prefix is held in similar esteem. Silent Knight was by Dutch Ch. Samoems Scorpion out of a Shalfleet bitch. His brother, Int. Ch. Samoems Sir Lancelot, sired the litter brother and sister Chs. Samoems Starboy and Sweet Valentine, both top winners on the Continent. Silent Knight quickly gained his title in this country winning 12 CCs in all and siring four English champions. On giving up her Shalfleet kennel to live abroad Mrs Wilton Clark returned Silent Knight to his breeder, Tim Teillir, but left behind in England his champion son from one of his first litters, Ch. Shalfleet Silent Wish (already the sire of Ch. Marshall's Milord at Faracre) and Mrs Thompson's Ch. Walkabout

147. *Ch. Dondelayo Ruanne of Charmoll. (Diane Pearce)*

Warrior King. Silent Knight's breeding is chiefly represented by the Walkabout, Ballagan, Astrophel, Ishkoodah and Faracre prefixes from whom a number of good winners of this breeding have appeared.

The disbandment of the Shalfleet kennel which has played such a part in the history of the breed is no less sad than the deaths of Mrs Knight (Dondelayo), Mr James (Samarkand) and Frank Moore (Allgarth) and all of them are very severely missed. The trend today would appear to be towards exhibitors rather than breeders and those kennels with long established lines of predictable type are very much at a premium. One cannot help wondering where solidly-bred foundation stock is now to come from and whether the jumble of bloodlines appearing in the ring is not to some extent responsible for the same jumble of breed types which presents such problems for judges, both Specialist and All-rounder.

The most potent Shalfleet sire was probably Shalfleet Skyliner who sired three champions and, as we have seen, Selinko Another Lady descends from him through his son, Ch. Shalfleet Sailing Free, whilst Royal Mint and Wanderer carry lines to his dam, Ch. Shalfleet Starstruck. A certain amount of Laguna breeding was incorporated into the Shalfleet bloodlines by Shalfleet Schelle (Int. Ch. Laguna Leisure-Ch. Shalfleet Starstruck) and by Selbrook Brandy of Shalfleet (Ch. Deepridge Mintmaster-Ch. Selbrook Bracelet) but the Shalfleets remained predominantly Allways in both breeding and type. Like Ch. Nimrodel Ruff and Ch. Tweseldown Whinchat, Ch. Sequence of Shalfleet was one of the few really big winners (15 CCs) during the period who did not carry either Tarragon or Ligonier in her pedigree, being by Ch. Shalfleet Sailing Free (by Skyliner by Stargazer) out of Shadow of Andreovna (also by Stargazer). Bred by Miss Hall (Malbon) but campaigned by Mrs Wilton Clark, Sequence was a bitch who many thought to be a living embodiment of the breed standard. Schelle also proved a useful sire in producing Ch. Ballagan Flighty and Ch. Shalfleet Silver Knight of Shalfleet, the sire of Mrs Jones' glamorous Group winning Ch. Welstar Minted Model, the dam of the record holder Royal Mint and Ch. Welstar Winning Dream, also a Group winner. Ch. Shalfleet Sailing Free was also the sire of the black Ch. Poaching Black Jack who, in his turn, sired Ch. Martinsell Grand Slam, Ch. Curlands Night Dancer and Ch. Curlands Night Alert. Selbrook Brandy of Shalfleet whose breeding is above, was bred by June Selby whose Selbrook prefix was synonymous with quality over many years, and was purchased by Mrs Wilton Clark as an addition to her stud team where he more than earned his keep. He was the sire of Ch. Shalfleet Sequilla (out of Ch. Sequence), Ch. Deepridge Mosaic (out of Ch. Deepridge Minniva) and Ch. Shalfleet Story Writer (out of Shalfleet Storyteller).

Perhaps one of the most interesting developments in the last decade has been the great improvement in blacks and blues. These difficult colours, both to breed and to exhibit, have taken great strides forward in the hands of some very knowledgeable and dedicated breeders. The difficulties involved in getting to the top in these two colours are clearly demonstrated by the very few champions to gain their titles since the War; only five blacks and, so far as the records show, only one blue ever in the history of the breed. Of the two black dog champions, Ch. Ladiesfield Starturn sadly proved infertile and Ch. Poaching Black Jack was run over before he had time to cover more than a handful of bitches. Despite his limited stud career he left behind three champion progeny only one of which, however, was black, the lovely little bitch Martinsell Grand Slam. She too met a tragic end, being killed on the railway line together with her dam and half-sister, thus wiping out an entire bitch line representing years of planned breeding on the part of Joanna Russell and her sister, Caroline Brown (Martinsell). Grand Slam was only the third black champion bitch since the War, the other two being Ch. Poppy Tarquin, owned by Mrs 'Poppy' Martin and Ch. Seagift Black Diamond of Annalyn, bred by Mrs Peddie and campaigned in the Barnsley, Whitwell and Vaux partnership. Mrs Martin's Poppy prefix was one of the oldest in the breed and from 1922 onwards there have been Poppy champions both here and abroad. There can be few people in the breed who gave more to whippets than Mrs Martin; the Welsh Whippet Club, with which she was closely associated, owes much to her wonderful gift for sportsmanship and good fellowship.

In 1987 breed history was made when Ch. Martinsell Wild and Lonely gained his title, the first blue champion the breed has seen. Bred by Joanna Russell and

148. *Int. Ch. Charmoll Clansman. (Gilbert)*

149. *Ch. Charmoll Bonnie Prince.*

150. *Ch. Charmoll MacTavish.*

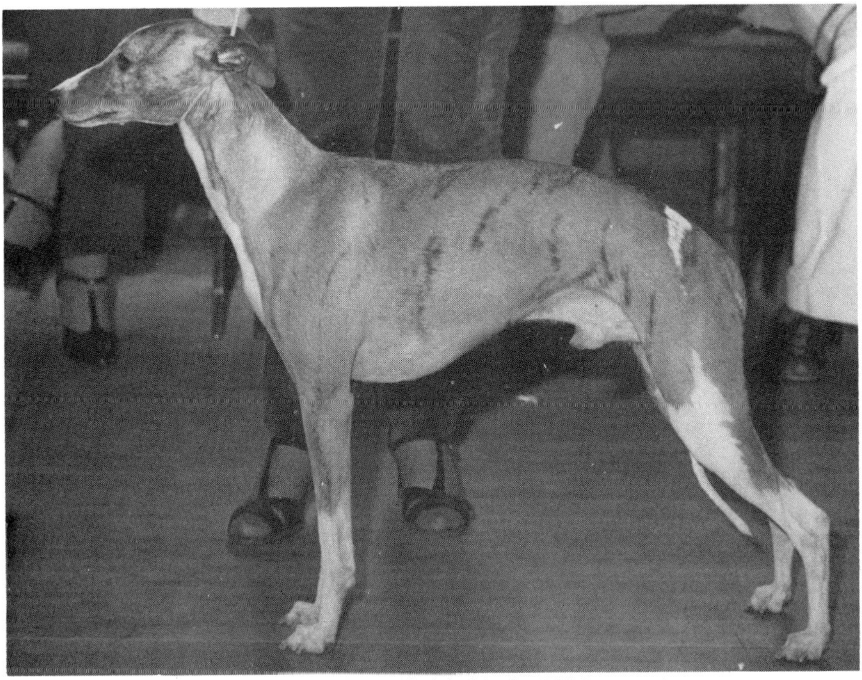

151. *Ch. Novacroft Madrigal. (Whimpanny)*

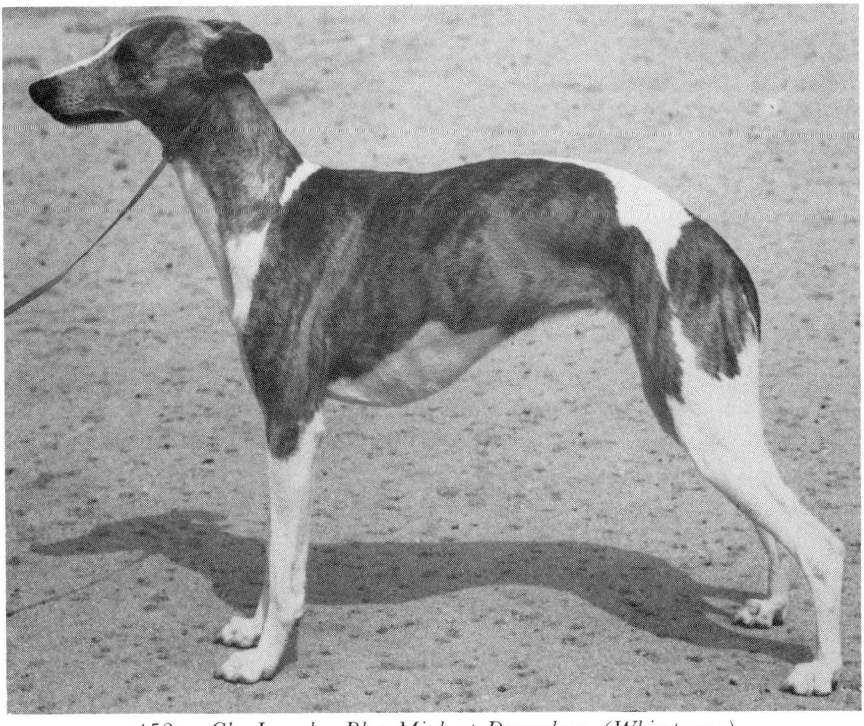

152. *Ch. Lowglen Blue Mink at Dennydene. (Whimpanny)*

Ch. MARTINSELL WILD AND LONELY	Rytstone Blue Magpie	Chatwig Charger	Selbrook Blue Print
			Kutak Wapiti
		Jenny Wren of Rytstone	Morgolok Taurus
			Trecarne Barbarella
	Martinsell Wild Rose	Ch. Nimrodel Wiveton	Bartonia of Brough
			Nimrodel Wissendine
		Martinsell Wild Teasel	Chisigo Ricky
			Shalfleet Sweet 'n Fair of Martinsell

Caroline Brown he is sired by Rytstone Blue Magpie, a CC winning blue dog with white trim. Magpie carried old fashioned Selbrook and Shalfleet lines together with some Martinsell/Ladiesfield colour breeding. Lonely's dam, Martinsell Wild Rose, was by Ch. Nimrodel Wiveton out of another CC winner, Martinsell Wild Teasel, Shalfleet and Dragonhill bred. This dog, who is the most beautiful pale lilac blue, is proving a very interesting sire and not only on colour lines though he throws a high proportion of blue puppies doubtless due to the recessive blue-dilute gene which is carried in most English bloodlines. Together with the dilute blue he throws a proportion of rich red fawns and as yet there seems to be no evidence of dilute pigment or eye colour, the fear of which has proved such a barrier to incorporating the dilute with American bloodlines. Amongst his progeny he already numbers two RCC winners and his influence on the breed might well prove consequential.

There have been so few CC winners amongst blacks and blues that it is worth listing them. Mrs Crocker's Crysbel Steel Blue (Seagift So Blue-Speedlite Panchino) was a CC winner and many thought unlucky not to gain her crown. Mrs Gaitskell's blue dog with white trim, Chancerick Kaspar (Ebzan Noudini Bey Noir-Chancerick Nimrodel Rosefinch), bred by Hilda Meek, won one CC and one RCC as did Silver Badger of Scarteen (Ch. Nimrodel Ruff-Mancot Rosaline) bred by Mr Millar and owned by Sally Edwards. The blue and white parti-colour Ch. Inadown Whispering Witch, bred by Mrs Kerr Pettersen, was one who did make it to the top, as did the very glamorous tri-colour Ch. Fleeting Spean La Calindra, bred by Mrs Shields and owned by Mollie Garrish. Laguna Christmas Carol,

Nimrodel Belladonna, Ousebank Morning Melody and Poachyn Blue Jeans at Laurelcote were blue RCC winners.

A number of blacks have won CCs and RCCs, notably Mrs Newton's Santune Harlem Rhythm (Black Brocade of Allways) and Mr Salter's Velocity Black Rod (by Inadown Black Watch by Brocade). Mr Silk has produced good blacks over several generations including two CC winners; Mrs Harris' Wyemere Black Gem (a great granddaughter of Bey Noir and Rosefinch, the mating which produced Chancerick Kaspar and the black Whippet Club Racing Association Ch., Chancerick Koh-i-Nor). Mrs Rigby, who has specialised in blacks of the highest quality over several generations, not only bred Ch. Poaching Black Jack but also Poaching Tadpole, a CC winner, and the RCC winners Poaching After Dark and Poaching Night Flight. Carol Neal's Stormalong prefix has also produced some nice blacks including the black RCC winner Stormalong Black Vizard to Belleek. The latest black to win a CC is Nimrodel Noir, a son of Woolsocks Summer Blaze out of a Ch. Poaching Black Jack daughter. Denhills Blackamour is another black who has notched up a couple of RCC. Anyone who has exhibited these colours will tell you how discouraging it can be when a judge kindly says how nice your dog or bitch is 'for a black/blue'. The fact is that a whippet can be any colour and until judges learn to put their prejudices aside and judge the make and shape of every dog regardless of colour, specialist colour breeders and exhibitors have a hard and lonely road to follow.

The top kennels of the last twenty-five years in terms of numbers of champions bred can be easily evaluated by studying Appendix 1. Mr N. Nicholson (Glenbervie) is still undoubtedly the leader in this field, having bred seventeen champions. Mrs Wilton Clark (Shalfleet) is a close second with Mr and Mrs Meakin (Oakbark) and Mrs Anne Knight (Dondelayo) not far behind. The Lowglen kennels are famous for the high quality stock they either campaign or breed. There are several other prefixes which, whilst they have never carried large numbers, have consistently produced winners on which the success of others has been founded, for example Newbold, Flarepath, Cockrow and Baydale. There are others who, whilst they have bred little have always had a good one to campaign. Mrs Roma Wright Smith piloted Ch. Beseeka Knight Errant of Silkstone to his many wins in this country, including the Hound Group at Crufts. Knight Errant was bred by Mesdames Lumb and Hughes by Oakbark Moonduster out of Newbold Madelina and was eventually exported to Mrs Khartsounis, whose South African kennels included such stars as Ch. Denorsi Moonduster of Glenbervie and S.A. Ch. Dondelayo Minette of Oldwell. It was in that ownership that he won the CACIB at the World Show at Verona. Although Miss Julie Smith was the official breeder of Ch. Jubilant Lady of Tygreen and Lowerdon the credit for breeding this outstanding bitch really belongs to Roma Wright Smith, who purchased her dam, Oakbark Minniva, especially to mate to Knight Errant. Jubilant Lady eventually ended up in the ownership of Mrs Sandra Marshall with whom she had a meteoric career, gaining her title very quickly and, in the course of doing so, winning BIS at

153. *Ch. Poltesco Peewit.*

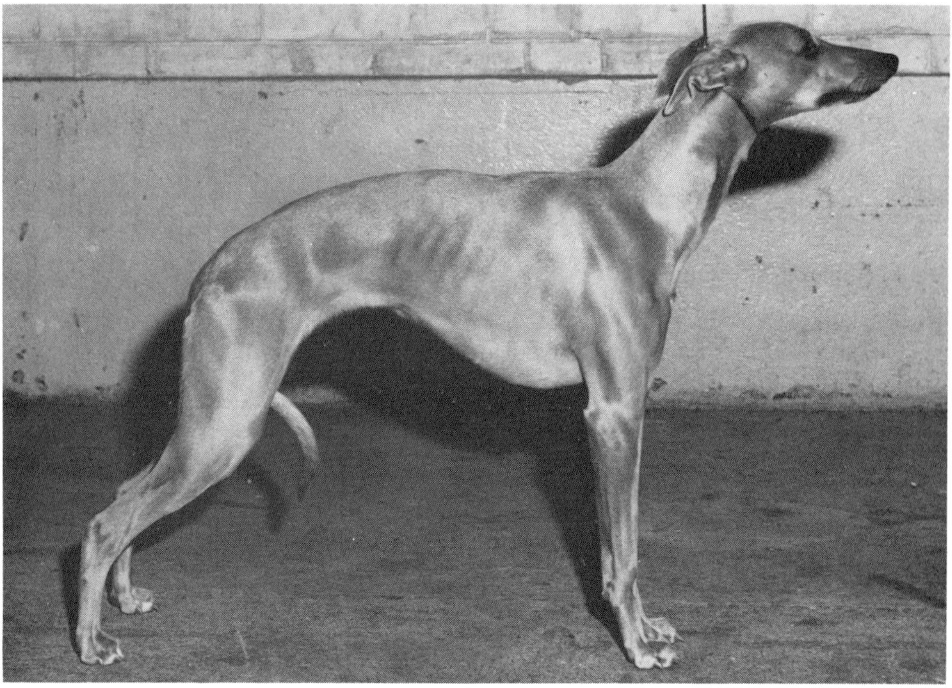

154. *Ch. Dragonhill Tawny Owl. (Cooke)*

155. *Ch. Nimrodel Ruff. (Diane Pearce)*

156. *Ch. Tweseldown Whinchat. (Lionel Young)*

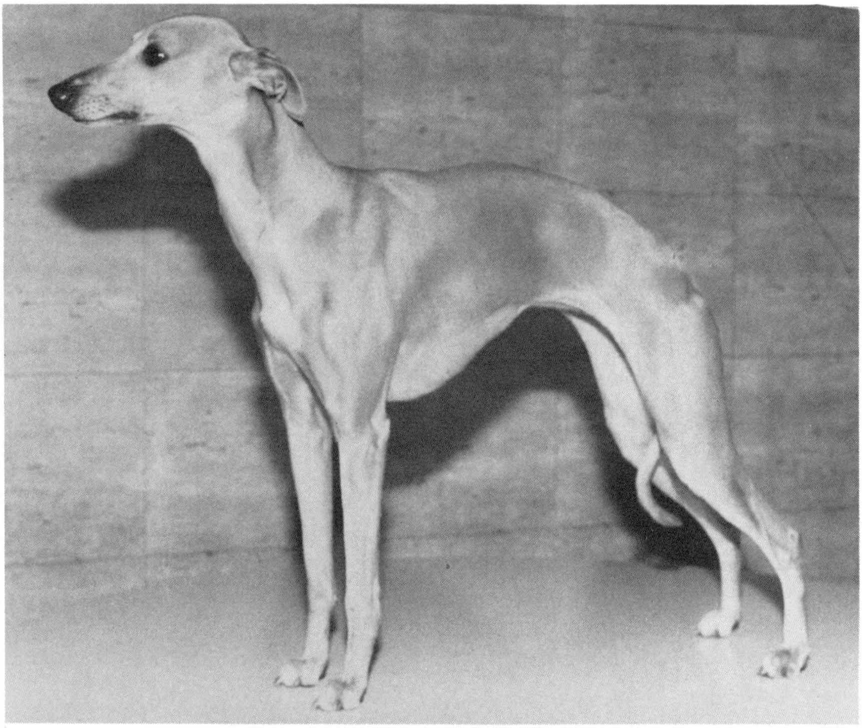

157. *Ch. Wipstych Courbette. (Whimpanny)*

158. *Ch. Wipstych Grandiflora. (Whimpanny)*

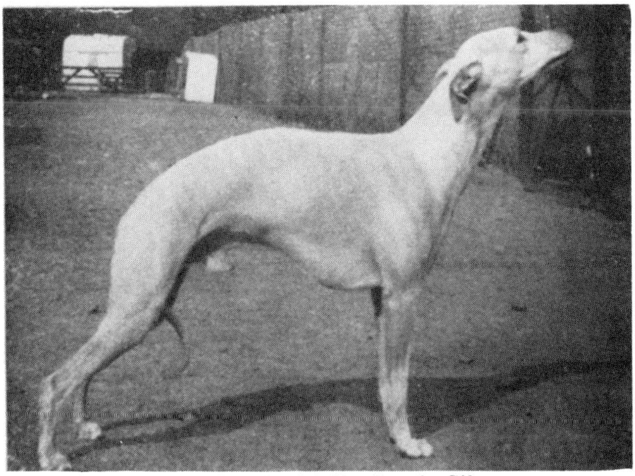

159. *Ch. Inniskelltr Lovely Silver.*

160. *Ch. Nimrodel Wiveton.*

161. *Ch. Mithrandir Gambit of Dhahran. (Whimpanny)*

162. *Ch. Welstar Minted Model.*

163. *Ch. Welstar Royal Mint. (Whimpanny)*

164. *Ch. Brough Lady Devine.*

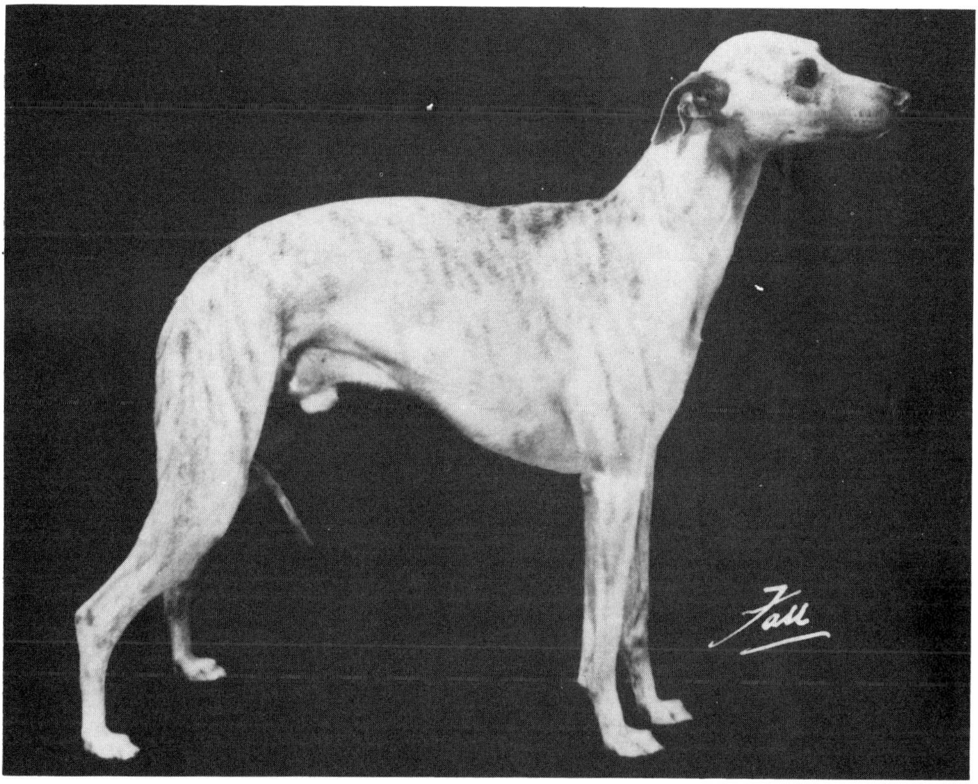

165. *Ch. Samoens Silent Knight of Shalfleet. (Fall)*

166. *Ch. Shalfleet Silent Wish. (Diane Pearce)*

167. *Ch. Selinko Another Lady. (Photographer not known)*

both Birmingham City and Darlington Championship shows. She won 12 CCs and the Hound Group at Crufts under Mollie Garrish who had given her her first CC. Roma Wright Smith's Silkstone prefix is responsible for winning dogs all over the world as she has always exported the best and her eye for good stock is perceptive. Her latest champion, Ch. Silkstone Astella (by Oakbark Mister Blue, sire of Ch. Cottonmere Monty of Oakbark and Ch. Cottonmere Personality of Oakbark) is now in South Africa.

Having looked at the leading sires from 1962 to 1989, and at their breeding, and at the chief winners and what lies behind them, one should, perhaps, take an overall look at the progress of the breed over the last twenty-five years. Some significant achievements have taken place. We have seen a whippet win Reserve BIS at Crufts (Ch. Dondelayo Duette), we have seen a whippet take the Top Dog in the Pedigree Chum competition (Ch. Nutshell of Nevedith); we have seen the crowning of the first blue champion (Ch. Martinsell Wild and Lonely), we have new records set up for both dogs and bitches (Ch. Nimrodel Wanderer and Ch. Selinko Another Lady). We have two bench champions winning the Moonlake Cup for dogs with the Whippet Coursing Club (Ch. Sound Barrier and Ch. Chyton Copy Press), we have English titles gained by two foreign champions for the first time (Ch. Samoems Silent Knight of Shalfleet and Can. Ch. Loricbrook Runaway of Shalfleet). Now we must ask ourselves what else we have seen.

168. *Ch. Nutshell of Nevedith. (Whimpanny)*

As a breed whippets (and sighthounds generally) are very free from problems of a hereditary nature; we do not have PRA or HD or a number of other problems one can think of. But there are one or two disquieting indications in the breed if one cares to look for them. Temperament is of vital importance and whippets should have steady temperaments, neither nervous nor aggressive. Yet there are dogs being shown in our whippet rings today that have to be doped before they can be handled and others who spend their time panting and shivering and showing other signs of distress. The Kennel Club would be better advised to run dope tests on show dogs instead of looking for chalk in their coats. This sort of temperament is very wrong in whippets and breeders must be careful about it and relentlessly reject it from any breeding programmes. A nervous show dog will probably produce a vicious pet dog and a breeder who will tolerate such a flaw for the sake of show success is unforgivable. The second slightly disquieting factor is the tendency, in the wake of the American Standard and their preference for a more exaggerated form of whippet, towards this same exaggeration in the breed here. Our Standard specifically says, 'all forms of exaggeration to be avoided ...', and exaggeration, especially over the loins and in the construction of the hind-quarters, gives first an appearance of weakness and subsequently can lead us in the direction of Hip Dysplasia. In America instances of this in whippets have been known and yet in this country Greyhound and Whippet skeletons are used as the norm against which

169. *Ch. Martinsell Wild & Lonely. (Whimpanny)*

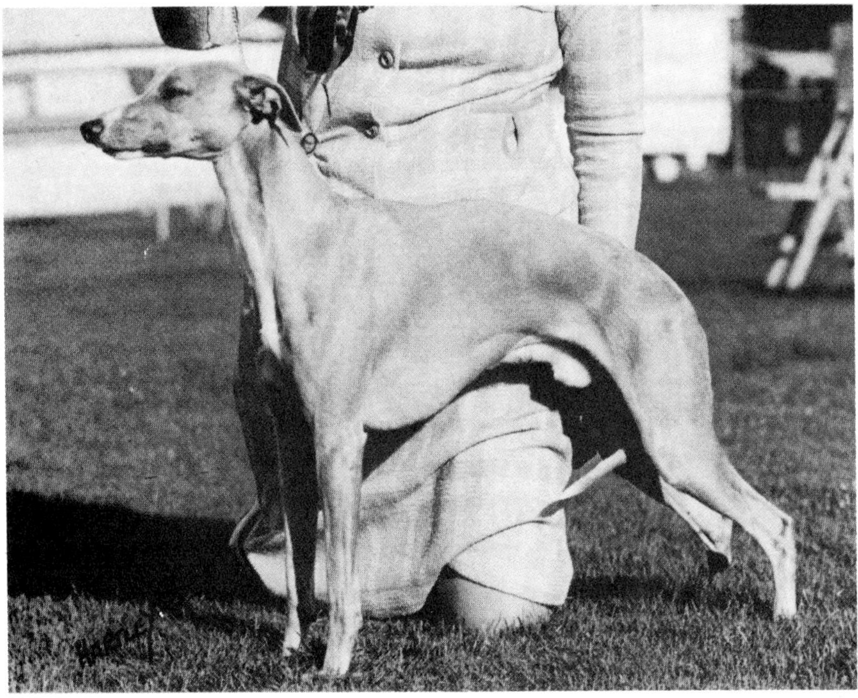

170. *Ch. Nimrodel Wanderer. (Hartley)*

to measure degrees of Hip Dysplasia in other breeds. It is vital for the future of our breed that breeders take care to safeguard the future of whippets in their breeding programmes and in their placements in the ring when judging. If we allow these abnormalities to creep into the breed we will have destroyed all the generations of lovely whippets which are our legacy from the past and which it is our duty to hand on to our heirs in the future.

To this end, the Breed Council, now well into its stride, has been running 'Teach-Ins' for aspiring judges and others interested in the breed and these functions, which have been held all over the country, have been very well attended and have proved a fascinating forum for discussion. We cannot hope that we will all agree over every detail concerning whippets but those of us who love and care for the breed and its future can do our best to breed selectively to the Standard, to breed sparingly – bearing in mind the huge number of whippets rescued each year by the J.R. Whippet Rescue – and, if we do so in good faith, we may hope to rival those great breeders of the past on whose integrity and expertise all our present day whippets are based.

APPENDIX 1

Index of Champions gaining their titles or winning CCs 1962/1989 listed under the PREFIX of both Owner and Breeder.
(X) Indicates double listing.
(CHs) Indicates other Champions bred or owned prior to 1962.

AKEFERRY	Mr S. F. R. Pendleton	Ch. Akeferry Jimmy (X) Ch. Tantivvey Akeferry Crusader (X)
ALLGARTH	Mr F. R. Moore	Ch. Allgarth Envoy Ch. Allgarth Eidelweiss (X) Ch. Deborah of Allgarth (X) Ch. Ambassador of Allgarth (X) Ch. Allgarth Atlantis of Sagewood (X)
ALLWAYS (CHs)	Mrs M. R. Cooke (formerly Mrs M. R. Jones)	Eng. and AUS Ch. Playmate of Allways
ALTYRE	Mrs M. Fell	Ch. Mr Softie of Altyre
ARMFIELD	Mr J. J. Armitage	Ch. Oakbark Armfield Joker (X)
BADGEWOOD	Mr & Mrs P. S. P. Fell	Ch. Badgewood Sewickly
BALDREY	Mrs J. S. White	Ch. Broughland Gina of Baldrey (X) Ch. Baldrey Limited Edition of Juneric (X) Ch. Baldrey Rainbow's End
BAIRD Miss S.		Ch. Nimrodel Wiveton (X) Ch. Sound Barrier
BALLAGAN	Lady Selway	Ch. Ballagan Prince Charlie of Briarcliffe (X) Ch. Ballagan Annie Laurie Ch. Ballagan Flighty
BARMOLL	Mrs B. M. McConkey	Ch. Barmoll Beelzebub Ch. Barmoll Beejapers

BARMOUD	Mr & Mrs J. Barker Mrs J. North Row	Ch. Barmoud Sungage
BAXENDALE	Lady Sarah Neill Fraser	Ch. Baxendale Coral Beauty Ch. Walkabout Whirlpool of Baxendale (X)
BAYDALE	The late Mrs Blair & Mrs S. H. Fenwick	Ch. Baydale Samfa Ch. Baydale Cinnamon (X) Ch. Baydale Royal Ascot (X)
BAYLISS Mr C.		Ch. Shalfleet Starstruck (X)
BESEEKA	Mesdames Lumb & Hughes	Ch. Beseeka Knight Errant of Silkstone (X)
BIRCONBRAE	Mr & Mrs R.J. & Miss B. R. Anderson	Ch. Nicely Naughty at Birconbrae
BLIK	Mrs I. Zurbriggen	Ch. Blik's Ringmore Bardolph (X)
BOUGHTON (CHs)	Miss M. Boggia Mrs A. Boggia	
BRIARCLIFFE (CHs)	Mrs C. Hodgson	Ch. Ballagan Prince Charlie Briarcliffe (X)
BREKIN (CHs)	Lady Dankwerts	Ch. Tranwell's Brekin Sally Lunn (X)
BONDICAR	Mr A. Freathy	Ch. Bondicar Blossom
BONLOUIE	Mrs L. D. Anderton	Ch. Bonlouie Abalon Star at Teisanlap (X)
BROUGH now BROUGHLAND	Mr & Mrs F. Hempstock	Ch. Brough Lady Devine Ch. Broughland Gina of Baldrey (X) Ch. Welstar Royal Mint (X)
BUCKLOW Mr E.		Ch. Danegeld Piper's Tune (X)
BUCHANAN Mr A.		Ch. Master Shoemaker of Oakbark (X)
CARLBAY	Mr & Mrs G. Barclay Hunt	Ch. Witch Hazel of Raddledandie (X) Ch. Twobridge Tiger Trap (X) Ch. Cider Apple of Carlbay

CARMODIAN	Mr & Mrs G. Carmichael	Ch. Carmodian Tawny Knight of Hutaka (X) Ch. Maximilian of Carmodian (X)
	(in partnership with Mr F. Nicholas	Ch. Black Knight of Carmodian (X) Ch. Lowerdon Soldier Blue (X)
CHANCERICK	Mrs H. M. Meek and Mrs S. Tyler	Ch. Nimrodel Rare Magic (X)
CHAPMAN Mrs K. (CHs)		Ch. Wingedfoot Tu Whit Tu Whoo (X) Ch. Playfair Ch. Interflora Ch. Telstar Moon Ch. Walhachin
CHARMOLL	Mrs C. Dempster	Ch. Dondelayo Ruanne of Charmoll (X) Ch. & USA Ch. Charmoll Clansman Ch. Charmoll Bonnie Prince Ch. Charmoll McTavish
CHATWIG	Mrs F. Charles	Ch. Houghtonhill Night Starry Sky of Chatwig (X)
CHERIBI	Mrs E. Collinge	Ch. Greenbrae Poltesco Dusky Maid (X)
CHILKA	Mr J. W. F. & Mrs W. P. Barker	Ch. Nutshell of Nevedith (X)
CHYTON	Mrs S. A. Rawlings	Ch. Chyton Copypress
COCKROW	Misses A. & E. Hudson	Ch. Cockrow Tarquogan of Glenbervie (X) Ch. Cockrow Pheasant
COLDSTONE	Miss J. Sladen	Ch. Tumbler's Clouded Buff of Coldstone (X)
CORNWATER	Miss J. Smith	Ch. Jubilant Lady of Tygreen and Lowerdon (X)
COTTONMERE	Miss D. M. Greenwood	Ch. Cottonmere Monty of Oakbark (X) Ch. Cottonmere Personality of Oakbark (X)
COURTENAY	Mr A. E. Halliwell	Ch. & USA Ch. Courtenay Fleet-foot of Pennyworth

COURTHILL	Mr R. Stock	Ch. Courthill Dondelayo Tiara (X) Ch. Courthill Coronet Ch. Shalfleet Showman of Courthill (X)
CRAWSHAW	Miss M. Wright	Ch. Pimlico of Crawshaw (X) Ch. Belinda of Hardknott (X)
CRYSBEL	Mrs M. Crocker	Ch. Tantivvey Diver (X) Ch. Crysbel Skylark Ch. Crysbel Skylight of Nevedith (X)
CREEDY Mrs		Ch. Othello of Velgra (X)
CURLANDS	Mrs P. Brown	Ch. Curlands Night Dancer (X) Ch. Curlands Night Alert
DAHRAN	Miss J. Munro	Ch. Mithrandir Gambit of Dahran (X)
DALEFORGE	Mrs B. Hartley	Ch. Daleforge Carmen Jones
DANEGELD	Miss B. Hinde	Ch. Danegeld Piper's Tune (X) Ch. Porthurst Atalanta (X)
DANROPA	Mr Daniels	Ch. Danropa His Lordship of Thurma (X)
DANSOL	Mr & Mrs D. Griffiths	Ch. Dansol Day Dreamer
DEEABLO	Mrs D. Cooper	Ch. Dondelayo Morning Mist at Deeablo (X)
DEEPRIDGE	Miss E. M. Hawthorne	Ch. Deepridge Masquerade Ch. Deepridge Mintmaster Ch. Deepridge Minstrel Ch. Deepridge Miniva Ch. Deepridge Mosaic
DENHILLS	Mr D. Hill	Ch. Denhills Delectabelle (X) Ch. Denhills Democrat (X)
DENNYDENE	Mrs K. Sedgely	Ch. Lowglen Blue Mink at Dennydene (X)
DENORSI	Mr J. Peden	Ch. Denorsi Moonduster of Glenbervie (X) Ch. Denorsi Moon Dust of Glenbervie (X) Ch. Denorsi Quickmatch of Glenbervie (X)

DONDELAYO	Mrs A. R. Knight	Ch. Denorsi Rioch Ch. Denorsi Dancing Belle Ch. Denorsi Dixie Belle Ch. Swiftfoot Susanna (X) Ch. Oakbark Dondelayo Storming (X) Ch. Dondelayo Rue Ch. Dondelayo Roulette Ch. Dondelayo Buckaroo Ch. Dondelayo Duette Ch. Dondelayo Ruanne of Charmoll (X) Ch. Courthill Dondelayo Tiara (X) Ch. Dondelayo Bandalero (X) Ch. & AUS Ch. Dondelayo Statue Ch. & AUS Ch. Dondelayo Reinette Ch. Denshill Delectabelle (X) Ch. Dianne Dondelayo (X) Ch. Samarkands Beau Ranger (X) Ch. Samarkands Firewolf (X)
DRAGONHILL (CHs)	Mrs D. Cleeve	Ch. Dragonhill Curlew Ch. Dragonhill Woodpecker Ch. Dragonhill Tawny Owl
DUDDLESTON	Mr J. D. Gregory	Ch. Great Ovation of Fairfoot (X)
ELMANASH	Mr & Mrs F. J. Holland	Ch. Elmanash Signoretta
EXHURST & JUNERIC	Mr & Mrs E. Minns	Ch. Nimrodel Wanderer (X) Ch. Baldrey Limited Edition of Juneric (X) Ch. Gypsy Moth of Glenbervie (X)
FAIRCORN	Mrs D. Edgar	Ch. Faircorn Waggonmaster
FAIRFOOT	Mrs J. Rollason	Ch. Fairfoot Towercrest Encore (X) Ch. Great Ovation of Fairfoot (X)
FALCONCRAG	Mrs S. M. & Miss P. Marston	Ch. Another Rose of Glenbervie (X)
FARACRE	Mrs K. Thomas	Ch. Shalfleet Storywriter (X) Ch. Marshall's Milord at Faracre (X)
FLAREPATH	Mr & Mrs H. Wood	Ch. Ravensdowne Bright Star (X)

		Ch. Laguna Ravensdown Astri (X) Ch. Towercrest Flarepath Taurus (X) Ch. Flarepath Astrinomical (X) Ch. Flarepath Astrinaught of Lowglen (X) Ch. Gosmore Flarepath Auriga (X)
FLEETING	Mrs M. B. Garrish	Ch. Fleeting Spean La Calindra (X) Ch. Fleeting Flamboyant Ch. Fleeting Fulmar
FLINTBECK	Mr R. Pye	Ch. Gypsy Picture of Glenbervie (X)
FREAK Mrs G.		Ch. Acomb's Tostig (X)
GAMELEA	Mr B. Diaper	Ch. Gamelea Mr Tic Tack
GAINSCLIFFE	Mr J. V. Williamson	Ch. Gainscliffe Renown Ch. Gainscliffe Chase the Ace
GARGANEY	Mrs K. George	Ch. Garganey Mistletoe Ch. Garganey Bartmeus
GILLIANA	Mr & Mrs G. Thomas	Ch. Gilliana Gonzales (X)
GLENBERVIE	Mr A. B. Nicholson	Ch. Hillgarth Sunstar of Glenbervie (X) Ch. Cockrow Tarquogan of Glenbervie (X) Ch. Sky Gypsy of Glenbervie Ch. Gypsy Moth of Glenbervie (X) Ch. Gunsmith of Glenbervie (X) Ch. Pathway of Glenbervie Ch. White Frost of Glenbervie Ch. Skytime of Glenbervie Ch. Gypsy Picture of Glenbervie (X) Ch. Glenbervie Solid Silver Ch. Glenbervie Beacon Light Ch. Twigairy of Glenbervie Ch. Another Rose of Glenbervie (X) Ch. Another Love of Risepark (X) Ch. Denorsi Moonduster of Glenbervie (X)

		Ch. Denorsi Moon Dust of Glenbervie (X) Ch. Quickmatch of Glenbervie (X)
GOSMORE	Mrs A. Dallison	Ch. Gosmore Flarepath Auriga (X)
GREENBRAE	Mrs A. Yerburgh	Ch. Greenbrae Laguna Lucia (X) Ch. Samarkand's Greenbrae Tarragon (X) Ch. Greenbrae Free as Air
HAMMONDS	Mrs A. Randall	Ch. Hammonds Sebastian Ch. Norwill Barley at Hammonds (X)
HARDKNOTT	Mrs M. E. Bennett	Ch. Belinda of Hardknott (X) Ch. Hardknott Mystery (X) Ch. Hardknott Quadrille (X)
HARQUE	Mrs A. Argyle	Ch. Wingedfoot Tu Whit Tu Whoo (X) Ch. Runway Controller (X) Ch. Harque Conneil Carry On (X) Ch. Harque Conneil Crown Jewel (X) Ch. Harque to Gamecock Ch. Harque to Rosa Ch. Harque the Lark Ch. Harque to Pegasus Ch. Harque Yonder Ch. Harque to Copelia Ch. Harque to Equerry (X) Ch. Harque to Huntsman
HAZIRAN	Mrs J. Williams	Ch. Jeremy Fisher of Hardknott (X)
HILLGARTH (CHs)	Mrs M. F. Sheffield	Ch. Hillgarth Sunstar of Glenbervie (X) Ch. Roanbar Hillgarth Sweet Surprise (X)
HILLSDOWN	J. P. Moran Healey	Ch. Hilldsown Tobique Ch. & USA Ch. Hillsdown Repique Ch. Hillsdown Roisin Ch. Oakbark Middleman (X) Ch. Nutcracker of Nevedith (X)

HOUGHTONHILL in partnership with NEVEDITH	Mr R. Hill	Ch. Houghtonhill Night Starry Sky of Chatwig (X) Ch. Crysbel Skylight of Nevedith (X) Ch. Nevedith Bright Beret (X) Ch. Nevedith Hill Breeze (X)
HUTAKA	Mrs A. Beckett Bradshaw	Ch. Carmodian Tawny Knight of Hutaka (X) Ch. Sunsalve Holidaze at Hutaka (X)
INADOWN	Mrs Kerr Pettersen	Ch. Inadown Whispering Witch
INNISKHELLTR	Miss G. Ussher	Ch. Bromholm Jonquil of Allways (X) Ch. Inniskhelltr Lollipop Ch. Inniskhelltr Lovely Silver Ch. Marlin's Dusky Miller of Inniskhelltr (X) Ch. Inniskhelltr Make Believe
JARMANE	Mrs J. Norman	Ch. Jarmane Sahryssa
KARNAK	Mr & Mrs C. K. Thornton	Ch. Karnak Silver Tiger (X)
KILLIGREW	Mrs H. Bradley	Ch. Killigrew Quintus Ch. Newbold Muffinman (X) Ch. Killigrew Ambrosia
KNOTKNUM (CHs)	Mr J. Fisher	Ch. Fair Landing of Knotknum (X)
KNUZERY	Mr J. Parkinson	Ch. Knuzery Delightful
LADIESFIELD	Mrs M. Wigg	Ch. Ladiesfield Starturn Ch. Ladiesfield Topaz Ch. Ladiesfield Bedazzled
LAGUNA (CHs)	Mrs D. U. McKay	Ch. Laguna Ligonier Ch. Laguna Porthurst Moonlight Sonata (X) Ch. Laguna Linkway Ch. Greenbrae Laguna Lucia (X) Ch. Laguna Light Lagoon (X) Ch. Laguna Lunanute Int. Ch. Laguna Leisure
LINKNUMSTAR	Mrs C. Coller	Ch. Fairlanding of Knotknum (X) Ch. Carina Mia (X)

LONGACRES	B. Harness	Ch. Blue of Longacres (X)
LORICBROOK	Mr M. Magder	Ch. Can. & USA Ch. Loricbrook Runaway of Shalfleet (X)
LOUNELL	Mr G. L. Morris	Ch. Laura Love
LOWERDON	Mrs S. H. Marshall	Ch. Jubilant Lady of Tygreen and Lowerdon (X) Ch. Lowerdon Soldier Blue (X) Ch. Lowerdon I Can Boogie (X)
LOWGLEN	Mr F. Nicholas	Ch. Gilliana Gonzales (X) Ch. Flarepath Astrinaught of Lowglen (X) Ch. Lowglen Newbold Cavalier (X) Ch. Lowglen Holly Go Lightly Ch. Solera Scarlet Ribbons at Lowglen (X) Ch. Lowglen Singing Bede Ch. Allgarth Eidelweiss (X) Ch. Black Knight of Carmodian (X) Ch. Lowerdon Soldier Blue (X) Ch. Lowglen Blue Mink at Dennydene (X) Ch. Lowglen Magic Moments
MACFIELD	Mr A. Mackenzie	Ch. Jeremy Fisher of Hardknott (X)
MANCOT	Mr A. S. Lowe	Ch. Mancot Petruchio
MALBON	Miss M. Hall	Ch. Sequence of Shalfleet (X)
MARASH	Mrs A. Denton	Ch. Queen of the May at Marash (X)
MARLINS	Mr L. Blik	Ch. Marlins Dusty Miller of Inniskhelltr (X)
MARTIN Miss M. M.		Ch. Hino Legacy (X)
MARTINSELL	Mesdames Russell & Brown	Ch. Martinsell Grand Slam Ch. Martinsell Wild and Lonely
MISPICKLE Mrs S. Haywood		Ch. Mispickle Mazurka of Zarcrest (X)

MITHRANDIR	Mrs P. Macdonald	Ch. Mithrandir Gambit of Dahran (X)
MOORE Mrs M.		Ch. Capo di Monte Ch. Queen of the May at Marash (X)
MYBERINE	Mr & Mrs M. Coburn	Ch. Myberine Miss Honeypenny
NEVEDITH	Mrs E. Newton Reid	Ch. Akeferry Jimmy (X) Ch. Nutcracker of Nevedith (X) Ch. Ruegeto Nina of Nevedith (X) Ch. Nevedith Paperweight Ch. Nevedith Uptown Guy Ch. Huntress of Nevedith (X) Ch. Nutshell of Nevedith (X)
in partnership with Mr R. Hill		Ch. Crysbel Skylight of Nevedith (X) Ch. Nevedith Hill Breeze (X) Ch. Nevedith Bright Beret (X)
NEWBOLD	Mr & Mrs D. Howarth	Ch. Topall Newbold Miguel (X) Ch. Lowglen Newbold Cavalier (X) Ch. Oakbark Michaela (X) Ch. Newbold Kerry Gold Ch. Newbold Muffinman (X)
NIMRODEL	Mrs I. H. Lowe	Ch. Nimrodel Willow Daughter Ch. Nimrodel Ruff Ch. Nimrodel Wiveton (X) Ch. Wipstych Grandiflora (X) Ch. Ringmore Riff Raff (X) Ch. Nimrodel Wanderer (X) Ch. Nimrodel Rare Magic (X) Ch. Withaway Nimrodel (X) Ch. Nimrodel Peerless
NORWILL	Mr J. & Mrs E. M. Patrick	Ch. Norwill Barley at Hammonds (X)
NOVACROFT	Mrs Gardner	Ch. Novacroft Starlight Ch. Novacroft Madrigal (X)
OAKBARK	Mr & Mrs D. Meakin & Mrs J. Greenwood Meakin	Ch. Oakbark Dondelayo Storming (X) Ch. Oakbark Armfield Joker (X) Ch. Oakbark Melord Ch. Oakbark Movie Queen Ch. Oakbark Must Love Ch. Cottonmere Monty of Oakbark (X)

		Ch. Flarepath Tambillo Tarquin (X) Ch. Oakbark Michaela (X) Ch. Oakbark Merchant Prince (X) Ch. Oakbark Mr Magic of Silkstone (X) Ch. Oakbark Middleman (X) Ch. Cottonmere Personality of Oakbark (X) Ch. Oakbark Mary Rose Ch. Master Shoemaker of Oakbark (X) Ch. Oakbark Generation Girl
PALMIK	Mr M. Howgate	Ch. Palmik Starsign Ch. Palmik Starry
PARDEE	Mrs D. Bradshaw	Ch. Pardee Portland Pride
PEPPARD (CHs)	Mrs D. H. Gollan	Ch. Peppard Pied Piper Ch. Peppard Premium Bond Ch. Peppard Top Flight Ch. Peppard Winter Queen Ch. Peppard Faithful Flora (X) Ch. Peppard Highland Fling (X) Ch. Peppard Royal Victory
PEPERONE	Mrs J. McLeod	Ch. Peperone Plaything Ch. Peperone Pepper Ch. Peperone Papermate (X) Ch. Hardknott Quadrille (X)
POACHING now POACHYN	Mrs M. Rigby	Ch. Poaching Black Jack Ch. Poachyn Silver Flyer (X)
POLTESCO	Miss M. Ironside	Ch. Greenbrae Poltesco Duskie Maid (X) Ch. Poltesco Peewit Ch. Poltesco Periquita Ch. Poltesco High Seas Ch. Poltesco Chough
POPPY (CHs)	Mrs Martin	
PORTHURST	Mrs D. Ticehurst	Ch. Laguna Porthurst Moonlight Sonata (X) Ch. Porthurst Atalanta (X) Ch. Porthurst Martini Sweet
PUDDLECOCK	Mrs R. Flatt	Ch. Flarepath Astrinomical (X) Ch. Hardknott Mystery (X)

QUINLAN Mr		Ch. Deborah of Allgarth (X)
RADDLEDANDIE	The Misses Dinnis	Ch. Witch Hazel of Raddledandie (X) Ch. Samarkand's Sun Courtier (X)
RAVENSDOWNE	Miss E.J. Fair	Ch. Ravensdowne Bright Star (X) Ch. Laguna Ravensdowne Astri (X)
REARSBYLEA	Mrs J. Cox	Ch. Rearsbylea Ranjitara
RINGMORE	Mrs D. M. Skelley	Ch. Bliks Ringmore Bardolph (X) Ch. Ringmore Riff Raff (X)
RISEPARK	Mr P. Newman	Ch. Another Love from Risepark (X)
ROANBAR	Mr & Mrs E. Griffiths	Ch. Roanbar Star Ch. Roanbar Hillgarth Sweet Surprise (X)
ROANSAIR	Mr C.J. & Mrs R.J. Strutt	Ch. Roansair Sandpiper
ROLLE Mrs		Ch. Carina Mia (X)
RUEGETO	Mr & Mrs G. Topham	Ch. Ruegeto Gay Dawn (X) Ch. Skytime of Glenbervie (X) Ch. Ruegeto Nina of Nevedith (X)
RUSSETTWOOD	Miss B. Rooney	Ch. Russettwood Portia
SAGEWOOD	Mrs G. Sage	Ch. Allgarth Atlantis of Sagewood (X)
SAKONNET	Mr & Mrs J. Moody	Ch. Sakonnet Devil's Cub Ch. Sakonnet Sprig Muslin
SAMARKAND	Mr R. M. James	Ch. Samarkand's Greenbrae Tarragon (X) Ch. Samarkand's Sun Courtier (X) Ch. Samarkand's Subaru (X) Ch. Samarkand's Beau Ranger (X) Ch. Samarkand's Fire Wolf (X)
SAMOEMS	Mr T. Teillir	Ch. Samoems Silent Knight of Shalfleet (X)

SANTUNE	Mr G. Newton	Ch. Santune Witch's Witch (X)
SAVILEPARK	Mrs P. Robinson	Int. Ch. Savilepark Sweet Harmony Ch. Savilepark Summer Season (X) Ch. Savilepark Subastral
SEAGIFT (CHs)	Mrs D. Whitwell	
SELBROOK	Mrs J. Selby	Ch. Shalfleet Selbrook Daylight (X) Ch. Selbrook Bracelet
SELINKO	Mr & Mrs B. Kennet	Ch. Selinko Another Lady
SHALFLEET	Mrs B. Wilton Clark formerly Mrs N. Odell	Ch. Shalfleet Story Ch. Shalfleet Spellbound Ch. Shalfleet Selbrook Daylight (X) Ch. Shalfleet Swordsman Ch. Shalfleet Sultan of Sherrimere (X) Ch. Shalfleet Sailing Free Ch. Sequence of Shalfleet (X) Ch. Shalfleet Starstruck (X) Ch. Shalfleet Springtime (X) Ch. Shalfleet Sequilla Ch. Shalfleet Storywriter (X) Ch. Shalfleet Silver Knight of Skyeboat (X) Ch. Shalfleet Showman of Courthill (X) Ch. Samoems Silent Knight of Shalfleet (X) Ch. Shalfleet Silent Wish Ch. Shalfleet Shablis Can. USA UK Ch. Loricbrook Runaway of Shalfleet (X)
SHALLMOOR	Mrs N. Battershall	Ch. Curlands Night Dancer (X)
SILKSTONE	Mrs R. Wright	Ch. Oakbark Merchant Prince (X) Ch. Beseeka Knight Errant of Silkstone (X) Ch. Oakbark Mr Magic of Silkstone (X) Ch. Silkstone Astella
SKYEBOAT	Mr & Mrs M. Rakison	Ch. Peppard Faithful Flora (X) Ch. Shalfleet Silver Knight of Skyeboat (X)

SOLERA	Mr & Mrs C. Jones	Ch. Solera Scarlet Ribbons at Lowglen (X) Ch. Santune Witch's Witch (X)
SOLOTOWN	Mr & Mrs Riches	Ch. Solotown Simeon
SPEAN	Mrs Shields	Ch. Fleeting Spean La Calindra (X)
SQUIRRELWOOD	Mrs G. V. Bisset	Ch. Squirrelwood Sheer Folly
STABLEYARD	Mrs P. Stenborg	Ch. Saint Aimee of Stableyard (X)
STALYHILLS	Mrs F. Broadbent in partnership with Mrs P. Nicholas	Ch. Savilepark Summer Season (X) Ch. Novacroft Madrigal (X)
STANLEY Mrs		Ch. Black Knight of Carmodian (X)
STICKLEPATH	Mr C. Boundy	Ch. Sticklepath Saracen
SUCHINI	The Hon. Mrs M. A. van Raalte	Ch. Suchini Shimmer of Gold Ch. Suchini Sundancer
SUMMERBOURNE	Mr G. Hughes	Ch. Summerbourne Stargazer
SUMMERHAYES	Mrs L. Gilden	Ch. Summersway Silver Finch (X)
SUMMERSWAY	Mrs H. Worsfold	Ch. Summersway Silver Finch (X)
SUNSALVE	Mr T. Nethercott	Ch. Sunsalve Holidaze at Hutaka (X)
TAMBILLO	Mrs E. Ratcliffe	Ch. Flarepath Tambillo Tarquin (X)
TANTIVVEY	Miss I. B. Clay	Ch. & USA Ch. Tantivvey Diver (X) Ch. Laguna Light Lagoon (X) Ch. Tantivvey Akeferry Crusader (X)
TEIGHWAYS (CHs)	Mr F. Barnes	Ch. Teighways Tiger Tim Ch. Teighways Tasmin Ch. Teighways True Love
TEISANLAP	Mrs Beaumont	Ch. Harque to Equerry (X) Ch. Bonlouie Abalon Star of Teisanlap (X)

TEST (CHs)	Mrs D. Lewis	Ch. Dancing Girl of Test
THOMPSON Mrs L.		Ch. Hino Legacy (X) Ch. & Ir. Ch. Painted Pony (X)
THURMA	Mrs J. Rose	Ch. Danropa His Lordship of Thurma (X) Ch. Thurma Royal Event (X) Ch. Thurma Just a Rose
TILEGREEN	Mrs J. E. Smith	Ch. Tilegreen Musical Minx Ch. Tilegreen Tornado (X)
TINRIBS	Mrs Stancombe	
TOPALL	Mr C. Goldsmith	Ch. Topall Newbold Miguel (X)
TOWERCREST	Mrs E. Watson	Ch. Towercrest Flarepath Taurus (X) Ch. Fairfoot Towercrest Encore (X) Ch. Whichway Starlet (X)
TRADEWIND	Mrs C. Ledger	Ch. Acomb's Tostig (X)
TRANWELLS	Mrs K. G. Jackson	Ch. Tranwells Brekin Sally Lunn (X)
TREVELMOND (CHs)	Mr D. Armstrong	Ch. Trevelmond Masquerade Ch. Trevelmond Miss Masquerade Ch. Thurma Royal Event (X)
TWESELDOWN (CHs)	Lady Anderson	Ch. Tweseldown Whinchat Ch. Tweseldown Summer Chord
TWOBRIDGE	Mrs J. Oddy	Ch. Baydale Cinnamon (X) Ch. Twobridge Tiger Trap (X)
TRINITION	Mrs Dyer	Ch. Baydale Royal Ascot (X)
TUMBLERS	Mr & Mrs A. W. Raines	Ch. Tumbler's Clouded Buff of Coldstone (X)
VELGRA	Mrs J. Edwards	Ch. Velgra Terrence Ch. Othello of Velgra (X) Ch. Denhills Democrat (X)
VELROZA	Mr & Mrs D. Rolls	Ch. Velroza Pink Gin
WALKER Mrs		Ch. Ambassador of Allgarth (X)

WALKABOUT	Mrs S. Thompson	Ch. Walkabout Waggoner's Walk Ch. Walkabout Warrior King Ch. Walkabout Whirlpool of Baxendale (X)
WAYCROSS	Mrs C. Simmonds	Ch. Waycross Wishing Star
WELSTAR	Mrs L. M. Jones	Ch. Welstar Minted Model Ch. Welstar Royal Mint (X) Ch. Welstar Winning Dream Ch. Welstar White Wine
WHICHWAY	B. Spencer	Ch. Whichway Starlet (X)
WINGEDFOOT (CHs)	Mr & Mrs C. H. Douglas Todd	
WHIPAWAY	Mrs P. Sebley	Ch. Marshall's Milord at Faracre (X) Ch. Poachyn Silver Flyer (X)
WIPSTYCH	Dr E. Jones	Ch. Wipstych Courbette Ch. Wipstych Grandiflora (X)
WOODFLAME	Holm & Butler	Ch. Woodflame Wellington Boot
WOOLSOCKS	Mr & Mrs D. Mayger	Ch. Woolsocks Summer Blaze
WYEMERE	Mr G. Silk	Ch. Wyemere Regal Prince
YNYSFOR	Mr B. Morgan	Ch. Ynysfor Aphrodite
ZARCREST	Mr H. Boyle	Ch. Lowglen Cavalcade of Zarcrest (X) Ch. Mispickle Mazurka of Zarcrest (X)

APPENDIX 2

The two record-holding sires prior to 1962 —

Ch. WINGEDFOOT MARKSMAN OF ALLWAYS, sire of 10:

Ch. Allways Wingedfoot Running Fox X Perpetual Motion
Ch. Wingedfoot Wild Goose X Wingedfoot Lanette
Ch. Mistral's Mrs Miniver X Fleeting Frieze
Ch. Wingedfoot Ringmaster X Eh for Adorable
Ch. Wingedfoot Tu Whit Tu Whoo as above
Ch. Evening Star of Allways X Ch. Fieldspring Betony
Ch. Boughton Modra X Fawn Louise
Ch. Winpin Misty Moon X Golden Dawn
Ch. Shalfleet Spellbound X Wingedfoot Bartette
Ch. Tranwell's Brekin Sally Lunn X Brekin Fiesta of Fleeting

Ch. PILOT OFFICER PRUNE, sire of 10:

Ch. Flying Officer Kite X Solo Flight
Ch. Seagift Silly Symphony X Ch. Seagift Seraph
Ch. Peppard Pied Piper X Ch. Sweet Pepper of Peppard
Ch. Springmere Fanfare X Springmere Flare
Ch. Tea for Theresa X Springmere Spanish Rose
Ch. Rosa of Ballymoy X Hillgarth Senorita
Ch. Jay for Jewel X My Delight
Ch. Seagift Speedlite Mustang X Seagift Simplicity
Ch. Bellavista Barry X Brekin Bright Spark
Ch. Seagift Speedlite Stencil X Ch. Seagift Starturn

Sires of four or more Champions since 1962 —

Ch. LAGUNA LIGONIER, sire of 11:

Ch. Badgewood Sewickly X Badgewood Calamity Jane
Ch. Peppard Premium Bond X Peppard Tit Bits

Ch. Laguna Porthurst Moonlight Sonata X Porthurst Moonlight
Ch. Russettwood Portia X Russettwood Rythm
Ch. & USA Ch. Tantivvey Diver X Fleeting Fancy Free
Ch. Deepridge Mintmaster X Deepridge Juliet
Ch. Wyemere Regal Prince X Wyemere Miss Marilyn
Int. Ch. Laguna Leisure X Laguna Ravensdown Faerie Queen
Ch. Laguna Lunanute as above
Ch. Sticklepath Saracen X Sticklepath Sans Souci
Ch. Towercrest Flarepath Taurus X Flarepath Ravensdowne Vega

Ch. AKEFERRY JIMMY, sire of 10:

Ch. Baydale Royal Ascot X Baydale Sea Shanty
Ch. Pardee Portland Pride X Pardee Lanette
Ch. Nutcracker of Nevedith X White Bud of Glenbervie
Ch. Crysbel Skylight of Nevedith X Ch. Crysbel Skylark
Ch. Ruegeto Nina of Nevedith X Ch. Skytime of Glenbervie
Ch. Sakonnet Devil's Cub X Sakonnet Venetia
Ch. Sakonnet Sprig Muslin as above
Ch. Killigrew Quintus X Mulachre Dardanella
Ch. Mispickle Mazurka of Zarcrest X Mispickle Minivet
Ch. Harque to Equerry X Ch. Harque Yonder

Ch. COCKROW TARQUOGAN OF GLENBERVIE, sire of 9:

Ch. Sky Gypsy of Glenbervie X Ch. Hillgarth Sunstar of Glenbervie
Ch. Gypsy Moth of Glenbervie as above
Ch. Gunsmith of Glenbervie as above
Ch. Dondelayo Buckaroo X Ch. Dondelayo Rue
Ch. Dondelayo Roulette as above
Ch. Dondelayo Ruanne as above
Ch. Denorsi Moonduster of Glenbervie X White Gorse of Glenbervie
Ch. Denorsi Moon Dust of Glenbervie as above
Ch. Another Rose of Glenbervie as above

Ch. DONDELAYO BUCKAROO, sire of 10:

Ch. Laura Love X Dondelayo Lauretta
Ch. Gypsy Picture of Glenbervie X White Bridge of Glenbervie
Ch. Pathway of Glenbervie as above

Ch. White Frost of Glenbervie as above
Ch. Solid Silver of Glenbervie as above
Ch. Danropa His Lordship of Thurma X Dondelayo Coronette
Ch. Dondelayo Bandolero X Dondelayo Delia
Ch. Quickmatch of Glenbervie X Tarara of Glenbervie
Ch. & Aus. Ch. Dondelayo Reinette X Ir. Ch. Dondelayo Marianette of Seltaeb
Ch. Harque Yonder X Ch. Harque the Lark

Ch. LOWGLEN NEWBOLD CAVALIER, sire of 9:

Ch. & Aus. Ch. Allgarth Envoy X Shalfleet Stylish
Ch. Allgarth Eidelweiss as above
Ch. Solera Scarlet Ribbons at Lowglen X Springfleet Sweet Scarlet
Ch. Savillepark Sweet Harmony X Newbold Katerina
Ch. Savillepark Summer Season as above
Ch. Deborah of Allgarth X Garganey Charming Debutant
Ch. Ynysfor Aphrodite X Lowglen Donna's Daydream
Ch. Lowglen Cavalcade of Zarcrest X Tamaline of Lowglen
Ch. Lowerdon Soldier Blue X Newbold Startime

Ch. BELLAVISTA BARRY, sire of 8:

Ch. Laguna Leading Lady X Ch. Lily of Laguna
Ch. Laguna Ligonier as above
Ch. Bliks Ringmore Bardolph X Tweseldown Mimosa
Ch. Teighways Tasmin X Teighways Treacle Tart
Ch. Teighways True Love as above
Ch. Teighways Tiger Tim as above
Ch. and USA Ch. Courtenay Fleetfoot of Pennyworth X Myhorlyns Anita
Ch. Barmoud Sungage X Seagift Spode

Ch. CHARMOLL MacTAVISH, sire of 7:

Ch. Hillsdown Tobique X Denorsi Tinkermoon
Ch. Hillsdown Repique as above
Ch. Pepperone Pepper X Ch. Pepperone Plaything
Ch. Novacroft Madrigal X Novacroft Starlet
Ch. Oakbark Middleman X Oakbark Moving Picture
Ch. Peperone Papermate X Ch. Peperone Plaything
Ch. Tilegreen Musical Minx X Tilegreen Misty Morning

Ch. TOWERCREST FLAREPATH TAURUS, sire of 6:

Ch. Garganey Bartmeus X Garganey Jenny Wren
Ch. Oakbark Melord X Flarepath Aquaria
Ch. Oakbark Movie Queen as above
Ch. Great Ovation of Fairfoot X Duddleston Queen of Clubs
Ch. Faircorn Waggonmaster X Golden Delight of Faircorn
Ch. Flarepath Astrinomical X Ch. Laguna Ravensdowne Astri

Ch. NIMRODEL RUFF, sire of 6:

Ch. Wipstych Grandiflora X Ch. Wipstych Courbette
Ch. Ringmore Riff Raff X Ringmore Miss Polly
Ch. Woolsocks Summer Blaze X Welstar Amber Royale
Ch. Withaway Nimrodel X Ballagan Wishful
Ch. Poltesco Chough X Tweseldown Chicane
Ch. Welstar Winning Dream X Ch. Welstar Minted Model

Ch. SAMARKAND's GREENBRAE TARRAGON, sire of 5:

Ch. Cockrow Tarquogan of Glenbervie X Cockrow Lady Kate
Ch. Dondelayo Rue X Linknumstar Lizard
Ch. Samarkand's Sun Courtier X Samarkand's Sun Cloud
Ch. Dondelayo Duette X Ch. Dondelayo Roulette
Ch. Courthill Dondelayo Tiara as above

Ch. RAVENSDOWNE BRIGHT STAR, sire of 5:

Ch. Laguna Ravensdown Astri X Little Loo of Laguna
Ch. Gosmore Flarepath Auriga X Dorville Blue Penny
Ch. Flarepath Tambillo Tarquin X Ballagan Shining Star
Ch. Topall Newbold Miguel X Newbold Samena Queen of Diamonds
Ch. Fairfoot Towercrest Encore X Towercrest Firedancer

Ch. DEEPRIDGE MINTMASTER, sire of 5:

Ch. Deepridge Miniva X Deepridge Miss Mink
Ch. Deepridge Minstrel as above
Ch. Harque to Pegasus X Harque to Image

Ch. Oakbark Armfield Joker X Pat Jo Madam
Ch. Peppard Royal Victory X Peppard Preston Pans

Ch. BAYDALE CINNAMON, sire of 5:

Ch. Charmoll Clansman X Ch. Dondelayo Ruanne of Charmoll
Ch. Charmoll Bonnie Prince as above
Ch. Charmoll MacTavish as above
Ch. Twobridge Tiger Trap X Strayview Sophisticate
Ch. Black Knight of Carmodian X September Girl

Ch. POLTESCO PEEWIT, sire of 4:

Ch. Poltesco Periquita X Poltesco Quiz
Ch. Dragonhill Tawny Owl X Dragonhill Golden Plover
Ch. Nimrodel Willow Daughter X Willow of Allways
Ch. Nimrodel Ruff X Nimrodel Wintersweet

OAKBARK PYRAMID, sire of 4:

Ch. Oakbark Merchant Prince X Oakbark Michelle
Ch. Denhills Delectabelle X Rasaday Alisa
Ch. Newbold Kerry Gold X Ch. Oakbark Michaela
Ch. Newbold Muffinman as above

COCKROW PARTRIDGE OF CRAWSHAW, sire of 4:

Ch. Pimlico of Crawshaw X Kew Sally
Ch. Tantivvey Akeferry Crusader X Eegee Jane
Ch. Akeferry Jimmy as above
Ch. Belinda of Hardknott X Crystina of Hardknott

Ch. SAMOEMS SILENT KNIGHT OF SHALFLEET, sire of 4:

Ch. Shalfleet Silent Wish X Shalfleet Storyteller
Ch. Shalfleet Showman of Courthill X Courthill Chorus Line
Ch. Shalfleet Shablis X Shalfleet Sangria
Ch. Walkabout Warrior King X Shalfleet Spinning Torch of Walkabout

Appendix 3

The Whippet Breed Clubs

The Whippet Breed Council
Hon. Secretary: Mrs E. Newton
Nevedith Kennels, 244 Shuttleworth Road, Bolsover, Chesterfield S44 6PA

The National Whippet Association
Hon. Secretary: Mr M. Howgate
21 Heatherdown Road, West Moors, Wimbourne, Dorset BH22 0BX

The Midland Whippet Club
Hon. Secretary: Mrs W. Spencer
15 Mill Lane, Toft, Cambridge CB3 7RW

The Northern Counties Whippet Club
Hon. Secretary: Mr J. Parkinson
27 Low Road, Middleton, Morecambe LA3 3LG

The Whippet Club of Scotland
Hon. Secretary: Mrs J. R. McLeod
12 Livingstone Terrace, Dunlop, Kilmarnock, Ayrshire

The Whippet Club of Wales
Hon. Secretary: Mrs J. Poole
25 Bampton Road, Llanrumney, Cardiff, S. Wales

The East Anglian Whippet Club
Hon. Secretary: Mrs C. Neale
6 High Street North, Stewkley, Leighton Buzzard, Bedfordshire

The South Yorkshire Whippet Club
Hon. Secretary: Mrs D. Bradshaw
129 Musgrave Crescent, Shirecliffe, Sheffield

The Northern Ireland Whippet Club
Hon. Secretary: Mrs W. Sloan
41 Thornleigh Park, Lisburn, Co. Antrim BT28 2DD

The North East Whippet Society
Hon. Secretary: Mrs M. Gardner
83 Ewesley Road, High Barnes, Sutherland SR4 7RJ

Appendix 4

The Whippet Coursing Clubs

The National Whippet Coursing Club
Hon. Secretary: Miss S. Baird
Wyke Cottage, Queens Road, Crowborough, Sussex

The Whippet Coursing Club
Maj. Gen. P. J. Bush OBE
Thorndean, Boyndon Road, Maidenhead, Berks

The East of England Whippet Coursing Club
Hon. Secretary: The Hon. Mrs K. S. Richardson
Hungry Hall, Witham, Essex

The East Anglian Whippet Coursing Club
Hon. Secretary: Mrs Barron
Nicholls Farm, Lybury Lane, Redbourn, St Albans, Hertfordshire

The Woolley and District Whippet Coursing Club
Hon. Secretary: Mrs V. Hill
Shipton Grange House, Shipton-u-Wychwood, Oxon OX7 6DG

Appendix 5

Pedigree Whippet Racing

The Whippet Club Racing Association
Hon. Secretary: Mrs J. Henderson
41 Common Lane, Harpenden, Hertfordshire AL5 5DN

Appendix 6

Iconography

Frontispiece.

'Misse et Turlu', by Jean-Baptiste Oudry, (1686-1735). Two whippets belonging to Louis XV, signed and dated J. B. Oudry, 1725. In September 1725 it was reported that Oudry had been ordered by the King, Louis XV, to paint the portraits of some 'Levriers Anglois'. On Sunday, 10th March, 1726, Oudry presented the painting of 'Misse et Turlu, deux levriers Anglois' to the young King and Queen. The painting was 'very well received' and led to numerous subsequent commissions of the royal dogs. Misse and Turlu hung over the door of the king's chamber at Compiegne. It was sent to Fontainebleau, where it now hangs, in 1889. Although described as 'greyhounds', the word 'levrier' is also used to describe a whippet, and there is no doubt that both in relation to the roses, and in conformation, Misse and Turlu correspond to the present day whippet rather than greyhound. It is interesting that they had been imported into France and were described as English.
Reference: *J.-B. Oudry 1686-1755,* Galeries nationales du Grand Palais, 1 October 1982 — 3 January 1983, catalogue by Hal Opperman.

Plate 1.

'The 7th Earl of Northampton', by Pompeo Batoni, (1708-1787). Charles Compton, 7th Earl of Northampton, was painted in Rome in 1758 at the age of 21. He was to die five years later when he was English Ambassador in Venice. His full-length portrait has been in the Fitzwilliam Museum, Cambridge, since it was purchased in 1950. 'The dog is brown on a green chair' is the plain statement in the catalogue. It is included among the group of portraits which Batoni painted between 1753 and 1759 which 'will always number among the artist's most truly memorable works' and in which 'his vision and special poetry are nowhere more strongly present' (Anthony M. Clark). In the exhibition held at Kenwood in 1982, Edgar Peters Bowron rightly referred to 'the unusually intimate and touching relationship between man and dog'. Batoni was a consumate painter of dogs as well as their owners. Indeed, as Brinsley Ford observed nearly thirty years ago, 'dogs often accompanied their masters on the Grand Tour' in those days before the laws of quarantine. The scale and proportion of the dog in the portrait of Lord Northampton certainly puts it in the category of the small greyhound or whippet. As with 'levrier' in France, so 'levrieri' in Italian can be found in Roman statuary and are frequently encountered in Batoni's portraits of his English sitters, in those of Henry Pierse, Sackville Tufton, Lord Thanet, Sir William Knatchbull-Wyndham, Sir Sampson Gideon and his tutor and notably in that of Sir Humphrey Morris, described as 'a celebrated animal lover whose will allowed £600 a year to the care for the horses and dogs he left behind'. Also in the portraits of Sir William Watkins-Wynn with Thomas Apperley and Captain Edward Hamilton, where a dog is jumping up against Sir Watkins' right leg while another is curled up on the floor in a thoroughly whippet-like position.

The bust on the table on the left of the portrait of Lord Northampton derives from the full length statue of the Minerva Giustiniani which makes numerous appearances in other portraits by Batoni and was much visited by those on the Grand Tour. It may be that, just as the Minerva Giustiniani was native to Rome and appeared in numerous portraits by Batoni, the 'levriers' were also a part of his studio. Whether they were taken out by the English, or were native, the portrait of Lord Northampton demonstrates the point that we wish to make.

Reference: *Catalogue of Paintings, Italian Schools,* J. W. Goodison and G. H. Robertson, Fitzwilliam Museum, vol II, 1967, p.13, also to Anthony M. Clark, *Studies in Roman Eighteenth Century Painting (Batoni's professional career and style),* 1981, selected and edited by Edgar Peters Bowron, and the latter's catalogue of the exhibition *Pompeo Batoni and his British Patrons,* the Iveagh Bequest, Kenwood, 8 June-30 August, 1982, p.8-9, fig. 2 and also with gratitude to Francis Russell. Brinsley Ford's 'A Portrait Group by Gavin Hamilton's, was in the Burlington Magazine, December, 1955, p.378.

Plate 2

'A Nymph taking a Thorn out of a Greyhound's Foot', by Richard James Wyatt, (1795-1850). The marble group of a Nymph taking a thorn out of a 'greyhound's' foot was purchased by Lord Brotherton under the title 'Gratitude' and bequeathed to the Leeds City Art Gallery by his niece, Dorothy Una Radcliffe. It is one of a number of versions of the subject, another being at Leighton Hall, Liverpool, while a third belonged to Queen Victoria. It is not certain which of these, if any, is the one which Rupert Gunnis records as having been completed by John Gibson. However, both sculptors, Wyatt and Gibson, had met Canova in their early years and worked in his studio in Rome. Both settled in that city and spent the greater part of their working lives there. Wyatt became one of the most sought after sculptors in Rome. As Gunnis says, quoting Gibson, he 'acquired the purest style and his statues were highly finished. Female figures were his forte and he was clever in composition and the harmony of lines. No sculptor in England has produced female statues to be compared with those of Wyatt'.

Five years older than Wyatt, Gibson was also to live sixteen years longer. Both remained loyal to the precepts which they had absorbed in Canova's

studio, carrying the neo-classical taste well into the middle of the nineteenth century. Those standards of finish and precision can be relied upon in the same way as the examples of Oudry and Batoni provide evidence of type. These three illustrations are intended to make it clear that, in accordance with modern usage and definition, none of the dogs would be classified as a greyhound or Italian greyhound. Their poses are characteristic of whippets no less than their size in relation to the human body. The photograph shows the group at the bottom of the staircase in Temple Newsam, nr Leeds, Yorkshire.
See: Rupert Gunnis, *Dictionary of British Sculptors, 1660-1851.* We would also like to acknowledge the assistance of Dr T. Friedman.

Appendix 7

Bibliography

Whippets

Lloyd, Freeman
'The Whippet and Race Dog', (1894, 199pp). A contemporary description of the whippet, 100 years ago. Whippets had only just been recognised by the Kennel Club as a breed, rabbit coursing and rag racing were common sports in the north, there were classes for 'Rabbit Dogs' at shows and rough-coated whippets were still fairly numerous. Lloyd was mainly concerned with promoting whippet racing in the south and improving its somewhat doubtful image.

Fitter, B.S.
'The Show Whippet', (1947, 37pp). Whippets in a small nutshell. There are 12 pages of lists of winners and some fascinating advertisements showing dogs that are now 'pillars of the breed'. The first edition, of 1937, is very rare and very expensive.

Renwick, W. Lewis
'The Whippet Handbook', (1957, 93pp). The author was a very respected and knowledgeable breeder and judge, who had known many of the early breeders and their dogs. He wrote it when he was Secretary of the Whippet Club and it contains many interesting pedigrees and photographs.

Todd, C. H. Douglas
'The Popular Whippet', (1961, 193pp). The most comprehensive book on whippets to date. It contains a list of champions from 1946-60. The author was a very experienced breeder and judge.

Daglish, E. Fitch — *'The Whippet'*, (1964, 61pp). A slim volume with an interesting chapter on colour breeding. The author's genetic theories are arguable.

All the above books contain photographs, pedigrees and list of winners that are of interest to anyone wishing to learn about pedigree whippets.

Wilson, Pauline — *'Whippets; Rearing and Racing'*, (1979, 118pp). The author is Editor of *'Whippet News'*, the British Whippet Racing Association magazine, so the emphasis is on non-pedigree racing. There are two chapters on W.C.R.A. racing and 2½ pages on Rearing.

In addition, a chapter or section on whippets will be found in:

Drabble, Phil — *'Of Pedigree Unknown'*, (1964). Very good descriptions of working men's whippets and whippet racing in the Midlands.

Walsh, E. G. — In *'Coursing'*, (1975), the omnibus book on coursing, with contributions from some 30 people from all sections of the coursing world.

Russell, Joanna — *'All about Gazehounds'*, (1976). Each chapter contains the standard for the subject dog and it is interesting to compare the similarities and differences. The author is well-known as a whippet correspondent and breeder of black whippets.

Genetics and colour breeding:

Burns M. and Fraser, M. N. — *'Genetics of the Dog'*, (1967, 186pp)

Little, Clarence C. — *'The Inheritance of Coat Colour in Dogs'* (1957, 190pp).

Winge, Ojvind — *'Inheritance in Dogs'*, (1950, 145pp).

First Aid and Nursing, etc:

Pinniger, R. S. (ed) — *'Jones's Animal Nursing'*, (1972, 450pp). The handbook for those training as Animal Nursing Auxilliaries.

'T.V. Vet' — *'The T.V. Vet Dog Book'*, (1974, 205pp). General care and attention. Handy for quick reference, the photos leave little to the imagination.

Levy, Juliette de Bairacli — *'The Complete Herbal Book for the Dog'*, (1963, 200pp). A handbook on natural care and rearing for those who wish to know about such things.

Index of Persons

(To have listed all the dogs and kennel affixes mentioned in the text would have made the Index unwieldy. Kennel affixes held by people mentioned are shown in brackets; a full list of those kennels which have bred or made up champions since 1962 is given in Appendix 1 and a list of dogs which have sired more than four champions in the same period is given in Appendix 2).

Index of Subjects